CASE STUDIES IN LANGUAGE CURRICULUM DESIGN

Case studies are a powerful pedagogical tool for illuminating constructs and models in real-life contexts. Covering a wide range of teaching–learning contexts and offering in-depth analyses of ESL/EFL language curriculum design issues, this casebook is distinctive and unique in that each case draws on and is clearly linked to a single model presented in Nation and Macalister's *Language Curriculum Design* (**www.routledge.com/9780415806060**), giving the book a high degree of coherence. A short commentary by the editors after each case highlights features of note and/or issues arising from it. This is a versatile text, designed to work as a companion to *Language Curriculum Design* (adding meaning and depth to the model presented there by relating it to a range of applications), as a stand-alone text, or as a resource for language teacher trainees, teacher educators, practicing teachers, program administrators, and materials writers in the field.

John Macalister is Senior Lecturer at Victoria University of Wellington, New Zealand. He specializes in the fields of language teaching methodology and curriculum design and draws on experience in teacher education and curriculum design in Thailand, Cambodia, Kiribati, Vanuatu, and Namibia.

I.S.P. Nation is Professor in Applied Linguistics at Victoria University of Wellington, New Zealand. In addition to books, his extensive list of publications on teaching and learning vocabulary, language teaching methodology, and curriculum design includes journal articles, book chapters, and book reviews. He has taught in Indonesia, Thailand, the United States, Finland, and Japan.

ESL & Applied Linguistics Professional Series
Eli Hinkel, Series Editor

*Visit **www.routledge.com/education** for additional information on titles in the ESL & Applied Linguistics Professional Series*

CASE STUDIES IN LANGUAGE CURRICULUM DESIGN

Concepts and Approaches in Action Around the World

Edited by
John Macalister and I. S. P. Nation

Routledge
Taylor & Francis Group

NEW YORK AND LONDON

First published 2011
by Routledge
711 Third Avenue, New York, NY 10017

Simultaneously published in the UK
by Routledge
2 Park Square, Milton Park, Abingdon, Oxon OX14 4RN

Routledge is an imprint of the Taylor & Francis Group, an informa business

Library of Congress Cataloging in Publication Data
Case studies in language curriculum design / edited by John Macalister
and I.S.P. Nation.
    p. cm. — (ESL & applied linguistics professional series)
   1. English language — Study and teaching — Foreign speakers.
   2. English teachers — Training of.   I. Macalister, John. 1956–
II. Nstion, I. S. P.
   PE1128.A2C368   2011
   428.2′4071—dc22

                                             2011002638

ISBN: 978–0–415–88231–6 (hbk)
ISBN: 978–0–415–88232–3 (pbk)
ISBN: 978–0–203–84785–5 (ebk)

Typeset in Bembo
by RefineCatch Limited, Bungay, Suffolk, UK

CONTENTS

PREFACE

Curriculum design may be a field of expertise but it would be a mistake to think of it as the preserve of experts with secret knowledge alone. Every classroom teacher who makes a decision about what to teach and when, or about the presentation of classroom activities, or about what to test, is in effect a curriculum designer. The decisions the teacher makes about what happens in the classroom are going to be informed by a variety of factors, such as knowledge of the students, the layout of the classroom, the availability of appropriate technology, and beliefs about what constitutes effective teaching. In making these appropriately informed decisions the teacher becomes an active participant in the curriculum design process.

The idea for this book arose from the wish to illustrate the breadth of curriculum design experiences, from the individual classroom teacher working within the constraints of a tightly-controlled national curriculum to the team of well-qualified experts beginning with a free hand and an open brief, and everything in between. An important purpose, therefore, is to make the process of curriculum design come alive through a wide variety of examples. The experiences reported in this collection remind us that curriculum design is very much a creative activity with its aim being better learning. By reading about the variety of situations described in the book and the range of responses to those situations, we hope that the curriculum design process will be exemplified in an engaging way, and that individual teachers will be encouraged to make their own individual curriculum design decisions.

CONTRIBUTORS

Andy Boon is Associate Professor in the Faculty of Humanities at Toyo Gakuen University, Tokyo, Japan. He is also Program Chair for JALT West Tokyo. He completed a Master's degree in TESOL from Aston University, UK in 2004. He has published articles on teacher development, methodology, and motivation. His research interests focus on professional development and action research in the classroom. Andy can be contacted at andrew.boon@tyg.jp.

Maria J. Coolican earned her PhD from the University of Michigan and works predominantly in the areas of teacher education, program design and development, and educational reform. She has taught at the University of Portland and the University of Notre Dame, and currently teaches at the University of Michigan. Some of her current work centers on re-examining the ways in which primary and secondary world languages teachers are educated and then inducted into the profession.

David Crabbe teaches and supervises in the School of Linguistics and Applied Language Studies at Victoria University of Wellington. He is currently Assistant Vice Chancellor (Academic) with a broader role in university teaching and learning. His research interests are in language curriculum development as a problem-solving activity, with a particular interest in learner autonomy. In his current role those interests are applied to tertiary education in the full range of academic subjects. He has previously lived and worked in France, Nigeria, the UK and Singapore.

Patrick Foss has taught in Japan for 15 years. He recently joined the faculty in the College of Liberal Arts and Sciences at Tokyo Medical and Dental University.

Derek Foster began working for the Curriculum Project in 2007 after two years of teaching English to refugees and exiles on the Thai-Burma border. He co-wrote General English Pre-intermediate, and has contributed to many other ELT and social science materials. He is currently working on other levels of the General English series, editing social science books, and planning a critical thinking course. For more information about the Curriculum Project, visit www.curriculumproject.org.

Donald Freeman is on the faculty at the School of Education, University of Michigan, where he works with undergraduate and post-graduate teacher preparation in all subjects K-12. He was for 25 years on the graduate faculty at the School of International Training, where he chaired the Department of Language Teacher Education and founded and directed the Center for Teacher Education, Training, and Research, a research and development unit that designed and implemented teacher education projects around the world. His research and design interests focus on creating new, atypical professional environments to support individual learning and institutional transformation.

Kathleen Graves is Associate Professor of Education Practice at the School of Education, University of Michigan. She has worked on curriculum renewal and language teacher education in the US, Algeria, Bahrain, Brazil, Japan, and Korea. Her research focuses on teaching and learning as the heart of a curriculum and supporting teachers' professional development as the key to successful educational and curricular reform. She is the editor/author of two books on course design, *Teachers as Course Developers* and *Designing language courses* and is the Series Editor of TESOL's Language Curriculum Development series.

Angela Joe is Director of the English Language Institute at Victoria University of Wellington. She has taught ESP and EAP courses for over 20 years. Her research interests include English for Professional Purposes, English for Academic Purposes and second language vocabulary acquisition.

Katie Julian has worked with Burmese populations since 1995 as a teacher, trainer and materials designer. In 1999 she was awarded Victoria University of Wellington's Applied Linguistics Prize and English Speaking Union Award. In 2002 she co-founded the Curriculum Project under Thabyay Education Network, and has been its Coordinator since 2004. She is currently working on a teacher training manual for Southeast Asian teachers of English.

Gi-Zen Liu received his Ph.D. degree in Instructional Systems Technology from Indiana University Bloomington in the U.S.A in 2003. He is the director of the Foreign Language Center, and is an associate professor of the Foreign Languages & Literature Department at National Cheng Kung University in Tainan, Taiwan.

His research interests include blended language learning, instructional system design, and technology enhanced language learning.

John Macalister is Senior Lecturer in the School of Linguistics and Applied Language Studies at Victoria University of Wellington. He is also President of the Applied Linguistics Association of New Zealand. He specialises in the fields of language teaching methodology and curriculum design and draws on experience in teacher education and curriculum design in Thailand, Cambodia, Kiribati, Vanuatu and Namibia. His most recent curriculum design experience has been for trainee seafarers at the Marine Training Centre, Kiribati.

Paul Nation is Professor of Applied Linguistics in the School of Linguistics and Applied Language Studies at Victoria University of Wellington, New Zealand. He has taught in Indonesia, Thailand, the United States, Finland, and Japan. His specialist interests are language teaching methodology and vocabulary learning. His latest books on vocabulary include *Learning Vocabulary in Another Language* (2001) published by Cambridge University Press, *Focus on Vocabulary* (2007) from NCELTR/Macquarie, and *Teaching Vocabulary: Strategies and Techniques* published by Cengage Learning (2008). Three books, *Teaching ESL/EFL Listening and Speaking* (with Jonathan Newton), *Teaching ESL/EFL Reading and Writing*, and *Language Curriculum Design* (with John Macalister) have recently appeared from Routledge.

Kevin Parent is faculty at Korea Maritime University. Born and raised in Chicago but living in South Korea since 1999 when he came over as an exchange professor, he has taught university students in both Korea and America and has conducted in-service teacher training for Korean teachers. His PhD examined second language learning and polysemy. His interests include exploring aspects of teacher development, alternative education, corpus linguistics and lexical semantics.

John Read is an associate professor in Applied Language Studies at the University of Auckland, New Zealand, where he teaches postgraduate courses in language assessment, vocabulary learning and teaching, and research methods. His primary research interests are in vocabulary assessment and the testing of English for academic and professional purposes. He is the author of *Assessing Vocabulary* (Cambridge, 2000), as well as numerous articles and book chapters in his areas of expertise. From 2002 to 2006 he was co-editor of the international journal Language Testing. He is serving as President of the International Language Testing Association in 2011 and 2012.

Nicky Riddiford is the coordinator and teacher of a workplace communication program for skilled migrants at Victoria University of Wellington, New Zealand. She is also a member of the Language in the Workplace Project (LWP) research team and is a key contributor to the research which is tracking the development of pragmatic competence of a group of skilled migrants in New Zealand. She is the co-author of a recent textbook, *Workplace Talk in Action: An ESOL Resource.*

Lizzy Roe is a Senior Tutor in the Department of Applied Language Studies and Linguistics at the University of Auckland. Lizzy has taught English for twenty years in New Zealand, the UK and France in a range of contexts including English for business, medical, and study purposes, and teaching young learners. She also has experience in language teacher education and practical teacher training courses. She currently develops and teaches Academic English courses for undergraduate EAL students. Her interests include teaching and learning methodology, academic literacy skills, discourse analysis, and assessing language proficiency.

Moses Samuel is Professor in the Department of Language and Literacy Education, University of Malaya, Malaysia.

Saratha Sithamparam is Associate Professor in Language and Literacy Education, Universiti Brunei Darusalam.

Susan Smith has taught English for Academic Purposes and English for Specific Purposes in the School of Linguistics and Applied Language Studies of Victoria University of Wellington for fourteen years. Prior to that she taught in workplaces in Japan and at the Pontificia Universidad Católica del Perú.

1

INTRODUCTION

Paul Nation and John Macalister

Curriculum, or course, design is essentially a practical activity. The result is going to be experienced by teachers and learners in the classroom. In order to arrive at that result, however, the course designer is integrating knowledge from many areas in the field of applied linguistics and this was described in our earlier book, *Language Curriculum Design* (*LCD*). Not everyone reading *this* book, however, will have read *that* book and so we begin with an overview of our language curriculum design model (Figure 1.1).

The model consists of three outer circles and a subdivided inner circle, all enclosed within one wider circle. Some curriculum designers distinguish curriculum from syllabus. In the model, both the outer circles and the inner circle make up the curriculum. The inner circle represents the syllabus.

The inner circle has goals as its center. This is meant to reflect the importance of having clear general goals for a course. The content and sequencing part of the inner circle represents the items to learn in a course, and the order in which they occur, plus the ideas content if this is used as a vehicle for the items and not as a goal in itself. Language courses must give consideration to the language content of a course even if this is not presented in the course as discrete items. Consideration of content makes sure that there is something useful for the learners to learn to advance their control of the language, that they are getting the best return for learning effort in terms of the usefulness of what they will meet in the course, and that they are covering all the things they need to cover for a balanced knowledge of the language.

The format and presentation part of the inner circle represents the format of the lessons or units of the course, including the techniques and types of activities that will be used to help learning. This is the part of the course that the learners are most aware of. It is important that it is guided by the best available principles of teaching and learning.

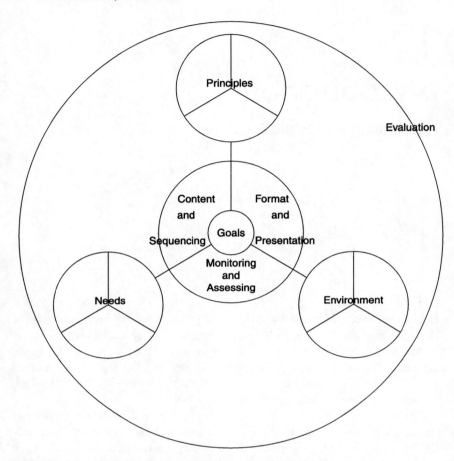

FIGURE 1.1 A model of the parts of the curriculum design process

The monitoring and assessment part of the inner circle represents the need to give attention to observing learning, testing the results of learning, and providing feedback to the learners about their progress. It is often not a part of commercially designed courses. It provides information that can lead to changes at most of the other parts of the curriculum design process.

The outer circles (principles, environment, needs) involve practical and theoretical considerations that will have a major effect in guiding the actual process of course production. There is a wide range of factors to consider when designing a course. These include the learners' present knowledge and lacks, the resources available including time, the skill of the teachers, the curriculum designer's strengths and limitations, and principles of teaching and learning. If factors such as these are not considered then the course may be unsuited to the situation and learners for which it is used, and may be ineffective and inefficient as a means of encouraging learning. In the curriculum design process these factors are considered in three sub-processes: environment analysis, needs analysis, and the application of principles.

Each of the inner circles can be segmented into three. For environment analysis (Figure 1.2) the segments provide information about the learners, the teachers, and the teaching–learning situation. The result of environment analysis is a ranked list of factors and a consideration of the effects of these factors on the design.

In needs analysis, the course designer considers the present proficiency, future needs and wants of the learners (Figure 1.3). The result of needs analysis is a realistic list of language, ideas or skill items that will be covered in the course.

The application of principles involves first of all deciding on the most important principles to apply and monitoring their application through the whole design process. The principles are supported by research and theory in the field. In the model, the three segments of the principles circle correspond with the three divisions of the inner circle (Figure 1.4). The result of applying principles is a course where learning is given the greatest support.

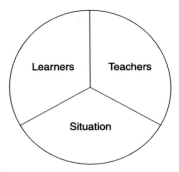

FIGURE 1.2 Factors in environment analysis

FIGURE 1.3 Three types of need

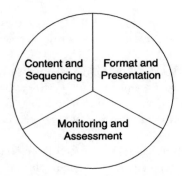

FIGURE 1.4 The subdivisions of principles

As well as the inner circle and the three outer circles, it is possible to imagine a large circle drawn completely around the whole model. This large outer circle represents evaluation. Evaluation can involve looking at every aspect of a course to judge if the course is adequate and where it needs improvement. It is generally a neglected aspect of curriculum design.

This, then, was the model that we introduced in our earlier book. The purpose of *this* book is to bring the curriculum design model to life through a collection of case studies drawn from different language learning contexts around the world. The different case studies are summarized in Table 1.1. We have matched the case study chapters to the chapters in *LCD* – aware, however, that many of the chapters draw on the whole design model – and provided suggestions for discussion or further work after each chapter.

The collection begins with a classic case study to provide an overview of the curriculum design model, Paul Nation and David Crabbe's survival language learning syllabus for foreign language learning.

The following three chapters focus on the outer circles. Environment and needs analyses provide important information for decisions about the inner circle; Katie Julian and Derek Foster describe considerable challenges in the design of a general English course for Burma and significant challenges also needed to be accommodated by Angela Joe in her design of language courses for tertiary level students in Oman. Paul Nation draws on principles to provide an answer to a question that many have hoped he would address – what his ideal vocabulary learning course would look like.

The focus of the next four chapters, chapters 6 to 9, is on the segments of the inner circle and on goals. Susan Smith found that the goals for Peruvian officials studying English in New Zealand needed to change from one course to the next. Nicky Riddiford drew on authentic workplace language for content in her course for skilled migrants, and Gi-Zen Liu considers issues of format and presentation in the information and communication technologies component of a hybrid

TABLE 1.1

Chapter	Title	Curriculum design focus	Language learning context	Learners	Teachers
2	A survival language learning syllabus for foreign travel	Overview	Any foreign language learning	Beginners	Non-native speaker
3	Design meeting context: A general English course for Burmese adults	Environment analysis	EFL	Post-secondary	Non-native speaker
4	Designing English language courses for Omani students	Needs analysis	EFL/EAP	Tertiary	Native and non-native speaker
5	My ideal vocabulary learning course	Principles	EFL and ESL	All levels	Native and non-native speaker
6	Opening the door to international communication: Peruvian officials and APEC	Goals	EFL/ESP	Adults	Native speaker
7	Helping skilled migrants into employment: The workplace communication program	Content and sequencing/Format and presentation	ESL/ESP	Adults	Native speaker
8	The blended language learning course in Taiwan: Issues & challenges of instructional design	Format and presentation	EFL	Tertiary	Non-native speaker
9	Designing the assessment of a university ESOL course	Monitoring and assessment	ESL/EAP	Tertiary	Native speaker
10	Refreshing a writing course: The role of evaluation	Evaluation	ESL	Tertiary	Native speaker
11	Localizing Spanish in the Ann Arbor Languages Partnership: Developing and using a "teachable" curriculum	Approaches to course design	Spanish as a SL	Elementary	Native and non-native speaker

(Continued)

TABLE 1.1 Continued

Chapter	Title	Curriculum design focus	Language learning context	Learners	Teachers
12	Learning to teach Spanish: Identifying, inducting, and supporting apprentice teachers in the Ann Arbor Languages Partnership	Introducing change	Spanish as a SL	Elementary	Native and non-native speaker
13	Negotiated syllabuses: Do you want to?	Negotiated syllabuses	EFL	Adult, post-secondary and tertiary	Native speaker
14	Enhancing consumerist literacy practices in an urbanizing community	Adopting & adapting	ESL	Lower secondary	Non-native speaker
15	The teacher as intermediary between national curriculum and classroom	Adopting & adapting	EFL	Middle school	Native and non-native speaker
16	Developing a blogwriting program at a Japanese university	Introducing change	EFL	Tertiary	Native speaker

course. John Read and Lizzy Roe engage with the difficult question of validity in the assessment of a university listening and reading course.

The large outer circle of the design model, evaluation, is considered in a number of the chapters but is the main focus of John Macalister's chapter, in which he reports on student response to a re-designed writing course in a university setting.

Chapters 11 and 12 are paired. Donald Freeman, Maria Coolican and Kathleen Graves report on the Ann Arbor Languages Partnership, an innovative collaboration between university and district with the aim of teaching Spanish to elementary school students. The first of their two chapters outlines their approach to curriculum design, and the second shifts the focus to training the teachers, the people responsible for introducing change.

The remaining chapters address important issues related to language curriculum design. Andrew Boon demonstrates the role of negotiation in different learning contexts in Japan, while Moses Samuel and Saratha Sithamparam draw on changes in the immediate environment to adapt coursebook exercises to make them more meaningful to the learners. Kevin Parent also looks at how teachers adapted the coursebook while working with a constraining national curriculum, a situation familiar to many teachers. In the final chapter Patrick Foss considers the introduction of change, in the form of a blogwriting component, in a Japanese university course.

The contents are summarized in Table 1.1, which shows the broad range of current curriculum design experiences drawn on by the contributors to this book. The range is more than geographical. It includes learners in foreign and second language settings, from no proficiency to advanced, from primary schools to the tertiary sector, from child to adult, and also includes both native speaker and non-native speaker teachers, working in environments that range from the resource-poor to the technologically privileged.

We are sure, therefore, that there will be much here to interest all those interested in the multi-faceted field of language curriculum design.

2

A SURVIVAL LANGUAGE LEARNING SYLLABUS FOR FOREIGN TRAVEL[1]

Paul Nation and David Crabbe

This chapter addresses a question that has been posed many times and for which many answers have been found. That question is: "What is the language knowledge that learners first need when they learn a language?" Previous answers to the question have generally focused on specific grammatical structures or vocabulary that were considered useful. The major exception to this is the Council of Europe work which has defined a Threshold level (Van Ek & Alexander, 1975), and a lower Waystage level (Van Ek, Alexander & Fitzpatrick, 1977), in terms of communicative function – what people need to do with language.

The study starts with the simple fact that millions of people throughout the world, in temporary informal social contact with speakers of another language, learn enough of that language to conduct initial communication. The study attempts to tap this phenomenon of successful initial language learning. Specifically, it asks what things do people typically need or want to say in the initial stages of contact with an unknown language and what resources serve them best?

We were particularly interested in the very first contact and how much learning could relate to that contact. This would apply to the language learning of many people – tourists in a country for a short time, professionals visiting a country for a short assignment. Such people often shy away from contact with the language, and yet if they learned a little, they would almost certainly profit more from their visit and would possibly be encouraged to take the learning further. We are thus looking at what guidance can be given to people who want to cross the very first threshold – the threshold of using the language for the first time.

A typical resource with which to approach this threshold is a book of useful words and phrases. Such phrasebooks are generally intended as reference books: a resource that you look up when you are in communicative difficulty. The aim of this study is to provide a list based on a principled approach that will give learners an immediate and useful return for the effort of learning. A quick survey of introductory course books indicates that their syllabus content provides a poor short-term return for someone with limited time to invest. There is usually too much material in the early lessons that is not relevant to immediate needs. The first chapters often deal with topics like the indefinite article, pronouns, or adjectives, before coming to something that can be immediately used. The following interview (Dickie, 1989) with a young foreign language learner highlights this.

> *Gareth is in his fifth month of learning Japanese in the first year of secondary school. He is speaking to the researcher.*
> "Tell me something in Japanese, Gareth."
> "OK. You ask me questions in English and I'll answer in Japanese."
> "Were you born in New Zealand?"
> "We haven't got up to 'yes' yet."
> "All right. I'll try something else. How old are you?"
> "Do you want me to say the whole sentence because I can only say the number?"
> "That's fine. Just tell me the number."
> "....."
> "That sounds good. Here's another question. What do you do at school?"
> "No, not that kind of thing."
> "Sorry. What sort of thing should I be asking you?"
> "Well, all the regular things like 'This is a pen' and 'The book is red'. That kind of thing."

The Purpose and Limits of the Survival Syllabus

The content of the present survival syllabus has been selected considering the situation of someone who is going to stay in another country for somewhere between one and three months. This is long enough to make it worthwhile learning something of the local language and yet not long enough to justify a sustained intensive course. No consideration has been given to special needs that the visitor may have as a result of the particular reason for visiting that country, such as to do academic research, to arrange a trade deal, or to get married. Rather, attention has been focused on survival, travel, and social needs which would be common to any visitor to another country. This includes getting the necessities at a good price and basic social courtesies (so you can get the necessities at a good price!). Pimsleur (1980, p. 16) describes this as "the 'courtesy and necessity' speaking level," and suggests that "this type of mastery can be achieved in less than sixty hours, which comes to only an hour a day for two to three months – an excellent return for a limited effort." This contrasts with the 240 hours needed to reach the elementary proficiency level in an "easy" language or 360 hours in a "hard" language (Pimsleur, 1980, p. 15).

The syllabus thus has two focuses

(1) a focus on spoken language on the assumption that in the mainstream tourist areas of a country communication will be in a spoken form.
(2) a focus on vocabulary. Research on vocabulary learning (Nation, 1982) has shown that it is possible to learn a large amount of vocabulary in a short time with good long-term retention. There is much more involved in language learning than memorizing words, but a carefully chosen vocabulary that takes account of the patterns words occur in can be an excellent basis for planning short-term learning. The size of the syllabus (approximately 120 items, consisting of roughly 150 words) takes account of learning rates revealed by this vocabulary learning research and Pimsleur's time limits, and makes it about one-quarter of the size of the Waystage syllabus prepared for the Council of Europe for initial language learning (Van Ek et al., 1977).

Table 2.1, using part of Munby's (1978) framework for needs analysis, shows how limited the communicative context is for the foreign traveler.

The Development of the Survival Syllabus

Criteria for Selecting the Communicative Content

The syllabus should contain useful items which also provide a good starting point for further learning and which are easy to learn. To make sense of this, criteria were set up to help decide whether an item should be included in the syllabus or not. Table 2.2 lists the criteria in order of importance. The second column shows

TABLE 2.1 The communicative needs of a temporary visitor

Purposive domain	Tourist, temporary visitor
Setting	Foreign city, used occasionally, culturally different, recreational, urban, unhurried
Interaction	Consumer, customer, non-native, guest
Instrumentality	Spoken dialogue, face to face.
	Very low on size of utterance, complexity, range of forms, delicacy, speed.
	Middling on flexibility.
	High tolerance of error, stylistic failure, reference to a dictionary, repetition, hesitation.

TABLE 2.2 Criteria for choosing content for the syllabus

Criterion	Source of information
Need	Needs analysis
Frequency	Eaton (1940)
Coverage and combinability	Viberg (1989), Substitution tables
Learnability	Higa (1963), Nation (1982)

what information was used to apply the criteria. The criteria and sources of information are discussed below.

Need

The first needs analysis was done by interviewing ten people who had recently returned from a visit to another country. Each interview took approximately three-quarters of an hour and required the interviewees to recall who they used the language with, in what situations, and what was said. After this open-ended interview each interviewee was asked to look through a list of words and phrases and to indicate whether they used any of the items in the list. This list was made by one of the researchers and was added to after each interview. This provided a good check on the information gained from the interview. All of the people interviewed were at a low level of proficiency in the language. Some had done a course before going to the foreign country; others had picked up what they could from phrasebooks and dictionaries. The countries visited included China, Italy, Japan, and Turkey.

The second needs analysis was done by surveying ten guidebooks which included lists of useful words and phrases. The guidebooks included some from the Lonely Planet series, Frommer's *Europe on $30 a Day*, Baedekker's *Japan*, APA Productions' *Thailand*, Cadogan's *Italy* and a range of other guides. Several guidebooks in the same series used the same list. In such cases the list was surveyed only once. Guidebooks were used because it was assumed that each one represented the experience of at least one well-traveled person. The information from the guidebooks was tabulated separately from the interview material, because guidebook lists can also contain items to consult in an emergency rather than to learn for everyday use.

An item was included in the first draft of the syllabus if it was mentioned by at least two of the people interviewed, or by one of the people as well as occurring in more than three of the guidebooks.

The third needs analysis involved one of the authors using the syllabus on extended visits to three different countries – Finland, Greece, and Thailand. During the visits (each longer than a month) a careful record was kept of what was used from the syllabus and what needed to be added.

Frequency

Frequency was checked by using Eaton's (1940) Word Frequency List, which collates the frequency of items in four European languages (English, French, German, and Spanish). Eaton found a very close correspondence in frequency level among the high-frequency words of those languages. For example 662 of the items which occurred in the most frequent 1,000 words of English corresponded to items in the most frequent 1,000 words of French, German and Spanish, and most of the remainder of the first 1,000 words of English occurred in the first and second 1,000 words of two of the three other languages in the study. The great majority of the words in the Survival Syllabus were in the first 1,000 words of Eaton's list. The age of the sources of Eaton's list accounts for some of the lower frequencies, such as *photo* (fourth 1,000) and *telephone* (fifth 1,000). Eaton's list is based on written text, which may account for the frequency of *Goodbye* (third 1,000). *Toilet* does not occur in Eaton's list!

Coverage and Combinability

Coverage is the capacity of a word to take the place of other words. A word which has good coverage can be used as a superordinate term in place of other words (*go* can be considered a superordinate of *run, walk, drive,* etc.), can be used to paraphrase or define other words (*thing* is an especially useful word in this respect), and can combine with other words to make new words (*foot* as in *footpath, football, footstep*). As Viberg (1989) shows, frequency is a close correlate of coverage. However, coverage can also be checked by comparing items in a list to see if one can replace others. This did not result in any changes to the syllabus, but it is a point to consider when the syllabus is translated into another language. For example, *How much?* in English can be used for both cost and quantity. It is more economical to learn this one item than two or three different ones.

Learnability

Higa (1963) investigated the effects on learning of the types of meaning relationships between words. He found that grouping synonyms, opposites, or free associates together made learning more difficult. The related items interfered with each other. The Survival Syllabus was checked to remove such items where they were not considered strictly necessary.

What the Syllabus does not Include

An item that only one person found very useful was not included. This is of course a reflection of the variation in circumstances in different countries, the variety of reasons why people go to another country, the variety of things that happen to them, and the many things they can do while they are there. Here are a few examples of excluded items: *Cheers! Are you married? I don't want meat* (for a vegetarian), *What is my size?* (for clothes), reporting a theft, dealing with illness, and talking to an official found searching your room. What is learned following this syllabus, therefore, will need to be supplemented by the use of phrasebooks and dictionaries to meet particular circumstances by almost all people who use it. But all the items in the appropriate sections of the syllabus will be worth learning and as a whole will put travelers over the threshold of initial communication.

Most people interviewed expressed the desire to be able to chat with people in the foreign country. This is an ambitious aim and is far beyond the goals of this syllabus. One of the people interviewed had studied the language for a total of more than 250 hours of class-time. In spite of this, he still found it very difficult to maintain conversations with three or more turns.

The Survival Syllabus

The syllabus has been divided into eight sections on the basis of information revealed during the interviews. The sections have been ranked and numbered according to the number of interviewees indicating that they used items in the sections divided by the number of items. So the section "Greetings and being polite" was the most useful one. Items which occur in more than one section are indicated by numbers in brackets. So, *I want* ... in Section 2 also occurs in Sections 5, 6, and 9. The slash (/) indicates alternatives.

1. Greetings and Being Polite

Hello/Good morning etc. + reply [there are many cultural variants of these, including *Where are you going?, Have you eaten?*]
How are you? + reply e.g. Fine, thank you.

Goodbye

Thank you + reply e.g. It's nothing, You're welcome.
Please

Excuse me [sorry]
It doesn't matter

Delicious (6)
Can I take your photo?

2. Buying and Bargaining

I want . . . (4, 6)
Do you have . . .?/Is there . . .?
Yes (8)
No (8)
This (one), That (one) [to use when pointing at goods]
There isn't any

How much (cost)? (5, 6)
A cheaper one (5)

NUMBERS (5, 7) (These need to be learned to a high degree of fluency)

UNITS OF MONEY (5, 6)

UNITS OF WEIGHT AND SIZE
How much (quantity)?
Half
All of it
(One) more
(One) less

Excuse me [to get attention] (4)

Too expensive
Can you lower the price? + reply (Some countries do not use bargaining. In others it is essential.)

NAMES OF IMPORTANT THINGS TO BUY (These may include stamps, a newspaper, a map.)

3. Reading Signs

Gents
Ladies

Entrance/In
Exit/Out
Closed

4. *Getting to Places*

Excuse me (to get attention) (2)
Can you help me?

Where is . . .? (5)
Where is . . . street?
What is the name of this place/street/station/town?

Toilet
Bank
Department store
Restaurant
Airport
Train station
Underground
Bus station
Hospital
Doctor
Police
Post office
Telephone
Market
I want . . . (2, 5, 6)
How far?/Is it near?
How long (to get to . . .)?

Left
Right
Straight ahead
Slow down (directions for a taxi)
Stop here
Wait

Ticket

When

5. *Finding Accommodation*

Where is . . .? (4)
Hotel

How much (cost)? (2, 6)
A cheaper one (2)

I want ... (2,4,6)
Leave at what time?
NUMBERS (2, 7)
Today
Tomorrow

6. Ordering Food

How much (cost)? (2, 5)
The bill, please

I want ... (2, 5, 9)

NAMES OF A FEW DISHES AND DRINKS

A FEW COOKING TERMS

Delicious (1)

7. Talking About Yourself and Talking to Children

I am (name)
Where do you come from?
I am (a New Zealander)/I come from (New Zealand)

What do you do?
I am a (teacher)/tourist

You speak (Chinese)!
A little/very little

What is your name? (Especially for talking to children)
How old are you? + reply
NUMBERS (2, 5)

I have been here ... days/weeks/months

I am sick

8. Controlling and Learning Language

Do you understand?
I (don't) understand
Do you speak English? (7)
Yes (2)
No (2)
Repeat
Please speak slowly
I speak only a little (Thai)

What do you call this in (Japanese)?

Organizing, Learning, Practicing

Clearly the syllabus simply identifies the knowledge or language resources required. The task of acquiring this knowledge in a way that would make it accessible in communicative situations is addressed briefly in this section. The following principles and suggestions are based in part on studies of the good language learner (Rubin, 1975; Rubin & Thompson, 1982; Naiman, Frohlich, Stern, & Todesco, 1978) and research on vocabulary learning (Nation, 1990).

Principle: Organize your Learning

Decide how many words or phrases can comfortably be learned each day. One effective way to learn the words and phrases in the list is to write them on small cards with a first-language translation on the other side. These are then carried in bundles of fifty or so and are looked through whenever there is a spare moment. First, the learner looks at each foreign word and phrase and tries to recall the translation, looking on the back of the card to see if the recall is correct. When this is easily done for a bundle, then the first-language items are looked at while trying to recall the foreign word or phrase.

Some care needs to be taken in grouping the items to be learned. Opposites like *exit/entrance, men/women, far/near, left/right* should not be learned together. This means that one of the items, say *exit*, should be learned first. When this has been learned satisfactorily the other item in the pair, *entrance*, can be studied. Similarly, words that are free associates or synonyms should not be learned together. Possible free associates in the Survival Syllabus include *bus/train*, names of foods, numbers, *today/tomorrow*, and *street/town*. This means it is more efficient to learn the numbers, for example, one by one and to group them in a series after they have been learned.

Principle: Learn Forms for Meanings Rather than Meanings for Forms

A basic principle behind all learning is that the quantity of learning depends on the quality of mental activity in the brain at the moment that learning occurs. This means that the more thoughtful and deep the learning activity, the faster and more secure the learning will be. The technique of using cards is one way of making learning deep because it encourages the learner to make an effort to recall the translation equivalent of each item. Another way to do this is to use the keyword technique or some variation of it. The research supporting these suggestions is reviewed in Nation (1982, 1990). In learning words and phrases it is particularly important to focus on meaning and visualize it in some way. Say the form as you do this. For example you may be learning how to say "too expensive." Imagine yourself in a market holding a piece of local cloth, looking at the trader and wanting to pay less than the price suggested. With that image in your mind, say the words "too expensive."

Principle: Get as much Practice as you Can

Learning the items in the Survival Syllabus does not guarantee that they will be available for use. To develop fluency, practice is needed. The essential element of fluency practice is that the learner should focus on the meaning of the message as suggested above and that there should be several repetitions of the activity.

It is particularly important that numbers can be dealt with fluently. Number dictation, where a speaker says a number and the learner writes it in figures rather than words, is an effective activity. This should be done many times and with increasing speed.

When a traveler arrives in the country there will of course be further and more meaningful opportunities for practice. The more practice there is beforehand, however, the faster the learning can be put to use.

Some Final Comments

This syllabus is reductionist in nature. Communication, even initial communication, is a complex phenomenon and the syllabus, like all content-based syllabuses, reduces that to a set of discrete items. Based on experience, however, we believe that by learning these discrete items, a traveler will be able to enter the complexity of initial communicative contact and have a sound starting point for further language learning if desired.

The syllabus is clearly oriented towards production. A traveler needs to maintain the initiative in communication and has little chance of playing a responding role in any extensive communication.

The main criteria of need should make the meanings in the syllabus applicable to all travelers, no matter what language is involved, although the specific items chosen would need fine-tuning for each language according to the other criteria. The phrases and words chosen are resources used in English to get a meaning across. Other languages may use different means. For example, "Excuse me" to get attention may in some languages simply require an honorific such as the equivalents of "Sir" or "Madam." For this reason, any translation of the syllabus into other languages should work from the functional meanings of the expressions and not the literal meanings.

Finally the authors would be interested to hear from anyone who tries out this list of resources in a new language experience.

Acknowledgement

My contribution to this chapter was completed while I was a visiting professor in the Department of English, Åbo Akademi, Åbo, Finland under a grant from the H.W. Donner trust. I am grateful for this generous support (Paul Nation).

References

Dickie, J. (1989). A case study of a language learner (unpublished course material). Wellington, New Zealand: Victoria University of Wellington.

Eaton, H.S. (1940). *An English-French-German-Spanish word frequency dictionary.* New York: Dover.

Higa, M. (1963). Interference effects of interlist word relationships in verbal learning. *Journal of Verbal Learning and Verbal Behaviour, 2,* 170–175.

Munby, J. (1978). *Communicative syllabus design.* Cambridge, UK: Cambridge University Press.

Naiman, N., Frohlich, M., Stern, H. & Todesco, A. (1978). *The good language learner.* Toronto, Canada: OISE.

Nation, I.S.P. (1982). Beginning to learn foreign vocabulary: a review of the research. *RELC Journal, 13,* 14–36.

Nation, I.S.P. (1990). *Teaching and learning vocabulary.* Boston, MA: Heinle Cengage Learning.

Pimsleur, P. (1980). *How to learn a foreign language.* Boston, MA: Heinle and Heinle.

Rivers, W.M. (1981). *Teaching foreign language skills* (2nd ed.). Chicago, IL: University of Chicago Press.

Rubin, J. (1975). What the good language learner can teach us. *TESOL Quarterly, 9,* 41–54.

Rubin, J. & Thompson, I. (1982). *Be a more successful language learner.* Boston, MA: Heinle and Heinle.

Schumann, F.M. (1980). Diary of a language learner: a further analysis. In Krashen, S.D. & Scarcella, R.C. (Eds.), *Issues in second language research* (pp. 51–57). New York, NY: Newbury House.

Van Ek, J.A. & Alexander, L.G. (1975). *Threshold level English.* Oxford, UK: Pergamon Press.

Van Ek, J.A., Alexander, L.G. & Fitzpatrick, M.A. (1977). *Waystage English.* Oxford, UK: Pergamon Press.

Viberg, A. (1989). A semantic field approach to vocabulary acquisition. (unpublished paper).

Comment

As noted in the introductory chapter, this case study has become something of a classic and, while it is the only case study in this collection that does not draw on recent curriculum design experience, is included here because of its clear demonstration of the curriculum design model. It also shows the dynamic nature of curriculum design, with one of the authors trialing the syllabus in different countries. While it would be a shame to lose such phrases as *We will take tea on the verandah* from phrasebooks available for travelers, if only for their entertainment value, there is no question but that a well-designed course such as this would meet the needs of modern-day travelers far better.

Tasks

1. This case study provides information about most parts of the course design model outlined in Chapter 1. Read the chapter again and analyze it in those terms.

TABLE 2.3

Parts of the course design process	Nation and Crabbe's procedure
Environment analysis	
Needs analysis	
Application of principles	
Goals	
Content and sequencing	
Format and presentation	
Monitoring and assessment	Not dealt with
Evaluation	

2. At the start of this curriculum design, Paul Nation and David Crabbe did a quick survey of introductory course books and found that the syllabus content was generally unsuitable for the type of learners they had in mind. Choose one or two recently published introductory course books, and examine the content of the first six chapters. Would recently published introductory course books meet the goal of quickly learning the survival vocabulary identified in this chapter?

3

DESIGN MEETING CONTEXT: A GENERAL ENGLISH COURSE FOR BURMESE ADULTS

Katie Julian and Derek Foster

> The further away the author is from the learners, the less effective the material is likely to be. (Jolly & Bolitho, 1998, p. 111)

Holliday (1994), Ellis (1996) and Jarvis and Atsilarat (2004), among others, address the question of appropriate contextualization. This is also discussed in Bax (2003a, 2003b), who argues for an approach that puts context at the centre of language teaching, and in the ecological approach recommended by Tudor (2002), which looks at the "various human and contextual factors which influence the use and likely effectiveness of the technology" – the approach, methodology, materials, and resources by which a course is designed and delivered.

In the past few years, context has been gaining ground as an important factor in English language curriculum development. Unfortunately, publishers are yet to catch up with this trend, presumably since commercial imperatives often work to the detriment of those who may benefit the most from a context-based approach – students and teachers in low-resource environments. These users, less likely to have the capacity to set up curriculum development and materials writing projects, are more likely to rely on (cheaply printed or photocopied editions of) international titles.

Bax (2003a, 2003b) discusses the issues involved in applying methodology to context. Methodology-driven and language-driven approaches to course design deprioritize context in their assumption that the *right* method, structural sequence, or lexis is what is required for successful language learning, regardless of the peculiarities of the situation. Even worse is the implication of context-neutrality often alluded to in the promotional blurbs of global commercial course materials, as in the following examples:

> *English for Life* recognises the international use of English. The **themes and characters** reflect situations that are **meaningful to everyone**. Contexts are chosen from a wide range of countries, not just the English speaking world.
>
> (Hutchinson, 2007, p. 6, original emphasis)

> *Language in Use* takes account of the fact that no two language classes are alike: students vary in level, ages and interest, and may have different cultural and learning backgrounds; classes vary in size, physical layout and formality; teachers have different teaching styles; and learners may have widely differing ideas about what and how they need to learn.
>
> (Doff & Jones, 1999, p. 3b)

While these are two of the less culture-bound series, they nevertheless contain much that many students in low-resource contexts would find irrelevant and perhaps confusing, such as people famous only in the West, opening a bank account, holidaying by plane, and features of a middle-class Western-style house. Also, the books are very expensive and the images do not photocopy clearly, the teacher's notes are in high-level English, and the methodology is confusing for teachers not immersed in the communicative language teaching (CLT) tradition.

Appropriate curricular training support is often beyond the means of many in the "expanding circle" of countries where English is not widely used as a second language other than by the urban elites (Kachru, 1985). Thus, low-resource countries such as Burma are in danger of being left behind in Graddol's (2006) influential World English Project, which predicts a scenario where English is a basic skill learned – not as a foreign language, but as a global lingua franca – from primary school. Other political, economic, and educational factors influencing this lack of support in the Burma context are too wide and varied for the scope of this chapter; a quick snapshot is presented in the next section.

Burma and its Diaspora: A Snapshot

Burma has been ruled by a military regime since the early 1960s. Every few years Burma makes international news headlines when sectors of its beleaguered population – students in 1988, monks in 2007 – attempt to express their discontent with this situation. The military's reaction has inevitably been to brutally suppress such expression, with substantial loss of life. The regime is also known for its disdain for international human rights norms, economic ineptitude, unbridled corruption, and negligible health and education spending. Many of Burma's ethnic minorities – most famously the Karen and Shan – have been engaged in a long-running civil war on Burma's mountainous borderlands. These adverse living conditions have resulted in millions of Burmese leaving Burma as political asylum seekers, refugees, and economic migrants.

Upwards of four million Burmese are living in neighboring countries: Thailand, India, China, Malaysia, and Bangladesh. Some are political asylum seekers, some are economic migrants, and some are fleeing war and ethnic persecution on Burma's borders. In Thailand these communities have variously established a government in exile, a number of ethnic-based de facto government departments, refugee camps, a thriving NGO scene, international lobbying mechanisms, networks of schools, clinics and welfare services, and a range of cross-border humanitarian support programs. The Thai government tacitly tolerates most of these most of the time.

The Curriculum Project and *General English*[1]

The Curriculum Project (CP) was formed in 2001 to develop curricula, materials, and teacher training to meet the needs of adult and post-secondary students from Burma. At that time, CP was working with three post-secondary schools[2] based in Karen and Karenni refugee camps,[3] and initial needs assessment focused on their requirements. These schools stated their most urgent need as being context-appropriate English teaching materials, as commercial materials available were very US and UK focused, and difficult to use in low-resource environments. Diagnostic testing indicated that early pre-intermediate[4] level was the most suitable place to start. As these schools were already using Cambridge University Press's *Language in Use Pre-intermediate*, it was decided that the most efficient way to get materials to these schools quickly was to design supplements to that course. These were released, module by module, from May 2002. By May 2004, 12

---

[1] Print copies of *General English* are available on request, and it can be downloaded free of charge at www.curriculumproject.org, along with CP's other ELT, social science, maths, and science materials.

[2] Post-secondary schools have been set up on Burma's borders as further studies options for high school graduates. Some are academic in focus, others vocational, and others have been set up by youth, religious and women's groups as training institutions for their constituents. As of May 2010, there were 43 of these on the Thailand–Burma border.

[3] The Karen are an ethnic group who have been fighting the Burmese military since 1948. They make up the majority of the populations of official refugee camps. The Karen Education Department functions as a government department for Karen communities in camps and in the parts of Karen State not under the control of the military junta. The Karenni are a smaller ethnic group in a similar situation. Political activists from Central Burma, and other ethnic groups such as the Shan and Mon, are not currently permitted to establish their own refugee camps in Thailand, so those fleeing Burma join the migrant worker population.

[4] There is no objective, universally accepted definition of 'pre-intermediate', but it roughly corresponds to the following standard measures of proficiency: A2–B1 on the Common European Frameworks; IELTS level 3; TOEFL score of 96–125 (http://en.wikipedia.org/wiki/Common_European_Framework_of_Reference_for_Languages, Thornbury, 2006).

General English modules, adapting and supplementing aspects of the *Language in Use* syllabus, had been completed.

Soon other schools and non-formal adult education programs were requesting this resource, so a stand-alone course was required. The modules were thus rewritten to obviate the need to teach them in parallel with *Language in Use*. In 2006 CP decided to edit the *General English* course for use inside Burma. As the Burmese government keeps tight control over print material used by their citizens, topics and language they may regard as subversive were taken out, and place names were changed to reflect official protocol.[5] This was necessary so as not to create problems for those using the book. Every attempt was made to keep a critical thinking and world knowledge focus, and to keep the content useful to the border community, many of whom are involved in overt anti-government activism.

Environment Analysis

> To achieve appropriacy we must investigate, try to understand, and then address whichever social context we are working in.
>
> (Holliday, 1994)

It may seem somewhat anomalous to go for a context-based approach – an approach usually characterized by principles of specific situational analysis – to the design of a coursebook intended for wide use in a relatively large number of different situations. Bell and Gower (1998) caution that situation-specific materials may discourage adaptation for particular groups of students. Nevertheless, we decided there was enough consistency of environment and needs (discussed later in this chapter) among our target groups to justify the development of a single course for them, so long as we made it as flexible as realistically possible.

Nation and Macalister (2010, pp. 16–17), Cunningsworth (1995, pp. 3–4, 149–50) and Richards (2001) provide useful checklists of environmental factors to inform and evaluate course design. The full list we adopted is extensive, and is summarized in Table 3.1.

Student Factors

General English's target audience is a broad range of students from Burma, namely any adult who has acquired an upper elementary level of English.

---

[5] Myanmar is the official government name for the country. Rangoon has been renamed Yangon, and a number of other place names were changed. Inflammatory terms such as "democracy" and "human rights" must be avoided, so rephrasing was required to retain key concepts.

TABLE 3.1 Questions asked in environment analysis

Student factors	What are their current language proficiencies?
	What are their prior language learning experiences?
	What are their interests?
	What are their expectations of the course?
	In what circumstances do they use English?
	What, and how strong, are their motivations for learning English?
	What lifestyle factors influence their study (time, work, etc.)?
	What beliefs and theories do they have about language teaching and learning?
Teacher factors	How much input do they have on curriculum, syllabus or materials selection and use?
	What training have they had?
	What is their English proficiency?
	How open are they to change?
	What lifestyle factors influence their teaching?
	What beliefs and attitudes do they have about language teaching and learning?
Situation factors	What are the current national/community language teaching policies, and how are they implemented?
	What impact will it have on different sectors of the communities who will use it?
	What are the physical environments in which the course will be delivered?
	What timeframe will the course be taught in?
	What is the relationship between the course and overall curricula?
	What language learning experience and traditions exist in the country?
	What are the views of relevant professionals?
	What are the views of employers, community groups and further studies programs where graduates of the course will go on to?
	What resources – human, financial and physical – are available to programs using the course?
Project factors	What are the underlying reasons for the project and who supports it?
	What resources – human, financial and physical – are available to the project?
	How much ongoing support can the project give to programs using the course?
	What research is relevant and accessible to the project?
	What beliefs and theories do project members have about language teaching and learning?

Some common characteristics of these students (although there are significant exceptions) include:

- having acquired an upper-elementary level of English, either through formal English language instruction or using English in daily and working life. The majority of pre-intermediate level students will have completed high school; many have Bachelor's degrees from Burmese universities.

- being familiar with grammar/translation methodology with an emphasis on rote-learning. Burmese school textbooks cover highly complex grammar points early on, and students are perceived as knowing them if they are able to reproduce the rules governing their form.
- having had limited exposure to the world beyond Burma or the border. Inside Burma, media censorship is tight and contact with visitors restricted. Refugee camps in Thailand do not allow unofficial visitors, and refugees are not normally allowed to travel outside the camps. Many programs are located in communities without electricity, computers, or telephones.

Questionnaires, discussions, and focus groups indicated a wide range of reasons for studying English: a desire to access higher education in English, employment in the service sector (particularly tourism), emigration to English speaking countries, understanding international media, and international lobbying were among the most common.

"The exploration of local cultures of learning" (Cortazzi and Jin, 1996), i.e. "students' habitual mode of learning, favoured study strategies, and their general ethos of study and learning, as well as the beliefs, attitudes, and expectations which underpin these behaviours" (Tudor, 2002) indicated dissatisfaction with the predominant (and required) methods used in primary-high school and reinforced in universities and private tuition classes inside Burma – rote memorization of prescribed texts, along with the answers to form-focused and comprehension questions. There is, however, widespread mistrust of techniques seen to emphasize fun at the expense of rigor. Explicit learning of grammatical forms is viewed by many as the cornerstone of a useful language learning experience.

Teacher Factors

In recent years more international assistance has been flowing into Burma and its borders, with an increase in the number of training opportunities for teachers, particularly working with migrant and refugee populations, monastery school networks, and urban community groups. These training workshops are usually run by expatriate trainers using language teaching methodologies developed in Britain, North America, and Australasia. Holliday (1994) points out that almost all the internationally established literature on English language education is published in these countries. This can have undesirable results, as the following comment from a CP trainer makes clear.

> I was puzzled by my senior teacher trainees' initial insistence on demon- strating activities requiring a lot of movement, noise, and competition, with only a tenuous relation to the lesson outcomes. When I asked them if they

would actually use these in their (large, fixed seated) classrooms, they indicated that this wouldn't be possible, but they thought that was what *student-centered, communicative* teaching was all about – what the foreign trainer wanted to see.

Teachers in Burma and along the border fall into four loose categories:

- Career educators aiming for best practice in their teaching. These teachers want to see clear progress from their students, are eager to explore different teaching techniques and are receptive to new ideas. Some have had formal teacher training either in-country or overseas. These teachers often start their own projects, or obtain responsible positions in NGOs and community schools.
- Those who are not teaching by choice. In many communities, educated people are expected to teach, as there are acute teacher shortages. As most teaching jobs are poorly paid, many hold down several jobs. With family and community responsibilities as well, lesson planning, marking assignments, and ongoing professional development are not high on their list of priorities.
- Experienced teachers who are skeptical of modern methodology. These teachers have had successful learning experiences themselves using more traditional approaches, often at mission-run schools prior to the military takeover in 1962. Many of these teachers hold senior positions in government schools and universities.
- Foreigners: volunteers or employees of NGOs and private language schools, with varying levels of experience and qualifications.

For every class where the enthusiastic, well-prepared, reflective, proficient English-using teacher works with a class of highly motivated, self-aware students, there are many more teachers with limited English proficiency, a skeptical attitude to unfamiliar teaching techniques, and neither the time nor the inclination to prepare lessons, working with classes who have little intrinsic interest in learning English.

Situation Factors [6]

English language learning is compulsory in Burma from kindergarten through to high school. In high school and at university, most subjects officially use English as the medium of instruction. In practice, this usually means that teachers explain the material in Burmese, and students rote-learn the English texts and repeat them verbatim in examinations. It is not unusual for students to graduate from

---

[6] For a comprehensive analysis of Burma's general education and of English language instruction traditions and beliefs see Thein Lwin (2007), Crismore (2002), and Maran Roi Ja (2007).

FIGURE 3.1 Post-secondary school in rural Karen State, Burma

university with only a very limited grasp of spoken English. All government schools and universities are tightly controlled, and there are few opportunities for outsiders to engage with them.

In Burma there are a number of independent language programs, which include small classes operating from teachers' houses, very large free or low-cost community-based classes, and courses offered by international organizations such as the British Council. CP prioritizes working with community-based not-for-profit classes, although our materials are made available to all. In addition, CP works with three independent, missionary-sponsored tertiary institutions, which are not subject to the same regulation or oversight as government ones.

Thailand has hosted political exiles from Burma since the 1960s, with the most recent wave entering Thailand in the wake of the 2007 uprising, and many belong to groups engaged in activism, development, and education. The Thai authorities tolerate their presence, but there is a constant fear of raids, imprisonment, and possible deportation to Burma. These groups view English proficiency as an essential skill needed to bring about positive social change in Burma.

On the Thailand–Burma border CP works with two main types of program: English classes set up by political exile organizations, and post-secondary schools based in refugee camps and in migrant communities. Six of the latter have standardized curricula under the jurisdiction of the Karen Education Department. The other thirty-plus are variously run by community, youth, women's, and religious groups. They aim to compensate for perceived shortfalls in the primary-high school system, equipping students with the skills they need to become effective community workers and/or access the limited tertiary study opportunities available. In most schools teachers are currently free to choose their own curricula, although there are moves to standardize this in line with Thai national frameworks.

All are funded externally, to varying degrees. Most camps have limited, expensive, and officially proscribed access to telephones and the Internet. Movement in and out of the camps is tightly restricted by the Thai authorities. Much of the camp population, particularly the more educated, is in the process of resettling to the US, Europe, and Australasia. The migrant population is very mobile, with high teacher and student turnover.

Most of these programs use English as a medium of instruction in content areas, as well as having English language instruction as one or more subjects. The rationale for using English to teach content, and problems associated with this, are discussed extensively in O'Brien (2004), Sproat (2004), Haikin (2007) and Thein Lwin (2007).

Currently, neither refugee nor migrant school graduates receive accredited qualifications, which is a major issue for them. Although the Thai education system is open to these communities at primary and middle school level, few students are sufficiently proficient in Thai. Both migrant and refugee post-secondary schools' policy is that all high school education should be English-medium; in practice few teachers and students have the language proficiency to enact this.

In the majority of English classes, the coursebook provides the prescribed or selected curriculum, syllabus, and materials. Some teachers are most comfortable teaching it from page 1 through to page 184; others will adapt, omit, and supplement.

Within the programs CP works with, both inside Burma and on the border, there is a wide range of physical conditions. Some common characteristics are crowded classrooms, fixed seating, and limited human and physical resources. Many schools and programs do not have electricity, and very few have computers on-site. Although CP works with a small number of well-resourced programs, the decision was taken to develop the course with the needs of the less-well-resourced in mind, in line with the aims of our project and the needs of the majority.

Project Factors

The Curriculum Project is a branch of Thabyay Education Network, which works to build the capacity of individuals within marginalized groups from all Myanmar's nationalities. Through the provision of integrated higher education services, Thabyay aims to equip these individuals with the knowledge, skills, attitudes, qualifications, and networks necessary to work effectively for social justice, human development, and reconciliation in Burma (Thabyay Education Network, 2009). Due to these goals, and those of funders and other key external stakeholders, the focus selected was English for community development, ethnic reconciliation, and positive social change in Burma.

Project factors have played an important role. First drafts of the course were researched, compiled, and implemented by one person, with assistance from two other project staff primarily engaged in other projects. By the third draft the project had acquired sufficient funding for an editor, a part-time illustrator, and an

FIGURE 3.2 Teacher Training Workshop, Karenni Refugee Camp, 2006

outreach worker with the remit to collect ongoing feedback and suggestions from teachers, students, and other stakeholders. Significant gaps in the expertise of project members included specialist knowledge of particular language areas, layout and design skills, IT, and audio engineering skills.

The extent to which CP is able to offer ongoing teacher and program support varies greatly from class to class and from year to year. Many users of *General English*, especially inside Burma and in areas difficult to access, have no contact with CP after receiving the materials. At the other extreme, some programs receive regular and extensive curriculum advice, monitoring, and teacher training.

Needs Analysis

Aims and Methods

The needs of our target groups were assessed primarily to identify the gap between what students are able to do and what they need to be able to do; this information would then inform the design of our own materials. However, further aims were to determine the extent to which existing courses adequately address these needs, and to provide us with evidence to justify our choice of language, content, skills, and sequencing to decision-makers who often themselves are grounded in a tradition of learning by rote, and as successful students are disinclined to change.

It would perhaps be misleading to describe this process as *a* needs assessment since it was carried out over many years and took many forms. One of the most influential components was CP's comprehensive diagnostic testing of students entering Post 10 programs in 2007. This process is discussed extensively in Julian and Foster (2007), and the results went some way to persuading unbelievers that pre-intermediate level was about right, indeed perhaps a little high, for the average 10th standard graduate. Other formal and semi-formal methods included teacher and student questionnaires, observing trainees in CP's teacher training workshops, observing classes, team-teaching, examining samples of students' work, gathering and analyzing data from written tests, interviewing teachers and students, analyzing textbooks commonly used by teachers in the target group, and surveying the available academic literature on relevant topics.

In addition, we spent much time over several years chatting to teachers, students, and other stakeholders, holding ad hoc meetings on related topics, and teaching English classes to our target groups. Such informal assessment may have had as much, or even greater, influence over the eventual content of the course.

Key Results

The assessment unsurprisingly highlighted a fairly diverse, and at times conflicting, range of needs across our target groups. In some cases the needs were not even immediately apparent, it being unclear in what circumstances certain groups of students would actually have to use English. Moreover, as the target groups for the course expanded and shifted since the first drafts of the course were written – the main change being a greater focus on community classes inside Myanmar as well as migrant, exile, and refugee communities on the border – goals, content, and techniques were reshaped a number of times.

Nevertheless, it was possible to identify a number of common threads. Prior learning usually focused on formulaic reading and writing, with an emphasis on correct production of grammatical form. Therefore, oral skills, wider reading and writing, usage, and fluency were seen as priorities. More fundamentally, rather than Auerbach's "neutral transfer of skills, knowledge or competencies," which acts in the interests of social institutions and ignores issues of power (1995, as cited in Richards 2001), educational needs assessment among Burmese communities has consistently indicated the need for curricula that encourage critical thinking, questioning, and greater awareness of local and global issues (Thein Lwin, 2007; Haikin, 2007; Thabyay, 2009). Indeed, many classes explicitly attempt to combine English language learning with development of critical thinking skills and understanding of important social issues.

As the target groups for the course are changing, goals, content, and techniques have been reshaped and redesigned since the first drafts of the course were written. Needs assessment is an ongoing process, and informs course evaluation feeding into future drafts of *General English*.

Challenges in Understanding the Context

Our assessment fell short of the ideal in a number of ways. Many important stakeholders were not included, or not to an adequate extent, due to communication or access difficulties. Some live in areas decreed off-limits by the relevant range of authorities.[7] Some are engaged in political activities which make contact too risky. Others live in places too remote to access easily. Their needs were often described by a third party or assumed; for example, one can easily assume that those living in remote rural areas do not want course components that require electricity to operate or pre-suppose familiarity with the Internet. The range of opinions canvassed was therefore narrower than desired.

To a large extent anecdotal evidence as to needs was biased in that some types of stakeholders had more influence than others. It was a challenge to extract meaningful comments from the majority of our core target group, partly due to the culture of deference towards those perceived to be in a position of authority, but also because many felt – accurately or otherwise – that they did not possess adequate knowledge or experience to make informed judgments on these matters. At the other extreme, one particularly influential group was foreign teachers – both volunteers and paid staff – working with Burmese educational and exile organizations. These people were more likely to have the time, confidence, and educational background required to offer opinions. As these are not a primary target group, we had to be careful not to give their views disproportionate weight, but the dearth of informative contributions from our core target group led to undesirably heavy reliance on such people.

Many teachers and other educational decision-makers had strong opinions about the levels their students should be studying which were at variance with the target students' proficiencies indicated by diagnostic testing. Some examples of views expressed:

> Students who have finished 10th standard should be studying at upper intermediate level.
> They have already done the present simple tense. They need to learn harder tenses.
> We need international level English so students can get into international universities.

Moreover, it must be borne in mind that needs are neither homogenous nor static. All stakeholders may have different views on what these needs comprise, and course designers must decide which stakeholders to prioritize. The needs of any given individual or group may also change in response to circumstances. For example, as large-scale resettlement took hold in the refugee camps on the border, the priorities of many students shifted from the language needed to work for Thailand-based NGOs and community-based organizations (CBOs) to that

---

[7]   Many programs are situated in areas where Burmese government forces and ethnic resistance groups are fighting, or under the shaky control of ceasefire groups. Access to these areas is tightly restricted.

which would be most useful for living and working in the west. Inside Burma, some students' work ambitions changed after Cyclone Nargis from, say, waiting tables at a restaurant in Singapore to assisting an INGO's relief and development operations.

Implementation

Principles

Underlying principles behind the development of *General English* were informed as far as possible by relevant research and expert opinion (particularly Nation & Macalister, 2010; Brown, 2001; Cunningsworth, 1995), modified by the specific needs and operating environment of the target audience. Aside from generalizable principles applicable to all good course design (e.g. Nation & Macalister, 2010, pp. 38–9), we specifically added the following:

- The course must be adaptable to and accessible in the range of situations in which it may be used. (Flexibility was key in the development of the course, given the wide range of environments, timeframes, teacher capacities, and resource availability of programs using the course.)
- The benefits and outcomes of the overall course, each unit and each activity must be clearly communicable to stakeholders. (Many teachers, students, and educational decision-makers have little confidence in unfamiliar method-ology (see Maran Roi Ja, 2007). Making the aims and rationale explicit throughout the course helps assuage this lack of confidence, and encourages teachers to select those parts most suitable to their situation. This consider-ation had to be balanced, however, with concerns of space and size. Although the approach taken would fall well within the CLT spectrum, it has taken elements from many approaches, and might be criticized for being overly eclectic (Brown, 2001).)
- The course must be self-contained. (In many cases, the course (and resulting teacher and student talk) is the only exposure to English available to the students. Therefore, it needs to be longer and more comprehensive in coverage than other courses of this type and to not require access to outside sources of input, output, or interaction.)

Content and Sequencing

As a result of these principles and the needs and environment analyses, the following decisions about the content of the course were made.

- Topics were selected based on the preferences of key stakeholders. While the majority of the course comprises the functional, day-to-day language that is unavoidable at this level, world knowledge, environmental, historical, and developmental issues are the focus of reading and listening texts and discussion activities. There is relatively little about celebrities, holidays, and teenage lifestyles.

- The structural syllabus was largely adapted from published courses, with particular elements added at the request of teachers and on analysis of areas of English language learning which people from Burma find difficult. For example, some pronunciation sections were designed to address the specific difficulties native speakers of Burmese (and some Burmese ethnic minority languages) often have when speaking English, such as sounding final consonants.

- Units of progress are structures and vocabulary, as opposed to the currently more respected outcomes, functions, or skills, as it was felt any other approach might prove too different from what teachers were used to (Maran Roi Ja, 2007). Grammar is treated in more detail than in most other general English courses as teachers and students are comfortable with this. However, there is more emphasis on use than form, in contrast to most students' previous experience of form-focused study.

- Diagnostic testing of key target groups informed the starting level of the course, which is a little lower than most other pre-intermediate courses.

- There is a heavy vocabulary load, which is listed at the end of each unit. This was provided to allow review of essential elementary-level words that students may have forgotten or never learned, and to allow coverage of more "worthy" issues without sacrificing core pre-intermediate language. Students and/or teachers can opt to spend more or less time on this, depending on class or individual needs.

- Attention was paid to ensuring students get rich exposure to key vocabulary and structures, which were recycled throughout the book.

- Each unit has a learner training section that looks at language learning and communication strategies and encourages a reflective approach to the learning process.

- Western sociolinguistic and cultural norms are treated as new information and explained in either the Teacher's or the Student's Book.

- The Teacher's Book includes extra activities, alternative activities for large classes with fixed seating, and provides guidance as to what can be omitted. No timing is suggested, as there is so much variation in teaching styles and frequency and duration of classes and courses.

- A variety of accents – native, expert and learner – were used in the audio recordings, reflecting the likelihood that most real-life English language interaction in Burma, the border, and places Burmese people are likely to migrate to does not involve native speakers.

Module Eleven

going to – the future – arrangements – geography – agreeing and disagreeing –
no + where/thing/one – word endings – argument – thinking about grammar

1. Future Plans

1.1 What are you going to do?

A. Look at this picture. These people are planning their futures. One is thinking of the short-term future, one is thinking of the medium-term future, and one is thinking of the long-term future. Which is which?

B. These people are also thinking of their futures. What are they going to do? Think of some ideas.

When I graduate, I'm going to...

Soon we're going to...

When I get out of here, I'm going to...

After the baby's born, I'm going to...

11.1 **C.** Listen to the audio. Were you correct?

41 Module 11

FIGURE 3.3 A page from the coursebook

Coursebook Format

Cost was a key factor in the design. Most programs CP works with have limited funding, and CP has a relatively small budget to give sets to programs for free. We therefore decided against some of the numerous components included in many published courses. *General English* has only one book for students, with workbook-like exercises at the end of each unit and revision material and a grammar reference at the end. The Teacher's Book contains placement and unit tests, and is interleaved with the body of the student's book material for ease of use (with the unfortunate consequence that the Teacher's Book is a cumbersome 523 A4 pages, and costs around twice as much to produce as a non-interleaved book). The accompanying CD contains audio in MP3 format, playable on almost all machines. The course is available either as one complete 12-unit course or in three parts of four units each.

Ease of reproduction by users was another factor. There are no color images or text (except on the covers), and line drawings were used rather than photographs where practical, which improves the quality of photocopying as well as keeping costs down. The CD includes PDF copies of both books, plus a number of CP's other resources, as well as the audio, and we actively encourage independent adaptation, printing, copying, and distribution. Editable versions of the course (in Adobe InDesign) are available on request.

Concerns

While the project can be considered a success overall, the finished product has a number of shortcomings. Some of these were unavoidable given the context; some were errors of judgment on the part of the writers; and many were caused in large part by the difficulties of operating with such limited resources.

- The course is significantly longer than commercial textbooks. Some structures and functions are covered in extensive, and arguably unnecessary, detail.
- The somewhat haphazard development process has led to parts of the course lacking: (a) consistency (in terms of the amount of focus given to each point, or the style of presentation), particularly the structural and functional syllabi; (b) completeness (i.e. the coverage of points expected in courses of this kind), particularly the reading and pronunciation syllabi; or (c) adequate integration into the rest of the course, particularly the pronunciation syllabus.
- As CP cannot afford to hire professional actors or audio engineers, the audio recordings are of varying quality.
- Many teachers may find it difficult to change their teaching style to the extent required in order to use this course effectively, or may be resistant to doing so.
- Many teachers will lack the language skills to give adequate feedback and mark open-ended activities, and in some cases even to understand instruc-

tions and explanations given in the Teacher's Book. It is difficult within the available space to give comprehensive guidance to teachers with very low English language proficiency.

Future Directions

Teacher support, training and evaluation of *General English Pre-intermediate* are ongoing, with a view to a future re-edit when funding and project resources allow. *General English Elementary* is in the planning and drafting stages, and is a focus for CP throughout 2010 and 2011, with beginner and intermediate levels scheduled for the more distant future depending on availability of personnel and funding.

In addition, supplementary materials on extensive reading and writing, persuasive writing skills, using movies in the classroom, and a guide to language learning activities have been produced, and a teaching skills curriculum designed to be taught by trainers in remote communities is in process. CP welcomes ELT professionals wishing to become involved with our projects.

References

Bax, S. (2003a). The end of CLT: A context approach to language teaching. *ELT Journal, 57*(3), 278–287.

Bax, S. (2003b). Bringing context and methodology together. *ELT Journal, 57*(3), 295–296.

Bell, J. and Gower, R. (1998). Writing course materials for the world: A great compromise. In B. Tomlinson (Ed.), *Materials development in language teaching.* Cambridge, UK: Cambridge University Press.

Brown, H.D. (2001). *Teaching by principles: An interactive approach to language pedagogy.* New York, NY: Longman.

Cortazzi, M. and Jin, L. (1996) in Tudor, I. (2002). Learning to live with complexity: towards an ecological perspective on language teaching. *System, 31*(1), 1–12.

Crismore, A. (2002). Perspectives on teaching English in Burma today and yesterday. *Asian Englishes, 5*(2), 58–63.

Cunningsworth, A. (1995). *Choosing your coursebook.* Oxford, UK: Heinemann.

Doff, A. and Jones, C. (1999). *Language in use beginner.* Cambridge, UK: Cambridge University Press.

Ellis, G. (1996). How culturally appropriate is the communicative approach? *ELT Journal, 50*(3), 213–218.

Graddol, D. (2006). *English next.* London, UK: British Council.

Haikin, M. (2007). Curriculum beyond borders (unpublished doctoral dissertation). Royal Melbourne Institute of Technology, Melbourne, Australia.

Holliday, A. (1994). *Appropriate methodology and social context.* Cambridge, UK: Cambridge University Press.

Hutchinson, T. (2007). *English for life elementary teacher's book.* Oxford, UK: Oxford University Press.

Jarvis, H. & Atsilarat, S. (2004). Shifting paradigms: from a communicative to a context-based approach. *Asian EFL Journal, 6*(4), 1–23. Retrieved October 13 2010 from <http://www.asian-efl-journal.com/Dec_04_HJ&SA.pdf>.

Jolly, D. & Bolitho, R. (1998). A framework for materials development. In B. Tomlinson (Ed.), *Materials development in language teaching* (pp. 90 – 116). Cambridge, UK: Cambridge University Press.

Julian, K. & Foster, D. (2007). Post-10 education on the border: English language proficiency of entry-level students. *School Education Research Journal, 5*, 121–138. Retrieved October 13 2010 from <http://www.nhecburma.org/publications/Education/PDF/SERJ5.pdf>.

Kachru, B.B. (1985). Standards, codification and sociolinguistic realism: The English language in the outer circle. In R. Quirk & H.G. Widdowson (Eds.), *English in the world: Teaching and learning the language and literatures* (pp. 11–30). Cambridge, UK: Cambridge University Press.

Maran Roi Ja (2007). Teaching English to Kachin youths in the Kachin area. *School Education Research Journal, 5*, 113–121. National Health and Education Committee. Retrieved October 13 2010 from <http://www.nhecburma.org/publications/Education/PDF/SERJ5.pdf>.

Nation, I.S.P. & Macalister, J. (2010). *Language curriculum design.* New York, NY: Routledge.

O'Brien, S. (2004). *Karen perspectives on schooling in their communities: Indigenous knowledge and Western models of education.* Toronto, Canada: University of Toronto.

Richards, J. (2001). *Curriculum development in language teaching.* Cambridge, UK: Cambridge University Press.

Sproat, R. (2004). Language use and policy in a linguistically fragmented refugee community (unpublished master's thesis). Macquarie University, Sydney, Australia.

Thabyay Education Network (2009). *Annual Report July 2008 – June 2009.* Chiang Mai, Thailand: Thabyay Education Network.

Thein Lwin (2007). *Education and democracy in Burma: Decentralization and classroom-level educational reform.* Retrieved October 15 2010 from <http://www.thinkingclassroom.org/Education%20Papers/8.%20Education%20and%20Democracy%20in%20Burma,%202007.pdf >.

Thornbury, S. (2006). *An A–Z of ELT.* Oxford, UK: Macmillan.

Tomlinson, B. (1998). *Materials development in language teaching.* Cambridge, UK: Cambridge University Press.

Tudor, I. (2002). Learning to live with complexity: Towards an ecological perspective on language teaching. *System, 31*(1), 1–12.

Wikipedia (n.d.). Common European framework of reference for languages. Retrieved May 13 2010 from <http://en.wikipedia.org/wiki/Common_European_Framework_of_Reference_for_Languages>,

Comment

This chapter has described an ongoing curriculum design project in a particularly challenging context. It is a project that appears to be seeking change in at least two areas – in people's lives, through giving people the language skills to access further educational and employment opportunities, and in Burma itself, through developing critical thinking skills. Most people would judge it an ambitious undertaking, not just because of the project's aims, but because of the challenges that the curriculum designers face in gathering information about the teaching–learning environment and the learners' needs. Katie Julian and Derek Foster have discussed this issue honestly, and provided us with a clear picture of the questions they were seeking to answer in their environment analysis.

One of the particular challenges inherent in this case study is the tension between what are sometimes referred to as BANA and TESEP (Holliday, 1994), with BANA being the approach to language teaching favored in Britain, Australasia, and North America, and TESEP that commonly found in tertiary, secondary, and primary teaching in the rest of the world. If curriculum designers are not aware of this tension in such situations, the introduction of a new curriculum can be a doomed exercise. Sue Leather's experience in the Republic of Georgia (Leather, 2001) is another case study that explores this issue.

Tasks

1. The information that we gather about teachers, learners, and the situation through environment analysis should influence the course's development. Read the chapter again and make notes about the effect of the environment analysis on the course.

TABLE 3.2

Environment analysis	Effect on course
Teachers:	
Learners:	
Situation:	

2. Environment analysis often produces a large number of constraints, and the curriculum designer should rank these so that the most important receive appropriate attention. Identify and rank the top three in this case study.
3. Once the important constraints have been identified, the course designer needs information in order to make decisions. This information may come from investigation of the teaching–learning environment, or from research and theory. For the top three constraints you identified in Task 2:
    a. what sort of information would you like to know?
    b. how did Katie Julian and Derek Foster gather their information?

Further Reading

Leather, S. (2001). Training across cultures: Content, process, and dialogue. *ELT Journal, 55*(3), 228–237.

4

DESIGNING ENGLISH LANGUAGE COURSES FOR OMANI STUDENTS

Angela Joe

This chapter reports on the development of an English for Academic Purposes (EAP) program as an integral part of four-year undergraduate degree programs for the Ministry of Higher Education in the Sultanate of Oman. The chapter first outlines a New Zealand-based course designer's approach to identifying key environmental factors in the Omani teaching and learning context, then describes how the course addressed contextual, learner and instructor needs.

Introduction

In 2005 the Ministry of Higher Education (MoHE) in the Sultanate of Oman undertook to transform six Education Colleges in regional centers into Colleges of Applied Science offering four-year undergraduate degrees in International Business, Communication, Design, and Information Technology. While the degrees were to be awarded by the MoHE in Oman, the content was to be provided by five New Zealand universities forming the New Zealand Tertiary Education Consortium (NZTEC).[1]

The Ministry originally contracted NZTEC to provide teaching and learning materials for two 16-week English language courses, of ten contact hours per week, for each year of the four-year degree. Each 160-hour English course aimed

---

[1] NZTEC is comprised of Auckland University of Technology (Communication and Design), University of Otago (Information Technology), Victoria University of Wellington (English language), University of Waikato (International Business) and the Academic Colleges Group (Board member). Each of the five subjects taught within the degree is led by a program coordinator from the respective New Zealand universities for NZTEC and a program director appointed by the Ministry of Higher Education in the Sultanate of Oman.

to provide further academic language development and language support for degree subjects studied concurrently.[2] Another tertiary institute had previously prepared all English course prescriptions but these were found to be at an inappropriate level and too narrowly focused on general English study skills. The Ministry stipulated that English language courses focus on English for Academic Purposes to support the concurrent majors at an appropriate level – hence the involvement of Victoria University of Wellington (VUW) in 2006.

The arrangement involved VUW preparing the curriculum and materials to be used in the course of instruction while the MoHE took responsibility for teacher recruitment, teacher training, course delivery, and the schedule of English language courses within the degree structure.

The first task involved writing eight English language course prescriptions aiming at a proficiency level equivalent to IELTS 4.0, with an increase of IELTS 0.5 each year. Most urgently, we had about a week to identify a suitable EAP textbook that could be used throughout the four years and would meet the needs of the learners and the context. A search of EAP course books led to the Garnet *Skills in English* series, which contains separate skills books at four different levels, from IELTS 4.0 through to IELTS 6.0.

After Ministry approval, work began on the design and development of the first 16-week EAP course. This was to be delivered to Oman within four months, followed by the second course four months later. The first priority was to undertake a situational needs analysis drawing on the experience of instructors of Omani learners and learners themselves.

Situation and Needs Analysis

Having never been to Oman nor having taught Omani learners, the greatest initial challenge was to quickly familiarize myself with the teaching and learning context at the Colleges of Applied Science and to analyze the factors which would impinge on the design of an English for Academic Purposes program. To do this, the following tasks were undertaken:

- meeting local teachers of EAP programs who had previously instructed college-age Omani or Emirati learners;
- meeting the newly appointed MoHE English Program Director who had assisted the Ministry in the delivery of the Foundation program and had run a large English language school in Muscat for three years;
- meeting an Omani high school teacher who had just completed an EAP program at Victoria University of Wellington;

---

[2] Subsequently, the provision of English language was limited to only the first two years of the degree.

- gathering written samples of Omani student work from the Foundation year;
- obtaining copies of IELTS test results from a sample of Omani students who were nearing the end of the Foundation year;
- obtaining a copy of the MoHE report (2006) on English language courses within the degree structure;
- gathering course outlines from the first-year degree courses studied concurrently with English.

The data gathering identified important situational, instructor, and learner constraints which are outlined below.

Situation

- The Colleges of Applied Science are in six different regional centres (Salalah, Sur, Ibri, Al-Rustaq, Nizwa, and Sohar) with differing demographics, resources, teaching and learning facilities, and specialist degrees offered.
- The Ministry purchases all English course books across all Colleges with the expectation that learners return the books in good condition at the end of the semester.
- The English Program Director and Deputy Director are based in Muscat, Oman with Heads of English and Coordinators reporting to them from each college.
- Oman is a predominantly Muslim society so materials writers used to conceptualizing teaching and learning tasks from a Western perspective need to reflect on the cultural and social implications of writing for a Muslim context.
- Women, in particular, are subject to social constraints outside of class which impact directly on independent learning opportunities.
- Learners typically do not have access to print or electronic learning resources beyond the Colleges and are not used to self-directed independent learning.
- Class sizes vary from 12 to 40 students.
- English classes are scheduled in two-hour blocks, five times a week.
- English is used as the medium of instruction throughout the degree program, with the exception of four or five College-required courses that are taught in Arabic; however, some lecturers use Arabic in classes to make the content more accessible.

Instructors

- In 2006, approximately 120 English instructors were employed at the Colleges.
- Instructors have a minimum qualification of a Bachelor's degree and the equivalent of a Certificate in Teaching English as a Foreign Language.

- Many instructors take holidays from the end of one semester to the next, which leaves little time for teacher training.
- One instructor teaches English to the same group of learners throughout the semester.

Learners

- Learners' English proficiency levels on admission to the first year of the degree ranged from less than IELTS 4 to 6, despite a minimum target of IELTS 4.0.
- Learners often perceive that course work from subject majors is more motivating and more valuable than English language courses.
- Learners' oral literacy is stronger than their written literacy.

Course Design

Having established the environmental constraints, the next step focused on working within and against them in order to move toward the goal of developing learners' academic language skills in ten hours a week over 16 weeks. With learners studying degree-level subjects alongside English, it was decided that using a content-based approach to learning English provided opportunities to model the kinds of learning tasks and strategies that learners could practice and apply to both English and degree-level study. In order to organize the time needed for language proficiency and to pursue topics of interest linked to the four subject majors the course was divided into two strands:

Strand 1 Developing and improving academic language and study skills via a content-based textbook.
Strand 2 Developing content-specific language and improving language performance related to specific disciplines via project work and integrated skills tasks.

Strand 1

With the target entry level of IELTS 4.0 from the bridging foundation year program to the degree, extensive development was needed in all four language skills in order to access important concepts covered in the four majors. For this reason, eight out of ten hours each week were devoted to intensive language and academic skills work based on *Skills in English*.[3] The course book had the advantage of being written for the Middle-Eastern market so that topics were culturally

---

[3] Based on the writing samples provided and the advice of the English Program Director, Level 2 of the *Skills in English* textbook was selected.

appropriate and it was expected to be available in large numbers for distribution across the Colleges. It also provided less experienced teachers with pedagogic support such as explicit notes drawing attention to differences between Arabic and English language features. Another feature to note is that the same topics appeared across respective units in the listening, speaking, reading, and writing course books, as well as respective units spiraling vertically up through the four levels. Despite these strengths, extra tasks were needed to target learners' areas of need.

Taking learners' general language proficiency as a starting point, a problem of low vocabulary levels and low general English proficiency levels pointed to the need for coverage of highly frequent general and academic language used across a range of topics.

Cobb and Horst (2001, p. 321) reported that Omani learners at Sultan Qaboos University in Oman from 1987 to 1990 had great difficulty comprehending reading texts because of "a lack of vocabulary." Although the *Skills in English* series highlighted vocabulary that occurred frequently in the texts as well as in general English use, these did not include the academic words occurring in the Academic Word List (Coxhead, 2000). Direct vocabulary learning tasks were therefore developed to notice, understand and use the forms and meanings of academic words found in course book texts as learners met them during the course.

To optimize opportunities to recycle language form, meaning, and use on familiar topics, additional receptive and productive tasks were provided for each course book unit. Short dictations were prepared based on 50-word extracts from texts learners had already encountered previously. Moreover, supplementary readings were provided. Some texts were intended for extensive reading or fluency development in which vocabulary was controlled, that is, 95 to 98 percent of the words were derived from earlier course work or from the first and second thousand most general words of English (Nation, 1986). Others were for intensive reading to extend the complexity of content and language available in the course book. The principle of creating repeated opportunities to consolidate and extend language use in multiple contexts was particularly important for lower proficiency learners who needed time to understand texts, notice language forms, and practice using them in meaningful contexts.

The final component that instructors were encouraged to incorporate into their program was guided independent language learning. At the most basic level this involved setting homework as preparation for an upcoming class. For those with students wanting a structured system for recording language goals and activities completed out of class, an independent learning record booklet was provided.

Strand 2

Strand 1 focused on improving general academic language development but did not address motivational issues related to the relevance of course content or the opportunity to review and direct their own learning through project or integrated skills work. Consequently, on the fifth day of the course, Strand 2 provided opportunities for integrated-skills, issues-based project work (Issues Logs (Watson, 2004), in which students collect and summarize articles on a current issue in the news). Originally, learners were to complete four Issues Logs, one for each of the four concurrent majors: International Business, Communication, Design, and Information Technology, with each one spanning four weeks. The rationale for organizing the Logs into four-week blocks was fourfold:

• It reduces the vocabulary learning burden because of substantial receptive practice, that is, key phrases are recycled, which leads to conceptual and linguistic enrichment through successive encounters over consecutive weeks.
• Greater attention can be focused on the form and meaning of language because students do not need to grapple with a new set of discrete vocabulary and concepts each week.
• Teachers can support productive language use and increase awareness of appropriate academic discourse and academic conventions through a reading to write model.
• Learners gain greater confidence in using language productively.

In practice, the goal of producing four Issues Logs in 16 weeks was unrealistic. First, because of national holidays and exam periods there are usually fewer than 16 full teaching weeks. Second, instructors could not fit in all the course-book work, the supplementary tasks, and the logs in the time allocated. Third, our expectation of the level of learners' independent research skills, experience in directing their own learning, and knowledge of Western academic writing was too high. Very few learners had experienced this kind of independent project work prior to the first year so a great deal of guidance and training was required to set out task expectations, select and shape topics, break the process down into realistic tasks, and direct learners to useful sources of evidence. In addition, we assumed too much shared knowledge of instructors' understanding about the logs when, in fact, a great deal more support was required. As a result, the number of Issues Logs was ultimately reduced to one. Problems with the time and the amount of support for the logs did not, however, affect the sequencing of logs in the broader program.

Together, the two strands contributed to course coherence and a predictable routine.

Horizontal coherence was achieved by the weekly cycle of guided course book instruction in Strand 1 and guided project work in Strand 2. In addition, four key components were included in the program: a) fluency work, b) focus on language form, c) focus on meaning in input, and d) focus on meaning in output. Another point to note is that recycling the same topics or themes from one course level to the next provided students with opportunities to further develop language, ideas, and skills related to those topics.

Year 1 Program Evaluation

The foregoing discussion outlines broad principles underpinning the curriculum design process based mainly on email communication and face-to-face meetings with selected individuals at the outset of the project. For the duration of this project annual visits have been scheduled between NZTEC and MoHE project team members but the following section briefly reports only on the inaugural visit of NZTEC program coordinators with MoHE team members in February 2007.

Nine months into the project, all stakeholders came together for the first time in Oman to review the two sets of first-year teaching and learning materials delivered to date. We were informed of changes to the structure of the degree program, which removed English language courses from years 3 and 4 of the degree and reduced the number of contact hours from ten to eight in the first and second semester in year two. In the final semester of English, instead of a general EAP course, ESP courses were to be written to help students manage the language demands of each of the four majors. In addition, rather than writing courses with the target of IELTS 4.0, we were to rewrite the existing course at IELTS 4.5.

Very importantly, visits to two Colleges were organized to meet key people, to better understand the context, the College infrastructure, and issues related to English language. Through brief focus group discussions, insights were gained into learners' and instructors' perceptions of materials written in New Zealand. Responses were mixed. Despite initial difficulties with setting up, scaffolding, and modeling Issues Logs, both instructors and learners felt that project work lent itself well to promoting research skills and directing independent learning on topics of interest to students. Responses to the course book, however, were less enthusiastic.

Although well received initially, the chosen course book proved problematic on a number of fronts. First, there were reported difficulties with the supply of textbooks in the numbers and time frame specified; second, mixed ability groups in classes resulted in the textbook catering well to the needs of lower level learners but less so for higher proficiency learners; third, many instructors perceived that the topics were repetitive and more challenging texts were required. While training in approaches to using the text to exploit the materials may have overcome the latter two difficulties, the English Program Director felt compelled to change the textbook.

Subsequently, an American EAP College series was selected. It aimed to socialize learners into the norms of a Western academic college context for students intending to embark on study in the US, but, not surprisingly, proved problematic in terms of cultural appropriateness. For example, one listening unit focused on music and dance. A comprehension exercise involved students in responding physically to directions by clapping a rhythm, holding hands, or showing partnership in some form, then dancing. Instructors in Oman stated that students would resist or refuse to participate in this type of activity. Difficulties were also encountered regarding coherence across different skills, inadequate authentic listening texts, and a writing course book that did not fit the needs of the learners. Needless to say, further changes were required to address these shortcomings.

Conclusion

The experience of analyzing contextual constraints and designing a program to meet the needs of various stakeholders both in New Zealand and Oman has highlighted the dynamic nature of the curriculum design process. Constant refinement and adjustment of the program has been needed in light of changing institutional requirements, practical concerns, and ongoing feedback from both instructors and learners. Had the New Zealand course designers been consulted about major changes to the curriculum and the learners' level of proficiency, and been better informed about the appropriateness of course materials early in the project, then fewer modifications would have been required. Crucially to the design process, and implicit in this project, has been the importance of establishing good working relationships, being flexible, and keeping open lines of communication.

References

Cobb, T. & Horst, M. (2001). Reading academic English: Carrying learners across the lexical threshold. In J. Flowerdew & M. Peacock (Eds.), *Research perspectives on English for Academic Purposes* (pp. 315–329). Cambridge, UK: Cambridge University Press.

Coxhead, A. (2000). A new Academic Word List. *TESOL Quarterly, 34* (2), 213–238.

Ministry of Higher Education. (2006). *English language courses to be developed by NZTEC.* Sultanate of Oman: Author.

Nation, I.S.P. (1986). *Vocabulary lists: Words, affixes and stems.* (Occasional Publication No. 12). Wellington, New Zealand: Victoria University of Wellington.

Phillips, T. & Phillips, A. (2005). *Skills in English.* Reading, UK: Garnet.

Watson, J. (2004). Issue logs. In J. Bamford & R. R. Day (Eds.), *Extensive reading activities for teaching language* (pp. 37–39). Cambridge, UK: Cambridge University Press.

Comment

The challenges for a course designer when faced with unknown students in an unfamiliar context are great, but are to some extent shared by every teacher preparing work at the start of the school year for students they have yet to meet. Just as Angela Joe has done here, in such situations teachers need to identify the sources of information and select the tools for carrying out needs and environment analyses. Once the analyses have been completed, decisions need to be taken to respond appropriately to the data gathered. For example, in this case study an important decision was to take a content-based approach to learning English, as the students were learning *in* English as well as learning the language.

As with other case studies in this collection, the dynamism of the curriculum design process is highlighted, for the original design had to change. The importance of developing and maintaining good relationships with the various stakeholders was critical here, and is an important consideration whenever a new curriculum is introduced. Good communication and good relationships greatly enhance the likelihood of successful uptake of what is new.

Tasks

1. Look at the tasks that were undertaken as part of the needs and environment analyses. For each task, suggest (a) the type of information that each might provide, and (b) the tool or tools you might employ in the analysis.
2. The selection of a suitable textbook was important in this English language course for Omani students. Bearing in mind the factors identified in the environment and needs analyses, design an evaluation form for selecting a suitable textbook in this context (see also *LCD* pp. 165–168). Be prepared to justify your evaluation form in terms of the environment and needs.
3. In your own teaching and learning context, how would you do an environment analysis to guide your course design for a class you had not yet met?

5

MY IDEAL VOCABULARY TEACHING COURSE

Paul Nation

This chapter attempts to describe my ideal vocabulary teaching course. This description has several purposes. Firstly, it provides a way of reviewing the current state of research on vocabulary as it relates to designing a vocabulary course. Secondly, it forces me to put my money where my mouth is and come up with the best suggestions I can for describing a course. Thirdly, it provides a basis for others to comment on and criticize with a view to improving such a description. Finally, it may eventually act as a model or at least a comparison for designing and evaluating vocabulary courses.

In the following description I will try to follow a rough general pattern for each part, firstly describing what I think should be done, and then describing the research evidence for such a decision. The overall plan of the course is based around the four strands (Nation, 2007) of meaning-focused input, meaning-focused output, language-focused learning, and fluency development. Meaning-focused input involves learning through listening and reading at a level which is suitable for the learner. Meaning-focused output involves learning through speaking and writing at a level which is suitable for the learner. Language-focused learning involves the deliberate study of language, in this case, vocabulary. Fluency development does not involve the learning of any new items but involves becoming very proficient at using what is already known. Fluency development needs to occur separately for each of the four skills of listening, speaking, reading, and writing.

Vocabulary Learning Through Meaning-Focused Input

A Substantial Extensive Reading Program

An essential part of any vocabulary course is a substantial extensive reading program making use of graded readers. Such an extensive reading program should actually fit into two strands of a course: the strand of meaning focused input when learners read material which is at the right level for them (Krashen (1985) would call this i+1), and the fluency development strand where learners read very easy graded readers, far below their usual meaning-focused input level, but read them very quickly. Extensive reading in the meaning-focused input strand should involve reading graded readers where around 2 percent of the running words are outside of the learners' present knowledge. This still means that there will be one unknown word in every five lines of the text, and between four and six unknown words per page on every page. This is still a heavy vocabulary load but is manageable. In such an extensive reading program, learners should be reading at least one graded reader every two weeks for the meaning-focused input strand (Nation & Wang, 1999). Initially such graded reading should be done quietly in class so the teacher can monitor that it is actually done and that the learners are truly engaged in reading English. After a month or two of such in-class reading, the graded reading can be increasingly assigned as homework. The hope is that by this time the learners will have discovered that they can be successful in such reading and that it is enjoyable (Takase, 2007).

During such reading learners may wish to use bilingual electronic dictionaries. This is perfectly acceptable as such dictionaries are rapidly improving in quality and some of them are now equal to, if not better than, some monolingual learner's dictionaries.

There is plenty of research which shows that vocabulary learning can occur incidentally from reading graded readers (Horst, Cobb, & Meara, 1998; Horst, 2005; Pigada & Schmitt, 2006). The Waring and Takaki study (2003) looked at the learning from one graded reader and found useful amounts of learning at three different levels of vocabulary knowledge. The classic book flood study by Elley and Mangubhai (1981; Elley, 1991) showed that an extensive reading program can result in a very wide range of different kinds of learning, and that the learning benefits of such a program are greater than those which come from a program of direct teaching.

Learning Through Listening

Learners should also receive a large quantity of input at the right level for them through listening. There are three major ways in which this could be done. One way is to make most of the classroom management occur through the medium of English. That is, English is used to tell the learners what to do, to control their behavior, to praise them for good work, to give them feedback on their performance, to explain why they are doing certain activities and what the benefit will be to them, and to generally motivate them. The success of this lies in the teacher's skill in finding comprehensible and consistent ways of doing these things through the medium of English. Ideally the language used for classroom management should come almost completely from the high-frequency words of the language.

A very engaging and useful technique for providing a reasonable quantity of listening is the activity called listening to stories. In this activity the teacher chooses a very interesting story at the right level for the learners. A source of such texts could be the award-winning readers listed on the Extensive Reading Foundation website (http://www.erfoundation.org). This activity has been described in other places (Nation & Newton, 2009), and simply involves the teacher reading the story to the learners in a serial form. That is, the teacher begins reading the story, repeating sentences where necessary and speaking at a slow enough speed for the learners to comprehend easily. After a few minutes of listening to the story, the teacher stops and tells the class that the story will be continued the next time they meet. In this way, bit by bit, the learners hear the story, become engaged in it, and find it easy to listen to because of their increasing familiarity with the characters and plot and the type of language used in the story. Where necessary, the teacher quickly writes up words on the blackboard to help the learners recognize them, and may give a quick explanation of the meaning if it is needed. This is an activity that learners look forward to, and its success depends on the quality of the story and the skill of the teacher in matching the speed and repetitions of the sentences to the level of the learners.

Research by Elley (1989) found that quickly giving attention to some of the words in the story increased learning by around 30 percent. Because graded readers use high-frequency words, they will be met very often and good conditions will be set up for learning them (Nation & Wang, 1999). Unpublished studies of graded readers show that new words at each level tend to re-occur in a variety of contexts that provide a rich range of associations that will help them stick in memory.

The third possibility for extensive listening is listening to the CDs that come with many graded readers. There are now computer programs available which can speed up or slow down a digital recording without altering the pitch, so that it still sounds natural. It is worth looking at these programs to see how well they can work with such CDs and whether they are helpful in developing the learners' listening skills. There are also small digital voice recorders which have this function. Extensive listening is not likely to be as big a source of vocabulary learning as extensive reading will be for learners of English as a foreign language. However, it is still a very important source of vocabulary learning and needs to play a substantial role in the meaning-focused input section of a language course.

Learning Through Meaning-Focused Output

From a vocabulary perspective, one of the most effective ways of providing both meaning-focused input and meaning-focused output is by having a content-based instruction focus in the course. Content-based instruction involves learning content matter while learning the language. In some countries where English is a foreign language, such as Malaysia, some of the school subjects such as mathematics and technology are taught through the medium of English. This has the dual goals of learning the subject and learning the language. Content-based instruction is used in some pre-university language courses by having themes that run through parts of the program.

At a more individual level, content-based instruction can occur when each learner has the opportunity to choose a topic that they will specialize in during the course. They then read a lot on that topic, gather information from a variety of sources about it, and report on this information gathering each week to a small group of fellow students. Eventually they will write a report on their data gathering and give an oral report to the whole class. It is important that there is work done on this topic every week so that learners gradually build up a substantial amount of knowledge about it, gain control of the vocabulary used in that topic area, and are able to talk, read, listen, and write about that topic with a reasonable degree of fluency.

Content-based instruction is particularly suited to vocabulary development for several reasons (Nation & Gu, 2007).

1   It reduces the vocabulary load which is created when learners jump from one topic to another during the course (Sutarsyah, Nation, & Kennedy, 1994).
2   It results in vocabulary occurring which is thematically rather than semantically related (Tinkham, 1997), and this makes vocabulary learning much easier in that the vocabulary items do not interfere with each other.
3   It provides good opportunities for vocabulary learning through linked skill activities, where learners deal with the same content material through a range of different skills. For example, they may read a text, then talk about it, and then write about it. The four skills of listening, speaking, reading, and writing can be combined in a very large variety of ways to provide many linked skill activities. When the same vocabulary occurs through each one of the three activities across the skills, there is a very high chance that it will be learnt.
4   Content-based instruction provides many opportunities for understanding ideas, applying the ideas, critiquing the ideas, and relating the ideas to various other kinds of knowledge. All of these types of activities encourage generative use of the vocabulary involved. Generative use involves meeting or using words in contexts which are different from those where they have been met before (Joe, 1998). Generative use has a very strong positive effect on vocabulary learning.
5   As learners engage in content-based instruction they develop substantial background knowledge of the material that they are working with. This background knowledge greatly increases the opportunity for guessing new words from context.
6   Speaking and writing activities in content-based instruction can readily draw on written input to the task. This allows the teacher to design vocabulary learning into the speaking task, by making sure that target vocabulary occurs in the written input to the task (Joe, Nation, & Newton, 1996; Newton, 1995).

The major problem in implementing content-based instruction where English is learnt as a foreign language is deciding on the content matter of such instruction. Most typically, topics like conservation, global warming, and current affairs are chosen for more advanced students. Topics need to be interesting for the students and to some degree familiar to the teachers.

Vocabulary Learning Through Language-Focused Learning

The language-focused learning strand of a course involves deliberate attention to vocabulary and other language features. A central activity in this strand is the deliberate learning of vocabulary using bilingual word cards.

Vocabulary Learning using Word Cards

Word cards are small cards which have a second language word or phrase on one side and its translation in the first language on the other. They are worked through whenever a learner has some free time. A reasonable goal for such learning is around 50 words a week, although this is about twice the learning rate found in language courses in Europe (Milton, 2009). In total this takes about two hours, including the time to make the cards.

This is a very effective learning procedure that is well supported by over 100 years of research (Griffin & Harley, 1996; Nation, 2001). There is now evidence that this learning directly contributes to implicit knowledge as well as explicit knowledge of vocabulary (Elgort, 2011, in press). This means that the kind of knowledge that is created by such learning is the kind of knowledge which is needed for normal language use. There are several computer programs which can be used for such learning, such as iKnow and WordChamp, and the best ones are those which can be used on a cell phone or an iPod so that the learner has flexibility in choosing when to do the learning (see Nakata (forthcoming) for a review). This kind of learning does not, of course, result in complete knowledge of the words, but results in an extremely important step forward in vocabulary knowledge. It needs to be supplemented by the other three strands of a course.

Strategy Training

Another very important part of language-focused learning is training in the strategies of guessing from context, learning using word cards, using word parts to help remember words, and using dictionaries to help vocabulary learning.

Such strategy training requires sustained attention to the strategies in class, so that learners gain guided practice in using the strategies correctly and eventually find it as easy to use strategies as to not use them. The dictionary-use strategy and the word-part strategy have not been the focus of very much research. There is, however, substantial research on learning from word cards and on guessing from context (Nation, 2001).

Multiword Units

There is value in giving attention to the analysis and memorization of multiword units. These are important in helping learners gain early fluency and accuracy in the language. It is important to realize, however, that most multiword units are not arbitrary combinations but follow normal grammar rules and the semantic constraints of the words that make them up. Giving deliberate attention to them, however, does provide a shortcut to early language use.

Boers and his colleagues (2006, 2007) have shown the effectiveness of giving deliberate attention to multiword figuratives. Research by Shin (Shin & Nation, 2008) has also provided a useful list of multiword units.

Intensive Reading

Intensive reading, of which the grammar translation method is a variant, is a useful way of giving deliberate attention to a range of language features within the context of language use. However, because it involves a lot of deliberate attention to language features, it is classified as part of the language-focused learning strand rather than the meaning-focused input strand. It involves the teacher and the learners working through a reading text, giving attention to useful and generalizable features of the language (Nation, 2009b, Chapter 3).

Fluency Development

Fluency development activities involve helping the learners make the best use of what they already know. Because of this, this strand of the course should not involve any new vocabulary or grammatical features, and should make use of texts and topics that are largely familiar to the learners. It is most effective to have separate fluency development for each of the four skills of listening, speaking, reading, and writing. Fluency development activities have the characteristics of being message focused, involving very easy material, involving some pressure to perform at a faster than usual speed, and involve reasonably large quantities of language use. Perhaps the strongest argument for having a substantial fluency development strand in the course is that learners' knowledge is not much use to them if it is not readily available when they want to use it.

Listening Fluency

The listening to stories activity described above begins by being a meaning-focused input activity, but by the time the learners are part of the way through listening to the story, it has probably changed to become a fluency development activity because of the learners' familiarity with the story, the characters, and the language used in the story. Shared book reading works in a similar way.

Listening to CDs of an easy graded reader either with or without the text is also a fluency development activity for listening.

Speaking Fluency

One of my favorite speaking fluency activities is the 4/3/2 activity. In this activity the learners work in pairs. Learner A in each pair talks to learner B about a very easy topic for four minutes. Learner B listens carefully, shows interest, but does not interrupt the talk at all. After four minutes is up, the teacher tells the learners to change partners, and learner A now delivers exactly the same talk to a new partner. After three minutes they change partners again and learner A now delivers the talk for the third time to a new partner for two minutes. The decreasing timeframe encourages learner A to speed up the delivery of the talk.

Research on this activity comparing the four-minute and the two-minute talks (Nation, 1989; Arevart & Nation, 1991) shows that this activity not only brings about increases in speed of delivery, but also a reduction of hesitations, and an increase in grammatical accuracy and grammatical complexity.

Reading Speed

Probably the most effective way of increasing reading speed is to have a focused speed reading course. Such a course involves the learners reading easy texts, recording their time, and answering comprehension questions on the texts. Their speed and accuracy of comprehension is recorded on graphs.

Such courses typically bring about an increase of between 50 and 100 percent in learners' reading speed for a small investment of class time (Chung & Nation, 2006). Another activity that can contribute to reading fluency is reading very easy graded readers. When learners read the very easy graded readers, they try to read as many as possible and as quickly as possible.

Writing Fluency

Ten-minute writing is a focused writing fluency development activity. In this activity two or three times a week the learners write for a strictly measured period of time of ten minutes on very easy topics. The teacher does not comment on the grammatical accuracy or the organization of the pieces of writing, but simply gives small amounts of feedback on the content, encouraging the learners to write more about that topic. The learners count the number of words that they have written in each piece of writing and record this on a graph.

This activity is under-researched. It is likely that the topic has a strong effect on the number of words written. It seems likely that increases in writing fluency will also be accompanied by increases in accuracy and complexity, even though no specific attention is given to these features. This would be a good focus for future research.

Linked Skills

Linked skills activities involve working on exactly the same topic using a succession of three of the language skills of listening, speaking, reading, and writing. For example, the learners may read about a topic, and then they talk to others about it, and finally they write about it. By the time they get to the final activity in the set of three, they are well in control of the language and content involved in the activity. They can thus perform the last of the three tasks at a fluent level. There are many possible combinations of the skills, and thus there are many possible linked skills activities. It is likely that the first of the activities in a linked skills series is meaning-focused input or output, perhaps with elements of language-focused learning. The second activity would be clearly meaning-focused input or output, and the last activity in the series would be a fluency development activity. Such activities require only a little teacher preparation and keep the learners usefully busy for a good period of time.

General Issues

The above description of the four strands of the course includes the activities that I think are the most useful for vocabulary development and language learning. Note that three of the four strands are meaning-focused, and one is language-focused. The principle of the four strands is that in a well-balanced course roughly equal time is given to each strand.

What is not in the Course?

A notable feature of the activities in the course is that only a small proportion of them involve a focus on the teacher. As a general principle, learners rather than teachers should be doing most of the work in a class. It is therefore always useful to make sure that the teacher is not working too hard fronting activities.

Table 5.1 contains a list of the activities mentioned in this chapter. They are classified according to whether they involve a focus on the teacher, individual work, or group work.

Table 5.1 shows that a reasonable number of the activities are still teacher focused, but they do not make up the majority of the activities in the course. Learners must eventually take responsibility for their own vocabulary learning, and individual work and group work provide good preparation for this responsibility.

TABLE 5.1 The top activities and their work focus

Activity	Focus on the teacher	Individual work	Group work
Extensive reading		√	
Classroom management	√		
Listening to stories	√		
Listening to CDs		√	
Content-based instruction	√	√	√
Using word cards		√	
Strategy training	√		
Intensive reading	√		
4/3/2			√
Speed reading		√	
10 minute writing		√	
Linked skill activities	√	√	√

Do we Need a Course Book?

A course book is a very useful part of a course but it is not an essential part. A course book is fine if it uses good principles of vocabulary selection, and if the teacher ensures that there is a balance of the four strands. Even with a very prescribed course, it is possible to balance the strands. There are several vocabulary exercise books available for teaching the high-frequency words of English (Nation, 2009a) as well as words from the Academic Word List (Schmitt & Schmitt, 2005). These could be useful as individual work or homework activities.

What Vocabulary?

So far we have looked at how vocabulary can be taught and learnt. However, a very important part of the vocabulary planning for a course involves making sure that the right vocabulary is being focused on. An essential part of good course planning involves testing the learners to find out their vocabulary size. There are several tests available to do this. The Vocabulary Levels Test (Schmitt, Schmitt, & Clapham, 2001) and the Vocabulary Size Test (Nation & Beglar, 2007; Beglar, 2010) are both available free from my web page at <http://www.victoria.ac.nz/lals/staff/paul-nation.aspx>. They allow teachers to find out whether the learners need to be focusing on high-frequency words, academic words, or low-frequency words (Nation, 2001).

High-frequency words need to be met across the four strands of a course. They deserve attention during class time. Low-frequency words on the other hand make up a large group of words which occur so infrequently that they do not deserve deliberate attention from the teacher during a lesson. Learners, however, need to learn these words once they know the high-frequency words of the language, and the teacher's focus should be on training the learners in the strategies needed to learn them. These strategies include, in order of priority, guessing from context, learning using word cards, using word parts as mnemonic devices, and dictionary use (Nation, 2008).

Principles

The design of this vocabulary course is based on several principles. The two that are most influential in the design of the course are the principle of the four strands and the frequency principle. The principle of the four strands is a format and presentation principle. It ensures that there is a good balance of learning opportunities throughout the course.

Four strands: A well-balanced language course has four equal strands of meaning-focused input, meaning-focused output, language-focused learning, and fluency development.

Each of these strands can also be stated as a principle.

Comprehensible input: Learners should have the opportunity to learn through message-focused listening and reading (meaning-focused input) where around 98 percent of the vocabulary is already familiar to them.

Output: Learners should be pushed to produce language through speaking and writing.

Fluency: Learners should become fluent in using what they already know in each of the four skills of listening, speaking, reading, and writing.

The principle guiding what vocabulary to learn is the frequency principle. This is a needs analysis and a content and sequencing principle, because it strongly affects what is learnt and in what order it is learnt.

Frequency: High-frequency items should be learnt before lower frequency items.

This principle needs to be accommodated to the interference principle.

> **Interference:** The items in a language course should be sequenced so that items which are learned together have a positive effect on each other for learning and so that interference effects are avoided.

In this chapter we have looked at the importance of the learners working hard without the teacher doing too much work. This is more than one principle, because it includes the strategies and autonomy principle and the time on task principle.

> **Strategies and autonomy:** Learners should be encouraged to develop the skill and motivation to take responsibility for their own learning.

> **Time on task:** Learners should spend as much time as possible listening, speaking, reading, and writing.

The principles listed above are some of those that I consider most important in my ideal vocabulary course. There are of course other principles (see Nation and Macalister, 2010, pp. 38–39) and incorporating these in a course will improve its effectiveness.

References

Arevart, S., & Nation, I.S.P. (1991). Fluency improvement in a second language. *RELC Journal, 22*(1), 84–94.

Beglar, D. (2010). A Rasch-based validation of the Vocabulary Size Test. *Language Testing, 27*(1).

Boers, F., Eyckmans, J., & Stengers, H. (2007). Presenting figurative idioms with a touch of etymology: More than mere mnemonics? *Language Teaching Research, 11*(1), 43–62.

Boers, F., Eyckmans, J., Kappel, J., Stengers, H., & Demecheleer, M. (2006). Formulaic sequences and perceived oral proficiency: Putting the Lexical Approach to the test. *Language Teaching Research, 10*(3), 245–261.

Chung, M. & Nation, I.S.P. (2006). The effect of a speed reading course. *English Teaching, 61*(4), 181–204.

Elgort, I. (2011). Deliberate learning and vocabulary acquisition in a second language. *Language Learning, 61*(2).

Elley, W.B. (1989). Vocabulary acquisition from listening to stories. *Reading Research Quarterly, 24*(2), 174–187.

Elley, W.B. (1991). Acquiring literacy in a second language: The effect of book-based programs. *Language Learning, 41*(3), 375–411.

Elley, W.B., & Mangubhai, F. (1981). *The impact of a book flood in Fiji primary schools.* Wellington, New Zealand: New Zealand Council for Educational Research.

Griffin, G.F., & Harley, T.A. (1996). List learning of second language vocabulary. *Applied Psycholinguistics, 17,* 443–460.

Horst, M. (2005). Learning L2 vocabulary through extensive reading: A measurement study. *Canadian Modern Language Review, 61*(3), 355–382.

Horst, M., Cobb, T., & Meara, P. (1998). Beyond a Clockwork Orange: Acquiring second language vocabulary through reading. *Reading in a Foreign Language, 11*(2), 207–223.

Joe, A. (1998). What effects do text-based tasks promoting generation have on incidental vocabulary acquisition? *Applied Linguistics, 19*(3), 357–377.

Joe, A., Nation, P., & Newton, J. (1996). Vocabulary learning and speaking activities. *English Teaching Forum, 34*(1), 2–7.

Krashen, S. (1985). *The input hypothesis: Issues and implications.* London, UK: Longman.

Milton, J. (2009). *Measuring second language vocabulary acquisition.* Bristol, UK: Multilingual Matters.

Nakata, T. (forthcoming) A critical investigation of flashcard software for second language vocabulary learning.

Nation, I.S.P. (1989). Improving speaking fluency. *System, 17*(3), 377–384.

Nation, I.S.P. (2001). *Learning vocabulary in another language.* Cambridge, UK: Cambridge University Press.

Nation, I.S.P. (2007) The four strands. *Innovation in language learning and teaching 1*(1), 1–12.

Nation, I.S.P. (2008). *Teaching vocabulary: Strategies and techniques.* Boston, MA: Cengage Learning.

Nation, I.S.P. (2009a) *4000 essential English words* (Books 1–6). Seoul, Korea: Compass Publishing.

Nation, I.S.P. (2009b). *Teaching ESL/EFL reading and writing.* New York, NY: Routledge.

Nation, P., & Beglar, D. (2007). A vocabulary size test. *The Language Teacher, 31*(7), 9–13.

Nation, I.S.P., & Gu, P.Y. (2007). *Focus on vocabulary.* Sydney, Australia: Macquarie University, National Centre for English Language Teaching and Research.

Nation, I.S.P., & Macalister, J. (2010). *Language curriculum design.* New York, NY: Routledge.

Nation, I.S.P. & Newton, J. (2009). *Teaching ESL/EFL listening and speaking.* New York, NY: Routledge.

Nation, P., & Wang, K. (1999). Graded readers and vocabulary. *Reading in a Foreign Language, 12*(2), 355–380.

Newton, J. (1995). Task-based interaction and incidental vocabulary learning: A case study. *Second Language Research, 11*(2), 159–177.

Pigada, M., & Schmitt, N. (2006). Vocabulary acquisition from extensive reading: a case study. *Reading in a Foreign Language, 18*(1), 1–28.

Schmitt, D., & Schmitt, N. (2005). *Focus on vocabulary: Mastering the Academic Word List.* New York, NY: Longman Pearson Education.

Schmitt, N., Schmitt, D., & Clapham, C. (2001). Developing and exploring the behaviour of two new versions of the Vocabulary Levels Test. *Language Testing, 18*(1), 55–88.

Shin, D., & Nation, I.S.P. (2008). Beyond single words: the most frequent collocations in spoken English. *ELT Journal, 62*(4), 339–348.

Sutarsyah, C., Nation, P., & Kennedy, G. (1994). How useful is EAP vocabulary for ESP? A corpus based study. *RELC Journal, 25*(2), 34–50.

Takase, A. (2007). Japanese high school students' motivation for extensive L2 reading. *Reading in a Foreign Language, 19*(1), 1–18.

Tinkham, T. (1997). The effects of semantic and thematic clustering on the learning of second language vocabulary. *Second Language Research, 13*(2), 138–163.

Waring, R., & Takaki, M. (2003). At what rate do learners learn and retain new vocabulary from reading a graded reader? *Reading in a Foreign Language, 15*(2), 130–163.

Comment

This chapter is almost the mirror image of a case study, in that it discusses what *should* happen rather than what *did* happen in the design of a language curriculum. At the same time, it demonstrates the value of applying research and theory about language learning to the practice of language teaching. Such principles provide a sensible basis to guide teaching and to help in the design of courses. They also allow teachers to vary their teaching according to the local context, and to be flexible in their approach rather than be bound by the strictures of any particular "method."

The principles discussed in this chapter (and those presented in *LCD*, pp. 38–39) are deliberately general, as they are intended for broad application. It is, of course, possible to produce sets of principles for particular uses, such as those for ICT in Gi-Zen Liu's chapter in this volume. Other examples of principles for particular uses that teachers and course designers might find useful are those for extensive reading (Day and Bamford, 2002) and learner autonomy (Cotterall, 2000).

Tasks

1. Paul Nation is describing his *ideal* vocabulary learning course. In the real world, however, contextual factors such as budget constraints may pose challenges for the teacher wanting to implement this ideal. Considering your teaching situation, or one with which you are familiar,
    a. What constraints can you identify?
    b. How could you work with those constraints to create the ideal vocabulary learning course?
2. Many teachers have been working with the same curriculum for a number of years or find that they must work with an already developed curriculum. Thinking of a curriculum with which you are familiar,
    a. Evaluate it against the suggestions made in this chapter.
    b. Identify places where ideas in this chapter could be incorporated.
    c. Choose one principle and say how you could apply it in that curriculum.
3. This chapter has focused on vocabulary learning. If it had focused on another aspect of language learning, such as reading or speaking, would it draw on the same principles?

Choose a different aspect of language learning and decide on the most important principles you would draw on. What type of classroom activities would you include as a result?

Further Reading

Cotterall, S. (2000). Promoting learner autonomy through the curriculum: principles for designing language courses *ELT Journal, 54*(2), 109–117.

Day, R.R., & Bamford, J. (2002). Top ten principles for teaching extensive reading. *Reading in a Foreign Language, 14*(2), 136–141.

6

OPENING THE DOOR TO INTERNATIONAL COMMUNICATION: PERUVIAN OFFICIALS AND APEC

Susan Smith

In 2008 it was Peru's turn to host APEC, the organization for Asia Pacific Economic Cooperation. APEC is a grouping of twenty-one economies in the Asia-Pacific region and numbers among its members such economic power-houses as the United States, China, Japan, Korea, Canada, Australia, and Russia. It currently accounts for over 40 percent of world trade and more than half of the world's GDP. Each year one of the member economies takes on the challenge of hosting several months of APEC committee meetings on a wide range of trade-related issues, culminating in the Leaders' Meeting for the Presidents and Prime Ministers of all the members.

One result of New Zealand's successful 1999 hosting of APEC was that officials from the New Zealand Ministry of Foreign Affairs and Trade were asked to share their APEC expertise with subsequent host nations. It was against this background that the Peruvian government asked the New Zealand government to provide an English language training course for thirty of its officials who would be playing a variety of roles in APEC meetings throughout 2008. The New Zealand government agreed to fund a 20-week program for two intakes of officials through NZAID, its overseas aid agency. NZAID appointed Victoria Link, a project management company associated with Victoria University, to design and manage a program for two intakes of Peruvian government officials between July 2006 and June 2007. Victoria Link set up a comprehensive program which included travel arrangements for the officials, a period of homestay accommodation, pastoral care, recreational activities, and language support in the form of two tutors who worked with the officials one-to-one during their independent study time and helped them with tasks that they were assigned by their teachers at the English Language Institute of Victoria University, which was contracted to design and deliver the language component of the program. Thus, five stakeholders were involved in what was known as the Pilot English Language Training Project (ELTP): the government of Peru; NZAID; Victoria Link; the English Language Institute (ELI); and the thirty Peruvian officials who were selected by their government to do the course.

NZAID's overall program goal was to assist in building Peru's capacity for good governance and its specific objective for the course was to enhance the capacity of the officials to develop the English language skills they required in order to be effective participants in APEC in 2008. The key indicators of achievement of this objective were that: (i) the course participants would improve their International English Language Testing System (IELTS) overall test scores by between half a band and one band from a starting point between 4.0 and 5.0 for the first group and 5.0 and 7.0 for the second; and (ii) the participants' learning objectives would be met.

Thus, the three-part challenge facing the ELTP course design team was to find effective ways to help the course members develop language skills for the APEC context, improve their IELTS scores and meet their learning objectives. In view of the fact that none of the members of the design team had any knowledge of APEC, this was a daunting task. However, they had the benefit of a model in the form of a highly successful program for Southeast Asian government officials, known as the ELTO (English Language Training for Officials) program, which the ELI had been running for many years. The ELTO program was also funded by NZAID and its goal was to help officials develop the English language skills they required to do their jobs effectively, particularly when representing their countries' views in international forums where the proceedings were in English. Improvement in the ELTO officials' IELTS scores was set down as one of the measures of the success of the program, so training in IELTS strategies had been incorporated as one strand of their course. The ELTO teachers regarded the ELTP as a companion program and readily agreed that the ELTP course members could take part in their IELTS classes. They also saw the combining of the Asian and Peruvian officials in IELTS classes as an excellent opportunity for a cross-cultural exchange.

With the issue of IELTS preparation resolved so satisfactorily, the ELTP teachers took a close look at the way that the ELTO program went about developing the English language skills of its participants. A content-based approach was used, with the content taking the form of sets of readings written by the teachers. Because the teachers prepared the readings they were able to use vocabulary and grammatical structures that were accessible to their students whereas authentic texts on the sorts of subjects that were the focus of the ELTO program, such as governance and sustainable development, tended to be far too complex for the officials and imposed a heavy learning burden on them. Another noteworthy feature was that the readings were published in booklets for the officials but the learning tasks which accompanied them were not. This was a departure from the study theme booklets of the academic English program taught at the ELI, in which tasks were presented together with readings. The benefit of the ELTO approach was that the teachers could easily vary the tasks for intakes of different proficiency levels, and, as the ELTP program would also have two quite distinct groups, the teachers decided to follow the ELTO model.

The ELTP team mapped out nine topics to be covered in three six-week modules, *An Introduction to New Zealand and to Language Learning, An Overview of Trade Policy and an Introduction to APEC*, and *Multilateralism and Preparing for APEC*, and aimed to complete the booklets for the first module by the time the ELTP officials arrived in New Zealand. Although it was risky to prepare a complete module before meeting the course members because it might turn out to be pitched at the wrong level, time constraints made this necessary. However, the teachers did have some useful information on which to base decisions about the first module. They knew, for example, that the members of the first intake were people in their thirties and forties who had completed their formal study at university some time ago and were now well established in their careers, so becoming a learner again would be a new experience. On that basis, they wrote readings and designed tasks for Module 1 that would introduce the officials to their new environment – not only New Zealand but also the learning environment – so that by the end of the first module they would feel at home in both contexts and be ready for the professional focus of Modules 2 and 3, during which they would be required to complete several of the course assessment tasks which were originally developed for the ELTO program. The vocabulary used in the readings for the first module was highly controlled to ensure that the texts would be accessible to the officials and ease them into the role of language learners, but it was intended that there would be much less control over the language in the readings for the other two modules. Another feature of the first module was its emphasis on helping the officials to develop their English language fluency. The teachers had been told that most of the officials did not use English in their workplaces and so anticipated (rightly, as it turned out) that fluency would be their top priority.

While the ELTP teachers were busy preparing the readings for the first module, NZAID undertook to find out about both the learning and content objectives of the first intake of course members by means of a questionnaire sent to them before they left Peru. This was the first phase of a needs analysis. What became clear at this early stage was that a significant proportion of the first group of officials did not work in areas associated with international trade or economics and had little or no knowledge of APEC. This meant that the readings for the second and third modules would need to provide a basic grounding in APEC's goals, practices, and culture. To write these modules, the teachers drew on the comprehensive information on the APEC website, academic articles on international trade issues and the support of officials from the Ministry of Foreign Affairs and Trade.

Once the course members were in New Zealand, the second phase of the needs analysis got under way. To gain a clearer idea of their expectations of the content of the course and the skills they thought it would help them develop, semi-structured interviews were held by the teachers. Two points emerged from these interviews. The first was that among the officials who had been told what their roles at APEC would be there was considerable diversity. Some had been assigned service roles, such as providing security or meeting the needs of their APEC visitors in terms of facilities, administration, translation, and information about Peruvian tourist sites and local products, while others anticipated that they would take part in the discussions and decision-making processes of APEC working groups and committees. The second point was that a sizable number of the officials did not know exactly what duties they would have. They had simply been shoulder-tapped for APEC duties in 2008. This new, and rather surprising, information gave the teachers pause for thought. It became clear that the curriculum would need to be broadened to provide practice in a wider range of skills than originally anticipated in order to meet as many of the potential needs of the course participants as possible.

The interviews also revealed that the officials wanted to meet with their professional counterparts in New Zealand government ministries and research institutes to discuss issues of common interest that were not related to APEC. Fortunately, this type of professional networking had been taking place on the ELTO program for years and the ELTP teachers had at their disposal the thoroughly trialed ELTO model of a research project with three linked tasks: formulating research questions, summarizing a source text, and writing a report on an interview with a New Zealand expert on the topic.

In terms of their language learning goals, the officials not only wanted to acquire language and skills for their APEC duties, whatever form they might take, but were also very keen to improve their IELTS scores because this would almost certainly enhance their career prospects. In fact, they candidly pointed out that an improved IELTS score would be of greater use to them in the long term than acquiring knowledge and skills for hosting APEC, which, after all, was an event that would occur only once in their working lives.

The information gained from the interviews was invaluable. Prior to the officials' arrival in New Zealand, the ELTP teachers were planning a course for people known only through their IELTS scores, job titles, and answers to a questionnaire about their goals for an APEC course at a time when APEC was largely unfamiliar to them, which made it difficult for them to give realistic responses. The interviews brought the course participants into focus and enabled the teachers to tailor the provisional, pre-arrival course into one which more closely matched the learners' needs. However, the tailoring did not stop there. It was an ongoing process throughout the course. For instance, the dichotomy between those officials who thought they might be given a logistical role at APEC and those who expected to play a part in negotiations on trade issues meant that the course members with a trade focus were pleased with the amount of reading and listening material on economics in Module 2, while those on the logistical side wanted rather less of economics. The teachers responded to this by ensuring that topics of more general interest were brought into various parts of the program, such as the daily fluency activities (Millett, 2008) and the listening materials. Also, in Modules 1 and 2 the teachers included a professional speaking strand in which the course members practiced the sort of small talk that plays an important part in official forums such as APEC, while in Module 3 an informal series of discussions with university staff and graduate students from seven Asian member economies of APEC was arranged so that the officials could learn about cultural dos and don'ts when interacting with people from those economies. The focus was on Asian cultures because the officials expressed concern about their lack of familiarity with them. These elements of the program were designed to be of use especially, though not exclusively, to those officials who might be given responsibility for meeting and greeting APEC visitors. Another element that was added to the program was a question-and-answer session with the official from the Ministry of Foreign Affairs and Trade who was in charge of New Zealand's hosting of APEC in 1999. He canvassed a wide range of practical issues, from seating arrangements to security, which helped to allay the concerns of those members of the group who anticipated being assigned logistical tasks.

Another way in which the course was tailored to meet the needs of the first group was the weighting that was given to the development of language skills. Extra listening classes were provided during the first module, as listening was an area of relative weakness for most of the officials and it was also a skill which all of them signaled as being important. On the other hand, writing requirements were scaled back after the majority of the officials said that they did not have a great need for writing skills. Indeed, one course member remarked that he wrote his scientific papers in Spanish and had them translated into English by means of a computer program.

Some more tailoring, in the form of well-intentioned social engineering, arose from the teachers' concern that, apart from shared IELTS classes with the ELTO officials, the ELTP group members spent most of their time in a monolingual and monocultural environment. This was not only during class time but also outside of it because, after an initial period in homestays, they were placed in shared apartments in the same building, with the result that they socialized with one another in Spanish. To introduce some variety into their class-based fluency activities, contact was made with a group of skilled migrants who were studying on a program designed to improve their knowledge of language and cultural practices in the New Zealand workplace (see Nicky Riddiford, Chapter 7, this volume). Like the Peruvians, the skilled migrants were professionals with well-established careers in their home countries, and the contact between the two groups was a source of much enjoyment as well as excellent language practice. However, an attempt to create links with another group of students at the university, New Zealand learners of Spanish, was less successful. When planning the course it had seemed natural that Kiwi students studying Spanish would welcome the opportunity to have language buddies who were native speakers of Peruvian Spanish. However, apart from a few ELTP course participants who organized regular out-of-class language exchanges with Kiwi students, very little resulted from this initiative, possibly because of age and stage-of-life differences.

At the end of the first program there was an opportunity for the teachers to take stock and make recommendations to the other stakeholders, particularly NZAID and the Peruvian government, about the future direction and management of the course. The sixteen officials in the first intake had diverse professional backgrounds and came from a wide range of ministries and local authorities and, as noted above, this meant that they had expectations that the program content would include, on the one hand, APEC goals and policies in the context of an exploration of international trade issues and, on the other hand, procedural information about how to successfully host APEC. The teachers' impression was that, although some of the officials found the materials on trade issues heavy going from time to time, they ultimately appreciated having an understanding of the economic fundamentals of APEC. However, the teachers recommended to NZAID that this diversity of expectations be factored into the planning for the next intake, either through the selection of candidates or by making it clear to course participants that, in terms of course content, a balance would be struck between the "what" and the "how" of APEC. As it turned out, though, the dichotomy which had been a feature of the first intake was non-existent in the second, with the officials saying that most of the logistical duties involved in hosting APEC were being contracted to firms in the private sector.

The teachers were not the only stakeholders who made a request for change. The Peruvian authorities asked that more content about APEC be included in the course for the second group of officials. Since the higher level of English proficiency of the second intake would enable the officials to cope with more listening input, the teachers increased the number of guest lectures about APEC and incorporated BBC and Radio New Zealand documentaries about international trade issues in the program.

In addition to expanding the APEC content, there was a greater focus on skills. For instance, the officials were given more opportunities to practice the formal speaking skills that they would need at APEC through discussion groups and the APEC simulation activity. Discussion groups were a weekly activity in which the person whose turn it was to be leader was responsible for choosing a topic and then guiding the group discussion by setting the parameters, making sure that all of the members made a contribution, keeping everyone focused on the topic and summing up the main points at the end.

Towards the end of the course the officials took part in a role-play activity designed to simulate an APEC meeting. This gave them an opportunity to practice the skills they had been developing in the discussion groups, but to do so in a context more closely resembling an APEC meeting in terms of its emphasis on consensus-building. A retired New Zealand diplomat who maintained close links with APEC was employed as a consultant to manage the various stages involved in this activity, culminating in the meeting simulation. His long experience as a facilitator of meetings on a wide range of topics and his particular experience with APEC were enormously valuable. Prior to the simulation the officials chose two issues which they wished to place on the agenda: farmer resistance to free trade reforms and a strengthened regional security network. They discussed the issues and wrote background papers on them. The consultant then prepared two proposals for each issue, which were to be the subject of discussion on the day of the simulation. The simulation was preceded by a lecture outlining the special nature of consensus-building in APEC and the integral part it played in the functioning of the organization. The consultant then chaired the officials' discussion, stopping it at critical points to give them immediate feedback on the way they presented their various positions on the issues and the extent to which they were operating in a way likely to achieve an APEC-style consensus. This practical advice from someone so familiar with APEC's modus operandi was extremely useful for the officials.

Another aspect of the increased focus on skills with the second intake was the training provided in writing APEC-style documents. The members of the first intake had not considered writing to be an important skill for them, but the second group of officials had a clearer idea of the duties that would be assigned to them at APEC and these included liaising with counterparts in APEC economies by letter and email, organizing meetings, and preparing a range of texts including meeting agendas, final reports, draft statements for inclusion in the final APEC declaration, memoranda of understanding, websites, media releases, and information about Peruvian projects.

An addition to the program which was made in response to a request from the officials was a workshop on techniques for working as a team so that, if called upon, they would be in a position to provide assistance to each other at APEC meetings.

One thing that did not change between the two courses was the IELTS factor. Despite the higher level of proficiency of the second group, IELTS cast an even longer shadow over Modules 2 and 3, when the IELTS preparation classes were held, than it had for the first intake. The officials were very anxious about the test and wanted to have as much practice as possible with IELTS-style speaking and writing activities, which made it difficult for them to give their full attention to other aspects of the course.

After the second ELTP course ended in June 2007 in a flurry of farewells and promises to meet again in Peru, teachers had time to reflect on the course. Had it achieved the aims of NZAID, the Peruvian government, and the officials themselves? There were many aims to consider, some publicly stated and others privately held. IELTS results were the most public of all, and they clearly showed that the program was successful. The majority of the course participants in both intakes obtained the increase in their IELTS scores specified in NZAID's indicator of achievement, with some of them going far beyond it. Generally, the participants in the first intake made greater gains than those in the second group, which was to be expected in view of the difference in their proficiency levels at the outset. The many years of experience of the ELTO program teachers with pre- and post-course IELTS tests has shown that learners who have reached the level of proficiency of the ELTP officials in the second intake tend to make more incremental and less dramatic progress on the IELTS test than learners at lower levels of proficiency.

Was the officials' private objective of furthering their careers through an improved IELTS score met? It is difficult to say, but some officials were promoted when they returned home and it seems that their IELTS results played a part in this.

Were the officials' learning objectives met? Their responses on the end-of-course evaluation forms suggest that they were. The first intake gave the course a strongly positive evaluation and the second group indicated that the course helped them to learn while they were in New Zealand and stimulated them to go on learning in the future.

Did the course help the officials to have the English language skills they needed to be effective participants in APEC in 2008? Some anecdotal evidence about this made its way back to the teachers from the then-chairperson of APEC's Economic Committee, who is also a professor at Victoria University. He first met with the officials in Wellington and then saw them in Lima in 2008 when the APEC meetings were under way. He reported that the officials were very successfully managing Peru's hosting of APEC and were enthusiastic about the benefits the course had provided for them. It was gratifying to hear that the course participants handled their APEC duties well because this was the ultimate test of the appropriateness of the course design. It would have been interesting to have a detailed description of the actual duties the officials were given at APEC in order to compare them with the course content and find the inevitable gaps, but this would have been an exercise with no practical application to the stakeholders because it will be another twenty years before it is Peru's turn to host APEC again, and thus there was no possibility of funding for such an undertaking.

And what of NZAID's overall goal of assisting in building Peru's capacity for good governance? This is a complex question which goes well beyond the domain of course design and delivery and ultimately is for diplomats, politicians, and specialists in development issues to determine.

Reference

Millett, S. (2008). A daily fluency programme. *Modern English Teacher, 17*(2), 21–28.

Comment

In this chapter Susan Smith has described a high-profile, well-funded, government-to-government language training course for officials, a course that gave participants access to "movers and shakers" in their field. As a result, it was also a relatively high-stakes undertaking. While the five different stakeholders would have had some differing expectations, one example of the importance attached to the course is that the participants' performance as English language speakers at APEC would potentially reflect on the host nation; in particular, if they performed poorly it would reflect badly on Peru.

In the initial planning of the course, participants had been expected to have defined roles at the Peru-hosted APEC meetings, and to share a set of very specific needs. Such an assumption would have facilitated planning. The needs and environment analyses did, however, throw up some challenges, such as the lack of knowledge about their roles at APEC, which meant that the course design was an evolving process.

A further challenge clearly arose from the shifting goals in the second iteration of the course, a result of changes in both the needs analysis and the student segment of the environment analysis. This was also complicated by the course designer's need to respond appropriately to stakeholder requests. Thus, providing a high-profile and well-funded course is far from being an uncomplicated exercise in course design.

Tasks

1. The focus of this chapter has been on needs analysis, but the curriculum was clearly designed on the basis of all three outer circles. Read the chapter again and identify the principles that appear to have been applied to the course for Peruvian officials.
2. Identify the key factors in the learning situation. What implications did these have for the curriculum?

TABLE 6.1

Learning situation factors	Effect on course
E.g. Course taught in capital city	Access to central government ministry officials

3. Change one or two of the key factors that you identified in Task 2. What changes in the curriculum would be necessary to respond to these changes?

7

HELPING SKILLED MIGRANTS INTO EMPLOYMENT: THE WORKPLACE COMMUNICATION PROGRAM

Nicky Riddiford

Introduction

Learning how to interact and communicate in appropriate ways in a new workplace is a challenging task for any new employee. This challenge is greatly increased when the interactions involve a language that is not the employee's first language. This chapter discusses the key elements of a program that is designed to help skilled migrants in New Zealand develop competence in the communication skills and workplace practices relevant to the professional workplace.

Background

The Workplace Communication Program for Skilled Migrants at Victoria University of Wellington, New Zealand (hereafter referred to as the skilled migrant program) was first established in 2005 and was designed to assist unemployed and underemployed skilled migrants to develop their communicative competence, in order to increase their chances of gaining employment in their chosen professions in New Zealand.

Needs of Skilled Migrants

Skilled migrants to any country face a sometimes bewildering array of challenges. It quickly becomes apparent to many that they lack key experiences that would facilitate their integration into the professional working community. Skilled migrants to New Zealand are no exception and the 2001 census figures showed that there were 2,000 skilled migrants, nationally, who were unemployed or underemployed. A lack of New Zealand work experience, a lack of awareness of and ability to use communication styles suitable for the New Zealand context, a lack of access to professional networks, a lack of contact with New Zealanders, and a lack of confidence are often cited as the areas of most concern.

Program Goals and Content

The program is designed to address these specific needs and aims to help skilled migrants:

* understand and develop appropriate communication skills in professional workplaces;
* gain New Zealand workplace experience;
* develop an understanding of New Zealand workplace practices in specific professional areas.

These very specific goals present a challenge as they are not easily achieved by classroom teaching alone and with this in mind the twelve-week program includes a six-week workplace placement. During this work experience component of the program, participants can put into practice the communication skills developed in the classroom-based instructional phase. Teaching in this phase of the course aims to develop awareness of characteristic features of communication in NZ workplaces, as well as develop analytical skills in identifying these features; skills which will empower migrant workers to make choices about how to interact in the workplace context. The classroom program includes a range of further topics to familiarize the participants with working in the New Zealand context, for example: cross-cultural awareness; CV and interview skills; information about New Zealand culture, history, politics, and employment issues; oral presentation; report writing; telephoning, emailing and meeting skills. The curriculum is flexible enough to allow for the addition of further topics in response to the needs of any particular group.

In the instructional component of the program, participants attend class for four hours per day. This time constraint influences how much class time can be devoted to each topic and the skilled migrant participants are required to spend a considerable time developing their skills outside the class.

Contributors

In order to meet the needs of the participants and to achieve the varied goals outlined earlier, the program relies on many contributors from different walks of life. The program is fortunate in having a number of key partnerships within the Wellington business community; in particular with the Rotary Club of Wellington and with an employment recruitment agency, the Johnson Group.

The Rotary Club of Wellington plays a significant role as a partner in the program and provides help in a number of areas: by providing volunteers from a range of professions to help as classroom tutors who carry out role-plays and mock interviews with the participants; by providing guest speakers on a range of workplace topics; by providing help with sourcing work experience placements; and by providing job mentors who assist the participants in their job search when they graduate from the program.

The Johnson Group, a recruitment agency, works alongside the program and has the role of sourcing the work experience placements from within the public and private sectors in Wellington.

Staff members at Victoria University contribute in a number of ways. The program is coordinated and delivered by teachers in the English Language Institute, School of Linguistics and Applied Language Studies. The Career Advisors from the Career and Development Service provide training and ongoing help with CVs and job interviews. In addition the course materials that focus on communication skills draw heavily on authentic workplace conversations recorded for the Language in the Workplace Project at Victoria University (LWP). Since 1996, the LWP has been developing a large corpus of transcribed recordings of workplace talk from a range of workplaces, and this material has been used extensively for research purposes. (See the Wellington Language in the Workplace Project website: www.victoria.ac.nz/lals/lwp/).

Another agency involved in the program is the ESOL Assessment and Access Specialist Service. Members of this service select and refer participants to the program and offer support to the participants as workplace consultants during their work experience internship.

Course Participants

The course is intended for skilled migrants who have gained permanent residency in New Zealand and have some experience in their profession; who have English as an additional language (at a level of IELTS 6 or higher); who have a Bachelor's degree or higher; and who are unemployed or underemployed. Participants have come to New Zealand from China, Taiwan, Russia, Singapore, Malaysia, Cambodia, Iraq, Brazil, India, Sri Lanka, Pakistan, Korea, Japan, and the Philippines. Their professional backgrounds include accounting, business analysis, financial analysis, insurance, public relations, medicine, office management, engineering, law, economics, banking, software development and testing, logistics, stock-broking, and information systems.

The selection criteria, goals of the program and the backgrounds of the course participants all have an impact on the content of the program. The high standard of English required allows the use of relatively sophisticated teaching and learning materials and activities. The goals of the program are all related to entering the professional workforce in New Zealand so the curriculum can be very focused. However, the range of professional backgrounds means that course material cannot be related to any one profession but rather, participants are given tools and frameworks which they can apply to their own specialist areas. In any one course there is usually a range of ages and length of professional experience but all the participants are highly motivated to improve their English language skills and their job search skills. The small size of the class (only 10 to 12 participants are accepted in each intake) allows for greater individual attention; attention that comes not only from the classroom teachers but from the agency involved in sourcing the work experience internships, from the workplace consultants who monitor and guide the interns' performance during their work experience, and from the volunteer tutors who visit weekly.

Needs Analysis

The program uses several processes to analyze the needs of each intake of partici-pants. On Day One of the program the skilled migrants survey their classmates in order to identify the particular needs of the group. On Days Two to Four of Week One the course coordinator (who is also the principal class teacher) interviews each participant about their particular needs. She then records the participants carrying out role-plays of a range of workplace scenarios and, immediately following this exercise, she carries out a retrospective interview with questions that are designed to elicit the thinking behind the role-play performances. Participants also complete written discourse completion tasks of the role-play scenarios and others. The role-plays and discourse completion tasks provide very useful snapshots of the level of communicative and pragmatic competence of each individual. In addition, in Week One, all participants are interviewed by The Johnson Group, who source the work placements, to establish abilities and preferred work goals.

Principles of Teaching and Learning

The acquisition of communication skills that are appropriate for different contexts (often described as pragmatic skills in the socio-linguistic literature) requires specific attention as these skills are often not picked up by simply living in a new society. Although second language (L2) learners are generally aware of pragmatic features and strategies in their own language (albeit often unconsciously), this awareness is not always carried over to their L2 production. This lack of awareness can have serious consequences for a new migrant as any inappropriate communi-cation can be regarded as being intentional (Riddiford, 2007).

According to Kasper (1996, p. 148) it is important to include certain elements in any instructional model that aims to develop pragmatic skills. These elements are: relevant input, opportunities for learners to notice the input, and opportuni-ties for learners to develop a high level of processing control of the language features. Bearing this in mind, the instruction module developed for assisting the participants in the skilled migrant program involved three components: authentic input; analysis and discussion of the input to encourage noticing; and many opportunities to develop control of the language features by practice with native speakers.

The Sequence of Instruction

Guided by the research on the value of authentic input, and bearing in mind the specific workplace focus of the instruction module, as mentioned earlier, authentic conversations from the Language in the Workplace Project, Victoria University of Wellington are used to illustrate certain communicative acts in a white-collar workplace context: requests, refusals, complaints, suggestions, and disagreements.

As discussed in Riddiford (2007) the steps in the instruction module employed in the program are as follows. First, the authentic conversations are analyzed in terms of the influence of socio-cultural factors on the language choices that the speakers had made, as well as in terms of the language forms themselves. For example, learners' attention is drawn to the significance of familiarity, status, and degree of imposition in each situation and how these factors influence the way people speak. As Schmidt observed (1995), both noticing the form and gaining an understanding of the socio-cultural elements involved are important in the development of pragmatic knowledge. After this analysis and discussion, the next stage entails opportunities for the learners to practice the language in role-plays with their classmates and with the native speaker volunteer tutors who visit the class weekly. The volunteer tutors, as mentioned earlier, are all from professional backgrounds and are ideally suited to provide feedback on the suitability of language choices and other features of the communication. The role-plays are also video-taped and, after class, learners are required to analyze their performance and reflect on what was successful or not in the interaction and the appropriateness of the language used. To encourage further noticing and reflecting, throughout the module learners are also required to keep a journal and record their observations of the use of speech acts in their lives outside the classroom and during the work experience period of the program.

An Example from the Requesting Unit in the Instruction Module: Asking for a Day's Leave

The example that follows shows in more detail the steps involved in analyzing an excerpt of an authentic conversation that involves asking for a day off.

Step 1: Relevant Input and Opportunities for Noticing

a. The context of the conversation is outlined (see below) and the participants' attention is drawn to the significant features of the context that will play a role in determining the language choices. For example the participants discuss their perceptions of the status/power relationship between the two speakers, how well they know each other and the level of difficulty of the task of asking for a day off.

The context

> Tom and Greg work in a government department. They have worked together for some time and know each other quite well. Tom wants to take Friday off and have a long weekend skiing. He goes to visit Greg.

b.   The participants are then given the two opening lines from the authentic interaction and are asked to role-play how they think the conversation would continue:

> Tom: Can I have a quick word?
> Greg: Yeah, sure. Have a seat.

c.   Having completed the role-play above, the participants read and listen to a reconstruction of the authentic dialogue and compare their role-played version with this.

The original conversation (from Holmes, 2000)

> Tom: Can I just have a quick word?
> Greg: Yeah sure, have a seat.
> Tom: (sitting down) Great weather, eh?
> Greg: Mm.
> Tom: Yeah, been a good week. Did you get away skiing at the weekend?
> Greg: Yeah we did – now how can I help you?
> Tom: I was wondering if I could take Friday off and make it a long weekend.
> Greg: I don't see any problem with that. You will have finished that report by then, won't you?

Step 2: Opportunities for Noticing and Reflecting

The participants then answer a series of questions that are designed to encourage noticing of linguistic features in the conversation, for example:

> Compare your conversation with the example. What differences did you notice?
> What words or phrases are used to make the conversation go smoothly?
> What phrase was used to make the request? Why was this phrase chosen?
> What words or phrases are used to soften the request?
> Are there any pauses? What is the effect of these?
> How does the dialogue begin? Where in the conversation does the request come?

How direct or polite was Tom?
Would the conversation happen in the same way in your country?

The participants then look at several more interactions involving requests in the workplace and analyze them using the steps outlined above.

Step 3: Opportunities to Practice and Receive Feedback

The participants then role-play several request scenarios with their classmates, with the teacher and with volunteer tutors. The role-plays are video-taped for later review. A final step involves the participants practicing making requests by email and by telephone and discussing the different style of language that these mediums require.

The Learning Cycle

As can be seen from the description of the instruction model and the example of the classroom materials above, the program provides many opportunities for learners to practice, reflect, observe, and receive feedback from teachers, from volunteer tutors, from workplace support personnel, and from managers during the work placement. The participants are often pushed beyond their comfort zone but as a result often make significant progress in a very short time. This cyclical process of learning is outlined in Figure 7.1.

Assessment

The progress that participants make is assessed during and at the end of the three-month course. There are a number of formal assessment tasks that the class is

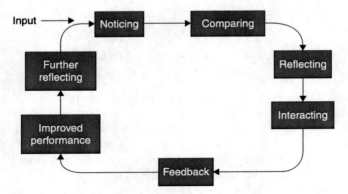

FIGURE 7.1 The cyclical process of learning

introduced to on the first day of the course. All the tasks are linked to the objectives of the program and this is made explicit in the course information booklet. The formal assessment tasks include:

- a professional portfolio containing a CV and cover letter, an email, a career plan, language learning goals;
- an oral presentation (10–15 minutes) that integrates understandings gained during the classroom phase of the course and the work experience component;
- participation in interactions during the course, for example, in mock job interviews;
- a self-evaluative reflective exercise where each participant summarizes their development of communication skills in English.

In addition each participant receives a report from their work placement manager, who comments on a range of features including the ability to work independently, communication skills, and how well the participant fitted into the team.

As can be seen from the discussion and model of the learning cycle above, there are also many informal assessment and feedback opportunities that occur throughout the course, for example, self-assessments of recorded interactions and mock job interviews, feedback from volunteer tutors, ongoing feedback from the teacher, and feedback from the workplace consultants.

Program Evaluation

Evaluation of the program takes a number of forms: an evaluation questionnaire completed by all graduating participants, a formal evaluation of the course and teaching carried out by the university, and informal debrief meetings at the end of each course with feedback from all contributors: teachers, workplace consultants and managers. In response to the suggestions raised in these different forms of feedback and evaluation the program is constantly being added to and improved.

In addition, several of the skilled migrant participants have also been involved in a research study that is currently being carried out by the Language in the Workplace research team at Victoria University. This study tracks the development of communication skills of course members during the instructional segment of the program and during the work experience period. The results of this research provide further valuable insights into the effectiveness of the teaching module and course materials.

Perhaps the most compelling insight into the value of the program comes from a survey of the employment outcomes for the graduates. To date approximately 79 per cent of the graduates of the program, from 2005 to 2009, have found employment in their professional areas.

Conclusion

This chapter has described a program designed to prepare skilled migrants for the professional workplace in New Zealand. Significant features of the program are the instruction in communication skills based on the analysis of authentic interactions; opportunities for participants to practice these skills with native speakers in the classroom and the workplace; and opportunities for participants to become aware of workplace practices in New Zealand by completing a six-week internship in their specialist areas.

References

Holmes, J. (2000). Doing collegiality and keeping control at work: Small talk in government departments. In Justine Coupland (Ed.), *Small talk* (pp. 32–61). London, UK: Longman.

Kasper, G. (1996). Introduction: Pragmatics in SLA. *Studies in Second Language Acquisition 18*, 145–148.

Riddiford, N. (2007). Making requests appropriately in a second language: Does instruction help to develop pragmatic proficiency? *The TESOLANZ Journal*, 15, 88–102.

Schmidt, R. (1995). Consciousness and foreign language learning: A tutorial on the role of attention and awareness in learning. In *Attention and Awareness in Foreign Language Learning* (pp. 1–63). Honolulu: University of Hawaii, Second Language Teaching and Curriculum Center.

Comment

This chapter has provided us with a concise description of a specific purposes course that has achieved remarkable results in moving skilled migrants into the workplace. The successful manner in which a number of people and organizations have worked together over several years is also a noteworthy feature of the program. Ultimately, however, the well-intentioned efforts of individuals and organizations would most probably have failed in meeting the program's goal if the course had not been appropriately designed.

The content of this course was clearly selected to meet the needs of the participants, which had in turn determined the course goals. The Language in the Workplace Project provided a rich resource of authentic workplace exchanges to draw on for teaching purposes, but having well-chosen authentic material for classroom use would not have been sufficient in itself. It was the tasks built around the available material that created the learning opportunities; in this case study, then, we have information both about course content decisions and about the format and presentation of the teaching material. These are important questions for teachers and course designers to consider, and the suggestions for further reading below explore them further.

Tasks

1. The content of a course should be related to the needs of the learners, and to who the learners are. Read the chapter again and make notes to complete the table below. As the example shows, not all needs in this case study may be language-related.

TABLE 7.1

About the learners	Learners' needs	Course content
Do not have New Zealand work experience	Experience of a New Zealand workplace	Work experience placement

2. Kasper's (1996) instructional model suggests three important elements, or principles, to draw on. Explain to a partner how these elements are included in the example from the requesting unit in this chapter.
3. This chapter has focused on how one pragmatic skill, making a request, was taught to the skilled migrants. Choose one other area of course content, from the table in Task 1, and consider a sequence of activities for teaching that. You might want to consider the principles that Nicky Riddiford mentions in this chapter, or draw on another set of principles.

Suggested Further Reading

Macalister, J. (forthcoming). Today's teaching, tomorrow's text: exploring the teaching of reading. *ELT Journal*.

Nation, P. (2007). The four strands. *Innovation in Language Learning and Teaching, 1*(1), 1–12.

Willis, J. (1996). *A framework for task-based learning*. Harlow, UK: Longman.

8

THE BLENDED LANGUAGE LEARNING COURSE IN TAIWAN: ISSUES AND CHALLENGES OF INSTRUCTIONAL DESIGN

Gi-Zen Liu

Introduction

Humans use language in various forms for communication for many purposes (Graddol, 2004; Szathmary & Szamado, 2008). We are living in a networked society in which information and communication technologies (ICT) are used in many situations, fields, and contexts to facilitate language learning, including the first and other languages. Technology enhanced language learning (TELL) is a trans-disciplinary field that has been influencing human language development in various academic subjects and areas for more than half a century. Since the 1990s, ICT-embedded language learning has been the most widely used form of TELL. In addition, the English language has been identified as "power on the Internet" (Flammia & Saunders, 2007), and in non-English-speaking countries English as a foreign language (EFL) or English as an international language (EIL) dominates the international use and spread of information and knowledge in many fields and contexts (Crystal, 2003; Graddol, 2000, 2004, 2006). Innovative ICT (Becta, 2004; Hill & Vasudevan, 2008) has opened the door for exploring culture-rich language learning materials, practicing receptive and productive language abilities, and promoting frequent language use in two-way communication.

ICT and Blended Language Learning

As Kern and Warschauer (2000) indicate, technology both serves and shapes new language teaching/learning paradigms. Hanson-Smith and Rilling (2006), Kern (2006), and Rozgiene, Medvedeva, and Strakova (2008) further identify the necessity and significance of using technology to facilitate language teaching and learning in this Internet Age. With the rapid development of ICT, both hardware (e.g. computers) and software (e.g. Internet-based communication systems) have increasingly become an integral part of language teaching. Since the 1990s, a hybrid course (Gould, 2003; Lawless & Pellegrino, 2007; Liu, 2003; Mayadas, Bourne, & Bacsich, 2009), which combines both the classroom and the Internet-based learning environment in delivering instruction, has been an innovative field that influences the way teachers facilitate students' learning. A hybrid course, or blended learning (Garrison & Kanuka, 2004; Macdonald, 2006), combines the advantages of online learning and teaching with face-to-face classroom instruction (Graham, 2006; Lawless & Pellegrino, 2007; Liu, 2003; Macdonald, 2006; Mayadas et al., 2009), and this way has become the prevailing language teaching trend with various applications of ICT (Liu, 2005). For example, Figure 8.1 shows a screenshot of various applications of ICT in English learning at National Cheng Kung University (NCKU).

As can be seen, the various ICT applications provided on the website for instructors and students of English include: (a) latest news concerning English learning activities on and off NCKU campus; (b) English learning platforms (including a Chinese-based NCKU learning platform and the multilingual learning management system, Blackboard); (c) several online self-testing systems of English (such as TOEFL and IELTS); (d) online materials for English learning (including Live ABC & CANDLE); (e) freely available online programs and lessons for developing various language skills and language study areas; and (f) freely available online resources for downloading Internet-based software and communications.

Echoing what Bax (2003) terms "integrated CALL" – which indicates the integration of various technology-based language learning applications – Liu and Chen (2007) identify three major types of ICT integrated into language curricula: (a) CALL programs with originally designed and embedded learning content (e.g. tutorials, testing, and games); (b) CMC tools without originally designed learning content but allowing users to provide language input (e.g. email, forums, chat rooms, Skype); and (c) learning management systems (or LMS, e.g. Moodle, Blackboard) with which instructors and students can upload, download, share, and retrieve a variety of electronic files, as well as do many other learning activities online. The use of ICT integration in both entirely online and blended learning contexts to promote and foster language development can be called blended language learning (BLL). However, BLL is still in development, and there are no standard forms (Andrews et al., 2007; Lamping, 2004; Leakey & Ranchoux, 2006; Stracke, 2007). Becta (2004) summarizes the research findings on effective ICT use in foreign language learning from the literature, identifying the ways that teachers and students can benefit from such practices when (a) instructors continuously develop professional knowledge of new ICT applications and regularly access ICT resources and integrate them into their teaching, and (b) students confidently use video-conferencing and other equipment in well-designed activities to engage in learning the target language. More importantly, how to make good use of ICT in language teaching and learning has

FIGURE 8.1 The various applications of ICT in English learning at National Cheng Kung University (NCKU)

become an important issue and a critical factor in the successful practice of TELL (Kern, 2006; Liu, 2005, 2008; Liu & Chen, 2007).

Soft Technologies and Hard Technologies in Language Learning

In this networked era, hard technologies may refer to both hardware (e.g. computer, cellular phone, and others) and software (e.g. email, blog, and others) (Jonassen, 2004; McDonough & Kahn, 1996) that people can use to learn new knowledge and skills independently or collaboratively in various wired and wireless contexts. Meanwhile, soft technologies refer to well-designed instructional techniques, processes, principles, or models that are developed based on specific behavioral and social methods or theories to enable learning individually or in groups (Heinich, Molenda, Russell, & Smaldino, 1999; Jonassen, 2004), with or without the use of hard technologies (Shoffner, Jones, & Harmon, 2000), to bring about the desired learning outcomes. The various forms of both hard and soft technologies (see Figure 8.2) have been evolving to meet the varied needs of stakeholders in corporate, military, educational, and research settings. In order to make the best use of the available information and communication technologies, practitioners and researchers need to develop and promote a series of best practices related to them (McPherson & Whitworth, 2008; Rushby, 2007).

While hard technologies may have instant and obvious effects in their applications, the importance of soft technologies to the vitality of such applications should not be underestimated (McDonough & Kahn, 1996), and the latter tends to be more powerful than the former in practices and in their impact (Burgess &

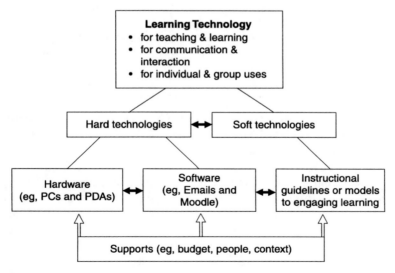

FIGURE 8.2 The interrelationship among various forms of Learning Technology

Gules, 1998). Even if a hard technology is able to operate independently, its value depends on how it can be used to facilitate human learning effectively and efficiently (Liu, 2008), and this phenomenon is obvious in language learning (Hoven, 2006; Lally, 2000). From the mid-1990s onwards, instructional designers of learning technology have been working with language teachers and/or computer programmers to develop numerous interactive websites and networked learning platforms (Becta, 2004; Colpaert, 2002; Levy & Stockwell, 2006; Liu, 2003) as either entirely online programs and lessons or as supplements to the face-to-face instruction provided in traditional classes (Ko & Rossen, 2001; Mayadas et al., 2009). Consequently, it is necessary to investigate how to make more effective use of hard technologies in language learning, as well as to discover the role and value of soft technologies, in order to understand both the potential and limitations of such technologies, so that they can be better applied in practice.

Integrating ICT into Language Learning and Teaching

Many language teachers and applied linguists have recognized that the use of modern technologies can help first language, second language, and foreign language learners develop their target language anytime, anywhere. CALL, also known as technology-enhanced language learning (TELL), is one of the promising academic areas within applied linguistics (Chapelle, 2001; Gruba, 2004; Levy and Stockwell, 2006). Researchers and practitioners of language instruction as well as applied linguists have realized that cutting-edge ICT, if guided or applied properly, can help all levels of learners develop their target language to a certain degree anytime, anywhere. Language learning and development in both CALL and non-CALL contexts foster the "dynamic, nonlinear, and open nature of complex systems" (Larsen-Freeman & Cameron, 2008, p. 200) for which many CALL researchers (e.g. Bax, 2003; Felix, 2008; Stockwell, 2007) have been attempting to propose means of identifying, exploring, and investigating the complicated attributes, processes, outcomes, impact, effectiveness, efficiency, and other aspects of CALL. Along with the evolution of various types of technologies applied to language learning (Liu & Chen, 2007), in this ever-changing, multidisciplinary field, there are several basic but important components that establish the "CALL equation" (Egbert, 2005). These components are adapted and presented in Figure 8.3, and include the learner (with his or her prior knowledge, experiences, motivations, behaviors, and others), the so-called "hard" technologies (hardware and software) and "soft" technologies (identified ways or methods for using hard technologies) (Jonassen, 2004), hyperlinked learning contents, and interactive learning tasks/activities, with or without the peer and/or instructor support.

For various levels of instructional design when integrating ICT into English teaching and learning, we may need to take these critical components into consideration in order to appropriately plan and develop the sequence of language learning in a hybrid course in an organized way.

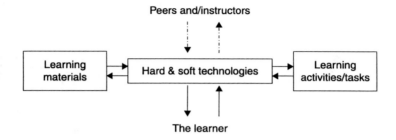

Context (physical, social, cultural, economic, linguistic and others)

FIGURE 8.3 A diagram adapted from Egbert's (2005) CALL equation

Levels of Instructional Design

Graham (2006) identified four levels of blended learning (a term used to describe the way a learner develops new knowledge and skills in both online and face-to-face learning environments) for interested researchers and practitioners to follow when arranging instructional materials and resources, as well as when designing learning activities and processes. The four levels, from top to bottom in terms of the nature of the blends in an organization or a company that learns, are (a) institutional level, (b) program level, (c) course level, and (d) activity level. Graham (2006) states that the learner usually has the right to decide which institution and program to attend, while the instructor and the instructional designer are supposed to take the responsibility to arrange meaningful learning experiences with appropriate materials and resources for the learner at the course and activity levels. I follow this well-developed perspective to identify the four levels of instructional design for integrating ICT into English teaching and learning in educational institutions (see Figure 8.4). Applying this perspective, at an educational institution there may be several language programs in which many different language courses are offered to the learners in order to develop the target language through well-designed learning activities that are conducted individually or collaboratively over a semester or a year.

Defining the Four Levels

It is important to clearly distinguish these four levels in order for the instructor and the instructional designer to better plan, develop, manage, implement, and evaluate the effectiveness and efficiency of integrating ICT into language teaching and learning in educational institutions. The definitions of the four levels are as follows.

a. At the institution level: the administrator (the president, chancellor, or principal) or the top-level committee at an educational institution must set up and

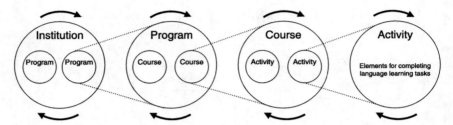

FIGURE 8.4 The four levels of integrating ICT into language teaching and learning

execute a university- or school- wide educational policy to formally recognize a blended learning or a hybrid course approach and increase its chances of success by giving the necessary administrative, financial, and technical support.

b. At the program level: the administrator (the chairperson or director) or the program-level committee at the department or discipline program must set up and execute a program-wide policy to formally recognize a blended learning or a hybrid course approach and increase its chances of success by providing the necessary administrative, financial, and technical support to the courses and instructors.

c. At the course level: the instructor or instructional designer of the course must prepare and execute a course syllabus that will aid the implementation of a blended learning or hybrid course approach by arranging learning and technical support for the learners.

d. At the activity level: the instructor or instructional designer of the course must prepare and undertake a variety of learning activities that will aid the implementation of a blended learning or hybrid course approach by arranging learning and technical support for the learners.

According to Thorne (2003), successful blended learning (combining face-to-face learning and e-learning) contains several important factors, such as (a) identifying the learning need, (b) setting up the level of demand, (c) recognizing and respecting different learning styles, (d) identifying learning goals with the current instructors, (e) presenting a friendly demonstration, (f) offering follow-up support, and (g) setting up a self-monitoring process. These methods should be helpful for instructional practitioners to integrate technology into human learning. In Taiwan, e-learning is supported by the government and there are some funding opportunities for the industry and the academic professionals to apply for innovative developments. Not only Taiwanese college students but elementary students are comfortable in the Internet-based learning environment, which is beneficial for Internet-enhanced language learning (Liu, 2005). However, there has to date been no large-scale, nationwide survey concerning the use, impact, and effect of Internet-assisted language learning and teaching in Taiwan.

Studies in Blended Language Learning, 2002 to 2008

To realize how ICT can be used in BLL, I first developed an instructional design theory (or IDT; Reigeluth, 1999) for teaching Freshman English in a hybrid course, following the designed case type of Reigeluth & Frick's (1999) qualitative formative research methodology (FRM). The two co-authors state that FRM was developed based on formative evaluation and case study research methodologies. For engaging students' language learning in this IDT, I used Omaggio-Hadley (2001) to combine the instruction of skills (speaking, listening, reading, and writing) and major language areas (vocabulary, grammar, and culture) into integrated, communicative language use with three communicative modes (NSFLLP, 1996) – interpretive, presentational, and interpersonal – to develop a design model (see Appendix A) with tentative guidelines for IDT. A first round of expert review then helped me to revise the model (see Appendix B) with improved guidelines, leading to the development of refined unit-based and project-based learning activities to foster language development in BLL. Fluency and accuracy of language use are the goals.

In the 2004–2005 study, I conducted the second round of expert review on the IDT, as well as putting the refined IDT into practice in two mid-proficiency-level classes of Freshman English at one university. Later, in the 2005–2006 research, I further identified effective ICT uses and benefits with the refined IDT in three Freshman English classes of three different proficiency levels (low, mid, and high) taught by three instructors at another university. In the studies, students and instructors were asked to reflect on BLL practices (using an LMS with self-chosen CMC tools and CALL programs) to see whether the chosen guidelines would work well in the instruction. Because the main concern of FRM is preferability, the criteria for evaluating the research were effectiveness, efficiency, and appeal (Reigeluth & Frick, 1999). Hence, the guiding research question for this work was "What are the synthesized principles for effective ICT practices in BLL?" To analyze the formative data in the studies, I used (a) emerging themes of the expert/instructor perspectives, (b) reasons and suggestions from the experts/instructors, and (c) my interpretations and decisions to revise the guidelines (Liu, 2003). In addition, I recognized the issue of situationality and replicated the study to increase the rigor of the results (Reigeluth & Frick, 1999). The major themes and findings of the studies are summarized in Table 8.1.

As mentioned above, expert review played a role in the refinement of the BLL principles described below. Established experts are capable of using their expertise and experience to identify possible problems in advance and recommend improvements (Flagg, 1990). However, Flagg argues that the disadvantage of expert review is "dependency on their particular experiences, biases, and values" (1990, p. 170). With this in mind, I carefully selected experts in March 2008, as I did for the previous two rounds of expert review. I invited five BLL experts with at least six years of teaching and research experience in Taiwan to participate in this work, and three of the five agreed to contribute to this research by providing their feedback on the principles contained in the research documents. Once the analyses were completed, I sent them

TABLE 8.1 A summary of the studies contributing to the continuous refinement of the BLL principles

	2002–2003
Research site	Indiana University, USA (the PhD thesis)
Major research work	The creation of the IDT; the first-round expert review on the guidelines in the IDT
Participants	Five EFL/ESL practitioners and researchers
Research purpose	To create the first IDT for teaching EFL in BLL with personal teaching and research experience and a literature review
Research instruments	The model and guidelines in the IDT; questions for expert review
Major research findings	A. The design model and the guidelines needed to be revised based on the experts' constructive comments B. The improved IDT includes the purpose, preconditions, rationale, features, learning theories applied to this IDT, criteria for the instructional guidelines and situations, terminology, cross-IDT guidelines, guidelines for unit-based learning, and guidelines for project-based learning (Liu, 2003) C. Each guideline is composed of the desired learning outcomes, methods and component methods, and when and how to use them
	2004–2005
Research site	Tunghai University, Taiwan
Major research work	The second-round expert review; guideline refinement; the practice of the IDT
Participants	Three senior EFL professors for the expert review; two EFL practitioners and two mid-level classes (30 and 26 students in each)
Research purpose	To further refine the IDT with expert review and put the theory into practice in two mid-proficiency-level classes of English
Research instruments	The model, guidelines and Blackboard.com; questions for expert review; standardized exams, teacher and student questionnaire
Major research findings	A. The expert review suggested that the guidelines needed to be refined with suggestions and tested in practice B. One EFL professor commented that "most guidelines would be useful, but some could be synthesized" C. The guidelines were further refined based on the comments D. Two EFL instructors used the guidelines in their classes. E. The two experiment classes performed better (57.04 and 55.65 each) than other mid-level classes (52.21 out of 70 on the average) in the exam
	2005–2006
Research site	National Cheng Kung University, Taiwan
Major research work	Three practices for the three proficiency-level classes of English

Participants	Three EFL practitioners and three proficiency levels of classes: 54 students in the high-level class, 48 in the mid-level, and 57 in the low-level
Research purpose	To further refine the guidelines and identify different practices for three different proficiency-level classes
Research instruments	The guidelines and Blackboard.com; teacher interview and student questionnaire after the practice (standardized exams were not taken as the three classes had different language levels).
Major research findings	A. The three instructors used some methods and component methods in the selected guidelines in the classes, and they all agreed that most of the guidelines were clear, useful and practical
	B. There was no agreement about the best ICT integration form based on participating instructors' experience and students' preferences
	C. The three classes were satisfied with their English reading ability and dissatisfied with their listening comprehension
	D. Two teachers commented the class size was too big to manage and suggested the classes should be made smaller to promote better learning outcomes
	E. The researcher deleted some component methods to make the remaining practical

2008

Research site	National Cheng Kung University, Taiwan
Major research work	A framework for ICT practice in BLL with expert review
Participants	Three invited scholars with at least six years of BLL teaching and research experience
Research purpose	To synthesize the principles for the three different proficiency-level classes with various ICT in BLL with latest literature and expert review
Research instruments	The synthesized seven principles for ICT practice in BLL with literature check; the questions for expert review
Major research findings	A. All three experts agreed that the seven principles are helpful and realizable. They also thought that various ICT tools had been included
	B. The three experts liked the educational values of the principles and commented that they "are meaningful and persuasive"
	C. One expert inquired if the principles had been used by other international BLL experts or language teachers of other popular major languages. She suggested this action needed to be undertaken to make the principles more refined.

the electronic file of the document by email to get their responses. This action provided triangulation of the data, and the experts' feedback was used to ensure accuracy of the data and trustworthiness of my interpretations (Stake, 1995). No further suggestions were given by the experts after this process had been completed.

Seven Principles for Effective ICT Practice in BLL

The seven principles – synthesized with a focus on ICT integration, language development and educational values – provide ways to successfully realize BLL for EFL classes of three language proficiency levels. The principles are described below and summarized in Table 8.2.

1. Infuse Systems Thinking into the Language Program and Course for BLL

We need to consider and integrate all components in the program and the course as a whole by taking a macro view to bring about successful design, implementation and evaluation (McPherson & Whitworth, 2008) in BLL, and this macro view emerges from a micro view of course development, material selection, learning activities and performance assessment.

2. Facilitate Written Communication Development Via Asynchronous Discussions

Students from all proficiency levels are allowed to have more time to think and reflect in writing than in speaking to foster meaningful discourse, so the discussion boards or forums in a CALL program, a CMC tool (e.g. email or wiki) or an LMS should be applied in a hybrid course with 25 to 30 students. However, it should be noted that while the real-time chatrooms and instant messaging are good CMC tools for typing practice, they do little for writing development.

3. Improve Oral Skills in Pairs or Groups by Means of Synchronous Interactive Tools

It was found that three to five students in the mid- and high-level classes, as suggested by Liu's IDT, performed well in role-plays when using NetMeeting or Messenger. With regard to the low-level learners, the use of pairs in dialogue practice with NetMeeting is a useful activity.

4. Promote Cultural Understanding with Guided Learning in CALL Programs

Students at all three proficiency levels can benefit from the instructor's guidance with specific cultural topics related to the lessons, such as festivals, restaurants, or

TABLE 8.2 The components and values of the seven principles for effective ICT practice in BLL

Seven principles for effective ICT practice in BLL	ICT integration	Skills and areas of language development	Educational value
Infuse systems thinking into the language program and course for BLL.	LMS (major) and CALL or CMC, depending on the needs and available ICT	The four skills (speaking, listening, reading, and writing) and the three areas (vocabulary, grammar, and culture)	Coherent structures and content within and outside the language class
Facilitate written communication development via asynchronous discussions	CALL, CMC, or LMS, depending on available ICT	Reading and writing development with the three language areas	Flexible time for allowing further thinking and reflection
Improve oral skills in pairs or groups by means of synchronous interactive tools	CMC video conferencing or synchronous chats in LMS	Listening and speaking development with the three language areas	Available time for stimulating reinforcement, recall, and meaning negotiation
Promote cultural understanding with guided learning in CALL programs	CALL (e.g. Live ABC or BBC English Learning) with search engines and YouTube	Listening and reading development with culture (mostly), vocabulary, and grammar	Real life of the target culture can be observed with sufficient resources
Use collaborative learning to enhance linguistic and communicative competence	Online community in the LMS and CMC (e.g. MSN Messenger or Skype)	Text-based or voice-based language capability with vocabulary and grammar	The help from more capable students is useful and promotes equality
Apply scaffolding to develop critical thinking with comparisons between native and target languages	CMC tools (email, forums), CALL programs, and hypermedia in LMS	Both the written and oral forms of vocabulary, sentences, and idioms	Understanding the differences and the similarities between the two languages
Utilize project-based learning to enhance language learning transfer	CMC tools (mostly forums and online communities) embedded in LMS with search engines	Oral and written communication	Providing more opportunities for engaging language use and discovery

ICT, information and communication technologies; BLL, blended language learning; CALL, computer assisted language learning; CMC, computer mediated communication; LMS, learning management system.

movies. The instructor then needs to survey a range of CALL programs to find videos that are suitable for these students and topics.

5. Use Collaborative Learning to Enhance Linguistic and Communicative Competence

Linguistic competence refers to the human capability of using vocabulary, idioms, and grammatical rules in two-way, interpersonal communication among multi-user groups and communities for various purposes. It is found that all three proficiency levels of students can develop their language skills to a certain degree in this way, with three students in a group for oral and written communication as the best practice for this.

6. Apply Scaffolding to Develop Critical Thinking with Comparisons between Native and Target Languages

Students perform well when guided to use vocabulary, idioms, or sentence translation to develop their understanding of the different nature, structure, and cultural concepts between the native and targeted languages through written or oral forms. During the analysis, reasoning, judging, and synthesis processes of transforming linguistic functions, critical thinking is promoted and enhanced.

7. Utilize Project-based Learning to Enhance Language Learning Transfer

This principle is effective when students engage in team-supported, project-based learning. All the instructors encouraged their students to explore more information about the topics they were considering in order to have more opportunities to transfer the acquired language into similar situations in their daily lives or into new study areas.

Recommendations for Future Research

Due to the rapid development of ICT and its impact on language learning and use (Graddol, 2004), "digital natives" (Bennett, Maton, & Kervin, 2008) and adults will learn to be multilingual in various workplaces and learning organizations in an increasingly globalized context. However, to make BLL more effective, we may need to undertake ethnographic research at the level of the individual in order to identify the relationship between computer and user, including both instructors and students, and also to conduct action research in individual contexts to discover problems and their related solutions (Bax, 2003). Therefore, I hope interested BLL researchers and language teachers (e.g., Spanish, Chinese, Arabic, French, and EFL) will apply the seven principles presented in this chapter and further refine them with research evidence (Becta, 2004).

Conclusions

The seven principles presented in this chapter cover the four levels of integrating ICT into English teaching and learning in educational institutions. However, there are still some challenges and concerns to which we need to pay attention when developing and promoting ICT integration in language teaching and learning, or blended language learning. With emerging ICT such as "context-aware ubiquitous learning" (Hwang, Tsai, & Yang, 2008; Liu & Hwang, 2010), BLL will remain a continuously evolving research topic (Stracke, 2007) and thus needs a process of professional development (Lawless & Pellegrino, 2007) as hybrid courses are likely to become the norm within a decade (Mayadas et al., 2009). Finally, more formative research is required in order to realize the specifics of *how-to-do* education in long-term studies of soft technologies to better exploit hard technologies.

Acknowledgement

This work is partially supported by the National Science Council in Taiwan (NSC 96–2411-H-006–030, NSC 98–2631-S-024–001 and NSC 98–2511-S-006–003-MY2).

References

Andrews, R., Freeman, A., Hou, D., McGuinn, N., Robinson, A., & Zhu, J. (2007). The effectiveness of information and communication technology on the learning of written English for 5 to 16-year olds. *British Journal of Educational Technology, 38*(2), 325–336.

Bax, S. (2003). CALL – past, present and future. *System, 31*, 13–28.

Becta (2004). *What the research says about using ICT in modern foreign languages*. British Educational Communications and Technology Agency, Coventry. Retrieved October 14 2010 from <http://partners.becta.org.uk/upload-dir/downloads/page_documents/research/wtrs_mfl.pdf>.

Bennett, S., Maton, K., & Kervin, L. (2008). The 'digital natives' debate: A critical review of the evidence. *British Journal of Educational Technology, 39*(5), 775–786.

Bonk, C.J., & Graham, C.R. (2006). *The handbook of blended learning: Global perspectives, local designs*. San Francisco, CA: John Wiley & Sons, Inc.

Burgess, T.F., & Gules, H.K. (1998). Buyer–supplier relationships in firms adopting advanced manufacturing technology: An empirical analysis of the implementation of hard and soft technologies. *Journal of Engineering and Technology Management, 15*, 127–152.

Chapelle, C.A. (2001). *Computer applications in second language acquisition: Foundations for teaching, testing and research*. Cambridge, UK: Cambridge University Press.

Colpaert, J. (2002). Editorial: The world of CALL. *Computer Assisted Language Learning, 15*(5), 437–439.

Cook, D.A. (2005). The research we still are not doing: An agenda for the study of computer-based learning. *Academic Medicine, 80*(6), 541–548.

Crystal, D. (2003). *English as a global language* (2nd ed.). Cambridge, UK: Cambridge University Press.

Egbert, J. (2005). *CALL essentials: Principles and practice in CALL classrooms.* Alexandria, VA: Teachers of English to Speakers of Other Languages (TESOL), Inc.

Felix, U. (2008). The unreasonable effectiveness of CALL: What have we learned in two decades of research? *ReCALL, 20*(2), 141–161.

Flagg, B.N. (1990). *Formative Evaluation for Educational Technologies.* Mahwah, NJ: Lawrence Erlbaum Associates.

Flammia, M., & Saunders, C. (2007). Language as power on the Internet. *Journal of the American Society for Information Science and Technology, 58*(12), 1899–1903.

Gagne, R.M. (1985). *The conditions of learning and theory of instruction* (4th ed.). New York: Holt, Rienhart, and Winston.

Garrison, D.R., & Kanuka, H. (2004). Blended learning: Uncovering its transformative potential in higher education. *Internet and Higher Education, 7*(2), 95–105.

Gould, T. (2003). Hybrid classes: Maximizing institutional resources and student learning. *Proceedings of the 2003 ASCUE Conference*, South Carolina, USA, 54–59.

Graddol, D. (2000). *The future of English? A guide to forecasting the popularity of the English language in the 21st century* (2nd ed.). London, UK: The British Council.

Graddol, D. (2004). The future of language. *Science, 303*, 1329–1331.

Graddol, D. (2006). *English next.* London, UK: The British Council.

Graham, C.R. (2006). Blended learning systems: Definition, current trends, and future directions. In C. J. Bonk & C. R. Graham (Eds.), *The handbook of blended learning: Global perspectives, local designs* (pp. 3–21). San Francisco, CA: John Wiley & Sons, Inc.

Gruba, P. (2004). Computer Assisted Language Learning. In A. Davies & C. Elder (Eds.), *The Handbook of Applied Linguistics* (pp. 623–648). London, UK: Blackwell.

Hanson-Smith, E., & Rilling, S. (2006). Introduction: Using technology in teaching languages. In E. Hanson-Smith & S. Rilling (Eds.), *Learning languages through technology* (pp. 1–7). Alexandria, VA: Teachers of English to Speakers of Other Languages (TESOL), Inc.

Heinich, R., Molenda, M., Russell, J.D., & Smaldino, S.E. (1999). *Instructional media and technologies for learning* (6th ed.). Upper Saddle River, NJ: Prentice-Hall.

Hill, M.L., & Vasudevan, L. (2008). *Media, learning, and sites of possibility.* New York, NY: Peter Lang Publishing, Inc.

Hoven, D.L. (2006) Communicating and interacting: An exploration of the changing roles of media in CALL/CMC. *CALICO Journal, 23*(2), 233–256.

Hwang, G.J., Tsai, C.C., & Yang, S.J.H. (2008). Criteria, strategies and research issues of context-aware ubiquitous learning. *Educational Technology & Society, 11*(2), 81–91.

Jonassen, D.H. (Ed.), (2004). *Handbook of research on educational communications and technology* (2nd ed.). Mahwah, NJ: Lawrence Erlbaum Associates.

Kern, R. (2006). Perspectives on technology in learning and teaching languages. *TESOL Quarterly, 40*(1), 183–210.

Kern, R., & Warschauer, M. (2000). Theory and practice of network-based language teaching. In M. Warschauer & R. Kern (Eds.), *Network-based language teaching: Concepts and practice* (pp. 1–19). New York: Cambridge University Press.

Ko, S., & Rossen, S. (2001). *Teaching online: A practical guide.* Boston, MA: Houghton Mifflin Co.

Lally, C.G. (2000). Emerging technologies, re-emerging techniques. *The French Review, 74*(1), 72–80.

Lamping, A. (2004). *Blended Language Learning: A report from BBC/LSC Get Talking.* Retrieved October 14 2010 from <http://www.bbc.co.uk/languages/tutors/blended_learning/blended_learning_report.pdf>.

Larsen-Freeman, D., & Cameron, L. (2008). Research methodology on language development from a complex systems perspective. *The Modern Language Journal, 92*(2), 200–213.

Lawless, K.A., & Pellegrino, J.W. (2007). Professional development in integrating technology into teaching and learning: Knowns, unknowns, and ways to pursue better questions and answers. *Review of Educational Research, 77*(4), 575–614.

Leakey, J., & Ranchoux, A. (2006). BLINGUA. A blended language learning approach for CALL. *Computer Assisted Language Learning, 19*(4), 357–372.

Levy, M., & Stockwell, G. (2006). *CALL dimensions: Options and issues in computer assisted language learning.* Mahwah, NJ: Lawrence Erlbaum Associates, Inc.

Liu, G.Z. (2003). An instructional design theory for teaching freshman English in a hybrid web-based instruction course in Taiwan (doctoral dissertation). Indiana University, Bloomington, IN.

Liu, G.Z. (2005). The trend and challenge for teaching EFL at Taiwanese Universities. *RELC Journal, 36*(2), 211–221.

Liu, G.Z. (2008). Innovating research topics in learning technology: Where are the new blue oceans? *British Journal of Educational Technology, 39*(4), 738–747.

Liu, G.Z. & Chen, A.S.W. (2007). A taxonomy of Internet-based technologies integrated in language curricula. *British Journal of Educational Technology, 38*(5), 934–938.

Liu, G.Z. & Hwang, G.J. (2010). A key step to understanding paradigm shifts in e-learning: Towards context-aware ubiquitous learning. *British Journal of Educational Technology, 41*(2), E1–E9.

Macdonald, J. (2006). *Blended learning and online tutoring.* Burlington, VT: Gower Publishing Co.

Mayadas, A.F., Bourne, J., & Bacsich, P. (2009). Online education today. *Science, 323*, 85–89.

McDonough, E.F., & Kahn, K.B. (1996). Using "hard" and "soft" technologies for global new product development. *R&D Management, 26*(3), 241–253.

McPherson, M., & Whitworth, A. (2008). Editorial introduction: BJET special issue on best practice or situated action: The organization of technology enhanced learning. *British Journal of Educational Technology, 39*(3), 411–421.

National Standards in Foreign Language Learning Project (NSFLLP). (1996). *National Standards for foreign language learning: Preparing for the 21st century.* Lawrence, KS: Allen Press.

Omaggio-Hadley, A. (2001). *Teaching language in context.* Boston, MA: Heinle & Heinle Publishers.

Reigeluth, C.M. (1999). What is instructional-design theory and how is it changing? In C.M. Reigeluth (Ed.), *Instructional-design theories and models: A new paradigm of instructional theory* (Vol. 2, pp. 5–29). Mahwah, NJ: Lawrence Erlbaum Associates, Inc.

Reigeluth, C.M., & Frick, T.W. (1999). Formative research: A methodology for improving educational theories and models. In C.M. Reigeluth (Ed.), *Instructional-design theories and models: A new paradigm of instructional theory* (Vol. 2, pp. 633–651). Mahwah, NJ: Lawrence Erlbaum Associates, Inc.

Rozgiene, I., Medvedeva, O., & Straková, Z. (2008). *Integrating ICT into language learning and teaching: Guide for tutors.* Altenberger Straße 69, 4040 Linz: Johannes Kepler Universität Linz.

Rushby, N. (2007). Editorial. *British Journal of Educational Technology, 38*(1), 3–4.

Shoffner, M.B., Jones, M., & Harmon, S.W. (2000). Paradigms Restrained: Implications of New and Emerging Technologies for Learning and Cognition. *The Journal of Electronic Publishing, 6*(1). Retrieved October 14 2010 from <http://hdl.handle.net/2027/spo.3336451.0006.111>.

Stake, R.E. (1995). *The art of case study research.* Thousand Oaks, CA: Sage Publications.

Stockwell, G. (2007). A review of technology choice for teaching language skills and areas in the CALL literature. *ReCALL, 19*(2), 105–120.

Stracke, E. (2007). A road to understanding: A qualitative study into why learners drop out of a blended language learning (BLL) environment. *ReCALL, 19*(1), 57–78.

Szathmary, E., & Szamado, S. (2008). Language: A social history of words. *Nature, 456,* 40–41.

Thorne, K. (2003). *Blended learning: How to integrate online and traditional learning.* London, UK: Kogan Page.

Appendix A

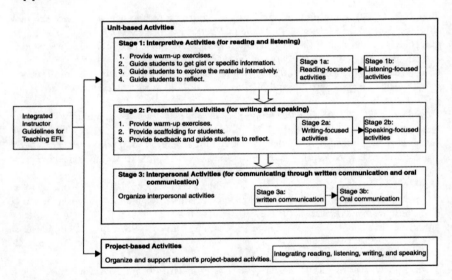

FIGURE 8.5 The Sequence of the Integrated Instructor Guidelines for Teaching EFL based on the Three Communicative Modes (Liu, 2003)

Appendix B

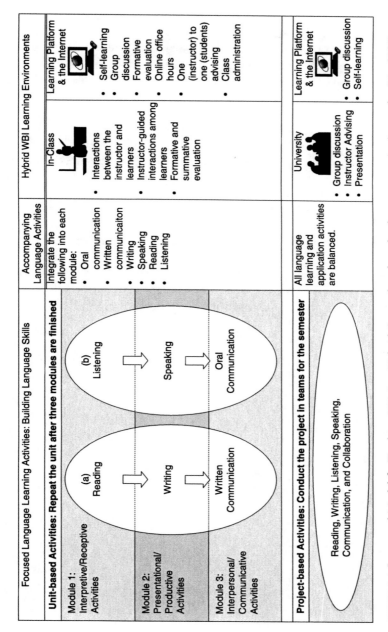

FIGURE 8.6 Integrated Model for Teaching EFL in a Hybrid Course based on the three communicative modes (Liu, 2003)

Comment

This chapter is very future-focused and anticipates a time – perhaps within ten years – when hybrid courses, or blended language learning, will be the norm. Gi-Zen Liu brings together several years' work to identify the principles that should inform the creation of ICT components in effective language learning courses. These principles are particularly relevant to format and presentation decisions, and have been arrived at through several cycles of evaluation. This iterative feature is typically a characteristic of robust curriculum design processes.

Tasks

1. Gi-Zen Liu proposes seven principles to apply to the introduction of ICT into language learning courses. To what extent do these principles differ from principles you might apply in a face-to-face teaching situation?
2. This chapter takes the view that hybrid courses will be the norm in the relatively near future. Consider your current teaching and learning situation, or one with which you are familiar, and whether hybrid courses are the future.
   a. To what extent is ICT currently incorporated into language teaching?
   b. What factors in the environment favor greater use of ICT in the future?
   c. What factors in the environment inhibit greater use of ICT in the future?

9

DESIGNING THE ASSESSMENT OF A UNIVERSITY ESOL COURSE

John Read and Lizzy Roe

Introduction

The focus of this chapter is on the Monitoring and Assessing component of language curriculum design. Many language teachers around the world are in a situation where the way in which their students are assessed is strongly influenced, if not completely determined, by external authorities such as the Ministry of Education, an examinations board or the administrators of their school. This can lead to the phenomenon of washback, where teaching and learning activities in the classroom concentrate on what the students need to do to pass a major external test or examination, rather than on the full range of learning objectives set out in the curriculum (Nation and Macalister, 2010, pp. 116–117). However, university teachers in countries like New Zealand have more freedom to plan the assessment of their courses in keeping with the principles of good curriculum design being exemplified in this book. Ideally, course assessment should be an integral component of curriculum planning, so that there is a direct relationship between the goals of the course and the criteria by which each student's achievement in the course is judged. Assessment has a significant role not just in the final result but also in monitoring learner progress during the course.

Given the embedded nature of assessment in the classroom, it is necessary to cover various aspects of the course design to provide a context for discussing the assessment procedures. The course we focus on here is ESOL 102, Academic English Listening and Reading, a first-year course for undergraduate students at the University of Auckland. It is one of a suite of six courses offered to students for whom English is an additional language, in order to enhance their study experience by developing their academic language skills. It is important to emphasize that this is not a remedial program. Like the other courses, ESOL 102 is for students who have been admitted to the university and who receive full academic credit for the course. This in turn places various constraints on course design and assessment, because the course must meet the University's quality standards and general expectations for degree-level study.

Learner Needs and Course Objectives

Learner needs can be determined only on a fairly generic basis for this course. Most of the students who enroll are from the Faculty of Arts, the Faculty of Science, or the Business School, with various intended majors such as sociology, psychology, politics, education, law, media studies, economics, marketing, computer science, statistics, and additional languages (e.g. Spanish, Korean). With such a wide range of subjects it is not possible to design the course to meet the specific needs of students entering a particular discipline or professional field.

In terms of Hutchinson and Waters' (1987) "necessities," it can generally be assumed that the students' academic listening needs centre on understanding what is said in lectures and tutorials, whereas in reading they need to understand textbooks, course notes, handouts, journal articles, reference works, and other assigned readings. The specification of necessities draws on the teaching experience of the ESOL tutors, plus the broader principles of best practice in English for Academic Purposes, as reflected in reference books, journal articles, and conference presentations in the field. With regard to learner "lacks" and "wants" (Hutchinson and Waters' other two areas of need), there is limited scope within a credit-bearing university course to tailor the syllabus or the teaching to the lacks or wants of particular classes from one semester to another – let alone negotiating the syllabus with the students at the beginning of the course. Nevertheless, at the first class every semester, students fill in a questionnaire which asks them to estimate how many hours a week they need to read and listen in English, and the types of texts and situations involved. They also identify the aspects of reading and listening which they find difficult. The tutors pay attention to this information as well as the comments in the course evaluations that are routinely administered at the end of each semester.

One particular lack which is well established from past experience is the learners' limited knowledge of academic vocabulary. It would be preferable to be able to assume that students entering the university were already thoroughly familiar with the word families in the Academic Word List (Coxhead, 2000), so that the course could concentrate on skills development, but the reality is that building the learners' lexical knowledge is an essential component of the course design. It thus features prominently among the main course objectives for ESOL 102:

- to develop listening, reading and note-making skills needed for academic purposes;
- to increase range and depth of English vocabulary in general and study topic areas;

- to develop awareness of effective reading, listening, and word attack strategies.

There is a fourth objective, which has a more direct bearing on the course assessment:

- to answer questions that show understanding of texts that have been read or listened to, during and outside of normal classroom hours.

From an assessment perspective, the last objective highlights the point that ESOL 102 and the other ESOL courses focus primarily on one – or, in this case, two – of the four macroskills. The division is somewhat artificial, given that successful academic study involves an integrated application of all four skills, but it is necessary for pedagogical purposes. This particular course deals with the receptive skills or, to put it another way, with input rather than output skills. In their other degree subjects, the students are typically required to demonstrate how well they have comprehended input texts through oral presentations and through essays, assignments, reports, and answers to examination questions. However, since the skills required for these output tasks are not among the objectives of ESOL 102 but of other courses in the ESOL program, it would not be appropriate to base the assessment of ESOL 102 on speaking or writing tasks of this kind.

Learning Outcomes

The four broad objectives for the course are further elaborated as learning outcomes, which are as follows:

- use strategies to make the reading process faster and more efficient;
- understand and identify or summarize the main ideas in an academic text (written or spoken);
- take notes from a text (written or spoken) in order to create an outline of key points;
- be aware of the author's purpose and identify issues arising from the content;
- answer questions relating to overall structure and detailed meaning of a text;
- know what to listen for in terms of the delivery of spoken information, i.e. word stress, intonation, lecturer's signals, predicting content, etc.;
- make the process of listening and note-taking faster and more efficient by using symbols, abbreviations, and labeling in their notes;
- have an increased vocabulary of academic words from the Academic Word List;
- guess the meaning of unfamiliar words by using "word attack" strategies, e.g. reference words, linkers, synonyms, word families (prefixes, suffixes), dictionary skills, etc.;

- look for relationships between words/ideas in sentences and across paragraphs.

This list of outcomes provides the basis for examining the content validity of the course assessment. In other words, if these are the particular kinds of knowledge and skill that the students are supposed to develop through taking the course and the purpose of the assessment is to measure the students' achievement, it should be possible to demonstrate that all of the stated outcomes are incorporated in a balanced way in the assessment procedures. It is beyond the scope of this chapter to present a detailed validation exercise of this kind, but the course outline distributed at the beginning of the course includes a checklist specifying which of the learning outcomes is assessed by each major component of the course assessment. We will comment further on content validity later in the chapter.

Course Content

Before discussing the assessment, it is necessary to give a brief account of the course content and how it is delivered. Proportionally, 60 percent of class time is spent on the reading skills component, and 40 percent on the listening skills. A coursebook of materials compiled from a range of sources is used in each class. The content of the texts is typical of the type of academic discourse that the students are required to process in their mainstream course subjects. For example, the reading texts are articles from serial publications, or extracts from chapters in prescribed course packs for subject majors. The listening texts are scripted 10-minute mini-lectures, based on similar academic sources. The lectures are written in-house and recorded in the University's professional recording studio. A range of topics is used so that students are not locked into a long theme-based unit of work that may not relate closely to their chosen field of study.

The course content is based on the analysis of academic discourse using a genre approach, and the development of skills and strategies for understanding academic texts. Each two-hour class centers on one or two different strategies, and every one to two weeks there is intensive study of a particular type of discourse. The discourse types increase in complexity as the course progresses, moving from exposition, exemplification, comparison–contrast, cause and effect, and problem–solution–evaluation through to generalization and evidence, argument–rebuttal, and research–evidence.

Initial classes familarize students with strategies and subskills to facilitate "top-down" processing of a text, so that they can broadly identify text organization and paragraph structure, as well as differentiating key concepts from supporting material. Another early focus is vocabulary and word attack strategies, which cover aspects such as common language markers in academic discourse, technical terms, affixation, and text cohesion. Vocabulary learning strategies are presented, and students are encouraged to work independently to build their vocabulary knowledge during self-study time. All input texts have been run through Haywood's (2007) *Highlighter* website to identify the words they contain from the Academic Word List, and follow-up tasks enable recycling of that target vocabulary.

Subsequent classes involve a combination of "top-down" and "bottom-up" meaning-building strategies for deeper processing of the text. Students use an approach of "while-processing" inquiry to monitor their understanding of the text as they read or listen. Led by the tutor, the class discusses any blocks to meaning, analyzes the cause, and identifies any remedial or compensatory strategies.

Assessment in the University

The assessment of ESOL 102 needs to be considered in relation to the principles and practices of course assessment in the University as a whole. For most university courses the final result is recorded as a letter grade (at Auckland: from A+ to C- for a pass; D+ to D- for a fail). The grade is in turn based on a percentage mark, with the minimum for a pass being 50 percent. The C- grade covers the range from 50 to 54 percent, a C grade is 55 to 59 percent and so on, in five-mark steps to A+, which is 90 to 100 percent. This kind of grading system is deeply embedded in undergraduate university education in New Zealand as in other countries and, until at least the 1970s, the grades were determined almost entirely by performance in written end-of-year examinations. Since that time, a wider range of assessment types – such as assignments, research reports, group projects, oral presentations, and portfolios – have become accepted and it is now a normal requirement to have a minimum of two assessments completed at different times during the course. Nevertheless, the system of grading remains and, for 100-level courses at Auckland, the regulations state that there should be an exam at the end of the semester worth at least 50 percent of the final grade.

There are two documents to guide teaching staff at the University in designing and carrying out their course assessments. Both documents are available in the public area of the University's website (http://www.auckland.ac.nz/uoa/home/about/teaching-learning/policies-procedures#s2c3). The first one, *Instructions to Examiners and Assessors*, emphasizes the regulations to be adhered to, the procedures to be followed, and the approvals to be obtained. It reflects the fact that there are quite high stakes involved for students in obtaining university qualifications, in terms of their future educational opportunities and employment prospects, and consequently there is an incentive for unscrupulous students to take short cuts and cheat as a way of improving their performance. Thus, the regulations are designed to promote equality of opportunity for all students, the security of examination materials, the confidentiality of results, and careful checking at each step in the process.

The second document, the *Assessment of Student Learning* policy, complements the first one by taking more of a student perspective and discussing how assessment procedures can contribute positively to student learning. The focus is on the validity of assessments as measures of learning outcomes for a course, as well as qualities such as clarity, transparency, and fairness, so that students know exactly what is expected of them. The policy encourages the use of a variety of assessment procedures appropriate to the discipline and highlights the value for students of timely and informative feedback on assessed work that they complete during a course. Therefore, whereas the first document imposes considerable constraints on the assessment of the ESOL courses, the second one offers scope for designing procedures that can measure to what extent the students have acquired the relevant knowledge and skills.

One interesting issue addressed in the policy is whether students should be assessed on a norm-referenced or criterion-referenced basis. The norm-referenced approach is defined as one in which students are ranked on a comparative basis in relation to one another, whereas with the criterion-referenced approach students are assessed according to how well their individual performance matches predetermined standards. The policy states that "within the student-centred learning ethos" that it promotes, "the primary model of assessment ... should be ... the criterion referenced standards based model." However, as Nation and Macalister (2010, p. 115) point out, the distinction between the two approaches is not so clear-cut when it is applied to university grading systems. In the Auckland case examiners are required to distinguish nine different levels of pass and it is inevitable that student performance will be judged comparatively to some degree. In addition, it is quite difficult to define performance standards except in broad terms, as you can see from considering how standards might be developed for each of the ten learning outcomes for ESOL 102 listed above. The assessments for this course are based to a large degree on marks accumulated in response to numerous comprehension items and tasks, and so the final result for each student is primarily the accumulated total mark from the various assessments, which we will now explain in some detail.

Assessment of ESOL 102

The components of the assessment for ESOL 102 can be summarized as follows:

TABLE 9.1

Coursework			50%
	Portfolio	20%	
	Test 1	15%	
	Test 2	15%	
Final examination			50%

The overall grade represents an even balance between the coursework, which is completed at various points during the 12 teaching weeks of the semester, and the required final exam, scheduled during a separate examination period one to three weeks after classes have finished. Although the coursework contributes to the final grade and is thus part of the Assessing function in the curriculum design model, it also has a Monitoring role in allowing the tutors to check on the progress of students in their classes and gain useful feedback on their teaching.

Let us now look at each component of the assessment in turn.

Portfolio

The portfolio consists of four activities (two for reading and two for listening) that the students undertake in their own time. Each pair of activities (reading and writing) is set two weeks before the completed work is due to be submitted, in Weeks 3 to 5 and 9 to 11 of the semester. For reading, the students are given a long text to read for understanding, together with some associated tasks, such as an academic vocabulary worksheet. They are encouraged to put into practice the strategies and skills presented in class, such as surveying the text for overall structure, taking notes from the text, checking dictionary meanings, and using a thesaurus for vocabulary extension. For the first portfolio reading, students produce an outline of the text structure, and a brief, paraphrased summary of the author's purpose and main ideas. The outline is marked using a criteria-based guide the students receive in advance. The second portfolio reading is to read and understand the text and take notes in preparation for answering comprehension questions in class. For listening, the students are required to go the University's English Language Self-Access Centre (ELSAC) to listen to a ten-minute pre-recorded lecture and take notes, before completing a follow-up outline task. This is also marked using a criteria-based marking guide.

The portfolio has several useful features. One is that it allows the tutors to set a rather longer reading text than would be possible to work with in class. It also introduces the students to the resources available at ELSAC, which may then encourage them to use the Centre to enhance their academic language ability in other ways, beyond just fulfilling the 102 portfolio requirement. Thirdly, in terms of the Monitoring function, the portfolio work provides a channel for written and oral feedback from the tutor. After each portfolio component is completed, tutors review in class the main ideas in each text and common problem areas are discussed. Follow-up practice activities may be recommended, using ELSAC resources. Finally, the portfolio activities encourage some independence among the students, in undertaking the activities out of class time and getting them done before the deadline. It could be argued that even more independence could be fostered by asking the students to find their own reading text, especially one related to another of their courses. This is an issue we will take up later in the chapter.

Tests

The second component of the coursework consists of two tests, each worth 15 percent of the final grade. They are given in class in Weeks 6 and 11 of the semester, and cover listening, reading and vocabulary use. In the listening test, students complete a gapped outline of a ten-minute, scripted, pre-recorded lecture on a general academic topic. For the first test the students fill in the gaps as they listen to the recording, whereas for the second test they take notes while listening to the lecture twice and are then given the outline to complete. The reading test is composed of comprehension and vocabulary questions based on an academic text of 10 to 12 paragraphs in length. A range of question formats is used to facilitate the deployment of different strategies such as recognizing text structure, identifying main ideas, understanding key vocabulary items, and inferring implicit information.

Like the portfolio tasks, the tests require the students to apply the strategies they have been taught in an integrated way to particular listening and reading tasks. It is not possible for the tutors to assess directly how well the students have put the strategies into practice. However, the tutors go through the answers to the tasks with the class when each test has been marked and explain how more accurate answers could have been achieved by using strategies and language analysis skills previously presented in class. It is hoped that this increased awareness will be reflected in improved performance by the students in subsequent course assessments – and of course in their study activities for other courses. This is where the Monitoring role of the tutors during post-portfolio and post-test class sessions becomes most valuable.

Final Exam

In the University's terminology, an "exam" is distinguished from a "test" in that it is scheduled in the period after classes end and is administered by the Examinations Office, which employs its own supervisors. Thus, the exam is a formal event, with its own set of rules and procedures for the students to comply with. It also means that all the exam material needs to be submitted to the Examinations Office about three weeks in advance.

The two-hour exam uses the same format as Test 2, that is, a listening and note-taking task, followed by a lecture outline completion activity, and a reading text with comprehension and vocabulary questions. Both texts represent typical academic discourse structures and contain many of the linguistic features highlighted during the course. To ensure that the listening component genuinely assesses listening comprehension ability, it is essential that the students are not given the lecture outline task until *after* they have listened to the lecture recording twice through. From past experience, the course convener has found it necessary to attend the first 30 minutes of the exam to ensure that this instruction is carried out by the exam supervisors.

The examination regulations require that the exam material should be kept secure until it is distributed in the exam room, so that none of the students has an unfair advantage by gaining access to the questions in advance. After the exam is over, the normal situation is that students can take their copy of the exam paper with them, and the paper for that semester is uploaded to the website of the University Library, where students enrolled in the course in future semesters can access it as practice material in preparing for their own exam. This is in keeping with the principle of transparency promoted in the University's *Assessment of Student Learning* policy. However, each of the exam papers for ESOL 102 involves an unusually large amount of preparation on the part of the course convener, in selecting and editing suitable oral and written texts as input, as well as setting the comprehension tasks. Thus, the Department has obtained special permission for the last several years to withhold the ESOL 102 papers and keep them secure, so that they can be reused in a future semester. To provide for exam preparation, there is a bank of materials which is made available to students in the last week of semester for study on a self-access basis. These include six listening and reading tasks from previous years which have been adapted to conform to the current exam specifications. Similar arrangements have been made to give the students access to preparation materials for Tests 1 and 2.

In discussing the marking of the exam and the other components of the course assessment, we first need to explain that the classes for ESOL 102 are organized in a different fashion from most 100-level courses in the Faculty, where each student attends two lectures a week plus a tutorial, which is a much smaller group of 20 to 30 students. In 102 and the other ESOL courses, there are no lectures: the students are divided into groups of up to 25 which meet twice a week for a two-hour class. Normally, there are about four groups each semester, taught by at least two different tutors, who mark the coursework of the students in their own group(s).

For the final exam, the marking is distributed among the tutors so that they do not mark any of their own students' scripts. The tutors meet prior to marking the exam and collectively mark a random selection of six scripts against the model answer guide. Most questions require short answers of one to five words taken directly from the input text, but a small number of questions allow for some personal interpretation by the students in their own words. The tutors discuss the answers and acceptable alternatives are added to the model answer guide. After marking, another meeting is held to discuss and resolve any problematic answers. The exam results are recorded for each individual along with their final grade for the whole course, and the course convener plus one other member of staff sign the final results sheet to confirm that they have carefully checked the accuracy of the grades. Thus, several procedures are followed to ensure the reliability of the assessment.

Monitoring the Quality of the Course

With regard to the Monitoring component of course design, the University requires that all courses have a student evaluation at least once every three years, but ESOL 102 has actually been evaluated most semesters. The evaluation instrument is the University's standard, computer-generated questionnaire, which is completed anonymously by students in class near the end of the semester. The questionnaire is in two parts: first, a fixed set of 11 core statements, plus others selected as appropriate by the course convener, with a Likert response scale for each one; and secondly, two open-ended prompts: "What was most helpful for your learning?" and "What improvements would you like to see?" There are procedures in place to ensure that tutors cannot influence the results and that individual student responses are kept anonymous. The forms go to the University's Evaluation and Scanning Centre, where the quantitative results are collated and made available on a secure website, not only to the course teaching staff but also the Head of Department and the Dean. After the grading period is over, the forms are returned to the course convener, who is responsible for collating the open-ended comments and taking follow-up action as necessary.

Student evaluations contribute to the routine monitoring of the course, but they had a particular role during a period in 2005 to 2006 when all courses throughout the University had to be reduced in scope as the result of introducing a new academic credit system. Up until then, the course content was based on six broad study themes, such as Health and the Environment, and Business and Technology. Student feedback indicated dissatisfaction with the limited relevance and large volume of the material, not all of which could be covered in the semester. Thus, the coursebook was redesigned to include a smaller number but wider range of texts, selected on the basis of text organization, cultural/academic relevance, and interest level for students.

Another area of concern was the course assessment. Before 2006, there were three tests and seven portfolio tasks in addition to the final exam, and students complained about an excessive workload. The tests have now been reduced to two and the portfolio tasks to four but, more importantly, the nature of the portfolio assessment has been changed, in two ways:

1) Previously, the out-of-class reading tasks were based on texts which the students chose from their subject courses, and the input for the out-of-class listening task was a lecture in another course. However, difficulties ensued when students presented reading texts that varied greatly in the type of discourse, the complexity of the ideas, and linguistic features such as lexical density and amount of linear text (as distinct from graphs or formulas). There was also a heavy marking load for tutors in determining how accurately each text had been summarized. Thus, the decision was made to pre-select texts that all the students would respond to, in the interests of greater reliability in the marking.

2) In the pre-2006 course, an attempt was made to assess strategy use by requiring the students to write a paragraph describing the strategies they had used to deal with the text, and to give a personal response to the text based on their own ideas and experience. However, there were indications from what the students wrote that they did not really understand the metacognitive dimension of the task. They tended simply to list the strategies in the coursebook, without explaining how they had applied them during the task. The feedback from tutors was that these components of the portfolio had to be marked quite subjectively. The tutors also raised the question (referred to above) as to whether it was fair to assess receptive skills through extended written discourse.

The change to the current type of outline task based on pre-selected texts for both the reading and listening activities in the portfolio has standardized the answer format and helped with marker reliability. Nevertheless, it can be argued that this emphasis on reliability has come at a cost to the content validity of the assessment. The teaching syllabus places a great deal of emphasis on the comprehension process and the application of effective strategies, and yet the course assessment is very focused on the outcome of comprehension, in the form of answers to questions and item formats that look very similar to those in a proficiency test like TOEFL or IELTS. This problem of dealing with the somewhat competing demands of reliability and validity is a familiar one in language assessment, but it is not easy to resolve.

At the time of writing, one fresh initiative planned by the teaching staff to address this issue is the piloting of a new version of the second portfolio reading task. The students will provide their own academic reading text (vetted for suitability by the tutor in advance), and then write a short (up to three-sentence) paraphrase of the main ideas and author's purpose, as well as an explanation of the reading process. The explanation will include how long the reading took, how easy the text was to understand, which parts proved difficult, and which reading strategies could be recommended to another reader to help understand the text. In this way, it may be possible to increase the validity of the assessment as a measure of the process dimension of the course syllabus.

Conclusion

In this discussion of ESOL 102 we have sought to emphasize how assessment should be an integrated component of language curriculum design, with a clear connection to the learning objectives and the way that the course is taught. Although the teaching staff have a considerable amount of autonomy in determining how the course is to be assessed, they also have to follow the regulations and procedures set by the University to ensure the quality of all its courses. The fact that this is a credit-bearing course raises the stakes of the assessment and it means that reliability is given a high priority. However, it is just as important, in the interests of validity, that the course assessment should show whether the students have achieved the target competence in academic reading and listening, as specified by the course objectives and learning outcomes.

References

Coxhead, A. (2000). A new academic word list. *TESOL Quarterly, 34,* 213–238.
Haywood, S. (2007). *The AWL highlighter.* Retrieved on October 14 2010 from <http://www.nottingham.ac.uk/~alzsh3/acvocab/awlhighlighter.htm>.
Hutchinson, T., & Waters, A. (1987). *English for specific purposes: A learning-centred approach.* Cambridge, UK: Cambridge University Press.
Nation, I.S.P., & Macalister, J. (2010). *Language curriculum design.* New York: Routledge.

Comment

John Read and Lizzy Roe have presented us with a very clear exposition of the issues surrounding language assessment. In particular, they have highlighted issues relating to validity, reliability, and practicality. The validity of assessing a course focusing on listening and reading using output measures – speaking and writing – is a brave issue to confront.

This chapter also reminds us of the relationship between the outer circles of the curriculum design model and the inner circle. Particularly important here are elements of the environment analysis, and especially the university's assessment regulations, and the application of principles relating to good assessment practice. It is, after all, decisions taken as a result of the outer circles that determine what happens in the inner circle.

Tasks

1. At the University of Auckland John Read and Lizzy Roe needed to consider the university's assessment requirements. Consider your own teaching and learning context and identify any constraints affecting assessment that may exist. In your context, how are these constraints worked with?
2. The "washback" effect of assessment on a course is well attested, and was clearly present in the course for Peruvian officials (see Chapter 6 by Susan Smith). Teachers have different views on "washback." Consider a situation where a curriculum has communicative goals but achievement assessment is a national examination with a focus on language knowledge, comprehension questions, and literature. With that situation in mind, work in a group of three, with each person suggesting (i) reasons in favor of the following positions and (ii) the likely effect of that position on teaching:
    a.   "Washback" is natural and isn't a problem.

    b.   "Washback" is natural but needs to be managed so that it doesn't clash with course goals.

    c.   Meeting course goals and developing language proficiency should be paramount.

3.   In the following table, identify the reliability, validity, and practicality issues in ESOL 102 assessment, and comment on how satisfactorily they have been dealt with.

TABLE 9.2

	Issues	Comments
Reliability		
Validity		
Practicality		

10

REFRESHING A WRITING COURSE: THE ROLE OF EVALUATION

John Macalister

A risk associated with courses that are offered year in, year out is that they may begin to lose their dynamism. Even when they perceive a need for changes to their teaching, teachers may not make them, and for very understandable reasons, such as workload pressure and time constraints. However, as a result, courses may begin to lose relevance for the learners, may not make most effective use of the class time available, and may not be delivering the best learning outcomes. One way to avoid this situation is to ensure that regular evaluation occurs. This chapter explores the changes resulting from evaluation of a university writing course and the evaluation of those changes.

Background to the Course

The course, which we shall call WRIT, exists to meet the writing needs of a body of students that shares only one common characteristic: all are non-native speakers of English. A second, near-universal characteristic is that almost all are students enrolled at university, but occasionally employees from the public service or private business enroll as a means of improving their written English skills, and at least one academic staff member from a non-English speaking background has taken the course. While most enrolled students are undergraduates, a few are post-graduate, including doctoral candidates, and they come from all the faculties in the university. Some were required to take the course, others chose it voluntarily, and a few admitted to taking the course as an "easy" option. Many are international students from East or South East Asia, but others may be exchange students from Europe or Latin America. A sizeable proportion, however, are either New Zealand citizens or permanent residents, and may come from Pasifika or refugee backgrounds. This group of students also contributes a number of "mature" students to the course. A further distinction is that while international students have had to meet language proficiency requirements for university entry, typically through IELTS testing, domestic students do not. The picture, then, is one of a diverse student body, with diverse needs. Perhaps, however, by enrolling in the course all are indirectly expressing a desire to be successful members of an academic writing community.

The Case for Change

WRIT has been offered as a 100-level or first-year course since the early 1990s, and while there have been changes from time to time, often coinciding with a change in the academic staff member coordinating the course, the changes have not been substantial. Partly this was because the evaluation measures in place did not indicate the need for significant change. Two of these measures – institutional evaluation measures and student comments in a non-assessed reflection writing exercise – indicated a good level of satisfaction with the course. The case for change, then, was driven by a third evaluation measure – staff observation.

Concerns about the course produced by observation fell into three main areas:

- Meeting student needs: While the course was presented as an academic writing course for non-native English speaking students, there were clear differences among the students in their needs, as indicated above. Some students, for example, needed to develop language proficiency rather than academic writing ability. As another example, the model of academic writing was a Humanities one and did not accommodate the writing needs of other disciplines, such as science reports or business proposals.
- Course structure: The course was structured so that there was a one-hour lecture each week for twelve weeks, and three hours a week of workshops for eleven weeks. While some teaching staff argued that the lectures provided the students with needed listening practice, and while it was clear from an organizational perspective that the lectures were designed to introduce the weekly workshop focus, the reality was that attendance at lectures fell off steadily during the trimester with the result that by the end of the course only around one-quarter of enrolled students were attending. No matter what the intention or the theoretical justifications, then, the lectures were not an effective form of instruction.
- Managing cognitive demands: The course required students to produce two essays on quasi-academic topics (such as renewable energy or sustainable tourism) based on a book of pre-selected readings. While care was taken to include readings that were (in the eyes of native-speaking instructors) well written and accessible, many students had difficulty understanding the texts.

This raised the uncomfortable question as to whether students who were being assessed on their writing ability were being penalized for a lack of understanding of the input provided.

A Response

As a result of these concerns, the university accepted a proposal to do the following:

- Redesign the 100-level course as a course for writing in English as a second language; this would remove the "academic" tag and allow a more effective response to the language proficiency development needs of some students, and would reduce the cognitive load so that writing ability was more clearly the focus.
- Introduce a new 200-level or second-year academic writing in English as a second language course, which would both provide a pathway for students wishing to develop their writing skills further, as well as an opportunity for students to work in discipline-specific genres.

The following sections of this chapter consider the re-design of the 100-level course, which is discussed in terms of the language curriculum design model proposed by Nation and Macalister (2010). In this model, decisions made in the three outer circles determine the nature of the inner circle. The discussion will begin with a brief consideration of those three outer circles, starting with environment analysis, and then move to the inner circle to show how the course responded to the outer circle factors. Attention is principally directed towards discussing changes to the existing WRIT, rather than to the considerable portion that was retained in the new course.

The Teaching–Learning Environment

As can be seen in Figure 1.1 (see page 2), each of the outer circles consists of three segments, or components, which, for the environment, are the learners, the teachers, and the situation in which the teaching–learning takes place. As mentioned above, the learners form a diverse body with correspondingly diverse needs. The teaching staff is also somewhat heterogeneous, but shares the characteristic of being native speakers. While the preference is for experienced teachers of English as a second or foreign language, graduate students with little or no language teaching experience are also occasionally employed. Learners and teachers come together on a 12-week course within a well-resourced university in an English-speaking country, placing relatively few limitations on the course. The way in which some of the important environmental constraints were accommodated within the course is shown in Table 10.1.

TABLE 10.1 Effect of outer circle factors on the course design

Identified factor	General effect	Specific effect examples
Learners enrolling in the course may not be well motivated	Tasks and texts that are chosen are likely to motivate the learners	Pre-reading activities to arouse interest in texts
Learners are studying in a university and need to write effectively in that environment	Tasks need to have face validity within that environment	Emphasis on analysis over description Use compare and contrast writing tasks
Learners may have little or no knowledge of NZ	Texts chosen provide opportunities to learn about aspects of NZ culture and society	Some use of texts by NZ authors, e.g. Witi Ihimaera
Learners come from a range of disciplines and have a wide range of English language proficiency	Individual differences need to be accommodated	Goal of course focuses on awareness Requirement for revision of writing allows individual needs to be addressed
Learners learn to write by writing	Many opportunities for writing need to be provided	"Write before you read" activities in class

Needs Analysis

The three components of the needs analysis circle are lacks, wants, and necessities. While no formal needs analysis is carried out, the *de facto* position is that learners need to write effectively within an academic environment. This, indeed, can be classed as a necessity for all students. It is likely that students want to write like native speakers, but the environmental constraint of a 12-week course means that this is unlikely to be achieved; thus it remains a "want" rather than a "necessity." In terms of lacks, while most students have met the university's formal language proficiency requirements, it is clear from their writing that a number of students do not have sufficient language skills for success in the university context.

Application of Principles

The application of principles is important to a course's design because it ensures that what happens in the classroom – captured by the inner circle of the design model – is informed by research about best practice. Three important principles (chosen from those presented in Nation & Macalister, 2010, pp. 38–39) were identified as being:

- time on task; in other words, as we learn to write by writing there need to be many opportunities for writing to occur;
- comprehensible input; the material that learners were being asked to read as a basis for responding in some way in writing should not over-burden them with cognitive demands; this principle relates to the concerns about language proficiency identified earlier;
- feedback; there should be repeated opportunities for learners to receive helpful feedback on their writing.

The "time on task" principle is related to another: the fluency principle or the idea that a language course should provide activities aimed at increasing the fluency with which the learners can use the language they already know, both receptively and productively, the importance of which was neatly highlighted by a student who wrote:[1]

> However, as I have no confident in my English writing, I end up write less to avoid mistake. As a result, I always fail to discuss my idea clearly.

A further principle underlying the course related to motivation. As much as possible, and especially perhaps for the students who were being required to take the course or were taking it because they saw it as an "easy" option, the learners should be interested and excited about learning about writing and they should come to value this learning.

Focusing on these principles also involved a response to some of the debates that have occurred in the field of second and foreign language writing, such as the role of literature (Hirvela, 2001; Horowitz, 1990; Spack, 1985; Vandrick, 2003), the attention that should be given to voice (recently, e.g., Matsuda & Tardy, 2007, 2008; Stapleton & Helms-Park, 2008), and the treatment of error (Ferris, 1999, 2004; Guenette, 2007; Truscott, 1996). The response to these debates included the use of literature, the attention to some voice issues, and the regular use of peer feedback.

The Goal of the New Course

The goal of the new course emerged principally from the needs analysis, but was also affected by environmental considerations. The guiding imperative, reflecting the necessity segment of the needs analysis circle, was more effective writing within a university context, but given the length of the course, the diverse student body, and

---

[1] The "voices" of eleven students are heard in this chapter. They include both female and male students studying at both under- and postgraduate levels, and are from different disciplines within the university, e.g. Science, Commerce, and Architecture. They also come from different parts of the world – Central, South-east and East Asia, the Middle East, and eastern Europe. Their "voices" have not been edited for linguistic correctness.

the variability of starting points in terms of writing and language proficiency, the goal needed to be expressed in developmental terms, rather than as a target. Thus the course was described as being designed to improve the writing of students for whom English is a second or other language. With the development of a 200-level course, the emphasis was on writing more generally than academic writing in particular.

As a way of operationalizing this goal, learners were introduced to and repeatedly reminded of the course "recipe:"

input + practice + feedback + reflection = awareness

The separate "ingredients" in this recipe are found in the other three segments of the inner circle, which cover content and sequencing, format and presentation, and monitoring and assessment. These are discussed below, and the effect of some of the key factors identified in the outer circles is shown in Table 10.1.

Content and Sequencing

One way of viewing the content is to describe it in terms of the input, or the texts that learners were required to read and respond to. In that sense, the course could be viewed as topic- or theme-based; the learners read and discussed (and were encouraged to re-read) a small number of texts on two different themes that provided the input for the two main writing tasks. The texts were mainly literary in origin, and were chosen as likely to be accessible and of interest to the learners. The comprehensible input principle was to the fore here, but the choice of texts, particularly for the first main writing task, also related to the motivation principle. For example, recognizing that the majority of students were non-New Zealanders, the first task had a New Zealand focus, allowing the learners opportunities to develop their understanding of the socio-cultural context in which they were now living. The assumption was that the learners would want to know more about that context.

Another way of viewing the content is to focus on the skills, sub-skills, and strategies that were introduced and practiced both in workshops and independently. The course used a process writing approach, and learners were taken through the stages from gathering ideas through repeated drafts to editing and publishing the final draft. As they worked through the writing process, there were multiple opportunities for feedback. Furthermore, as the learners were taken through the stages of the writing process twice, this provided repeated opportunities for practicing and understanding what was required.

While the comprehensible input and feedback principles were well served by the content and sequencing decisions described above, the time on task and fluency principles needed additional consideration. There needed to be regular, frequent opportunities for learners to write in class and this was principally achieved by pre-selecting a number of short texts that would serve as a stimulus for "write before you read" activities (Spack, 1985).

Format and Presentation

An early decision was taken to discard the weekly lecture and instead to increase the contact hours in workshops to 36; in other words, there would be three hours of workshops for twelve rather than eleven weeks. In part this was possible because of the nature of the teaching staff, as described earlier. Regular meetings and email communication ensured consistency across the different workshops, but the experience of the staff meant that decisions about actual classroom implementation, such as patterns of interaction, could be taken independently.

As the course was re-developed with a shift of focus from academic writing to writing more generally, this triggered consideration of a possible face validity issue. This was a credit-bearing university course being delivered to an audience of (almost entirely) university students; it needed, therefore, to appear relevant to academic life. This was achieved in two ways. First, there was an emphasis on an analytical response to the texts read, framed within a comparison and contrast rubric. For example, the first main assessable writing tasks required learners to compare, contrast, and suggest reasons for the differences between two versions of the same story, the second version deliberately re-written by the author thirty years after the first (Ihimaera, 1972, 2003).

The second way in which the face validity issue was addressed was to ensure that discrete sub-skills with obvious academic relevance received attention. A prime example of this was the use of references, which pick up on at least two of Casanave's (2002) writing games – blending voices, and making the paper look right. These were introduced as a focus for the second draft of the first main writing task and received repeated attention through feedback and through the second main writing task.

Monitoring and Assessment

The course was re-designed with six formal assessment points. Two of these were of the written product after learners were taken through the three- or four-week writing process, and two assessed responses to tutor feedback on those products (i.e. revisions); error correction was part of the feedback given by tutors. A further assessment was of an examination-type essay produced under time constraints. Although this sat a little awkwardly with the rest of the course it could be justified on two grounds. First, it provided learners with practice in an important genre of writing within the university context, and, second, it managed the risk of too favorably rewarding any students whose other assessed work, which was largely written outside of workshops, had been substantially contributed to by another person. The final piece of assessment was a reflection based on a small portfolio of the student's writing during the course. This, along with the two revisions of writing, were intended to focus on the "awareness" goal of the course recipe.

Opportunities for feedback were also an important consideration, and fitted well with the process approach taken. Learners provided peer feedback on each other's writing, the tutor provided feedback at different stages, and especially on the final product, and learners were expected to reflect on their own performance in terms of both product and process. Some time was devoted to training the learners in giving peer feedback, to ensure it was done effectively (Hansen & Liu, 2005; Rollinson, 2005). With the peer and tutor feedback in particular, a key idea was that learners needed to respond to it in some way. As Chandler (2003, p. 293) puts it, "What seems to be a crucial factor . . . is having the students do something with the error correction besides simply receiving it."

Evaluation

In Nation and Macalister's (2010) model of curriculum design, the process is bound within an outer ring of evaluation. This ensures that there are opportunities to evaluate whether the course is successful and to identify areas for improvement; it also ensures the course responds to changes in the teaching–learning context. Thus, evaluation involves more than "ongoing cycles of needs analysis" (Grabe, 2001, p. 37) and includes environment analysis and accommodation of new developments in relevant research and theory. The same evaluation tools that were available for the existing WRIT course were used for the new course, i.e. institutional evaluation measures, student comments in their reflection writing exercise, and staff observation. The institutional measures, which are essentially quantitative, indicated high levels of satisfaction, but evaluation of a more qualitative nature was provided by staff and students. Not all teaching staff were in a position to compare the old and the new courses, so comments were often on the effectiveness of components of the new course and in particular related to aspects of the assessment points, such as their relative weighting and the marking rubrics provided. In this section, student comment on the goal of the course and two of the principles underlying it will be presented.

Time on Task

The intention was to provide students with many opportunities to write, both in-class and out, in the belief that we learn to write by writing. Not all reading and writing were related to assessment points in the course. Opportunities to practice the strategy of predicting a text's content and writing those expectations before reading, followed by a written response to the text, occurred regularly. One student found this helped to minimize his anxiety about writing.

> The write before you read process is really helpful to achieve this goal. I realize that to overcome my anxiety is to write as much as I can. The more

I write I became more confident and be able to write without worrying about any mistake that I will make. Moreover, this process also helps me a lot in writing my first draft. This is because I just write what I have in mind as much as possible although sometime I am not sure about some fact that I wrote. I am not worry about making a mistake in writing the first draft is because it will be strengthen or fix in the peer response process.

Another student had returned to university after working "full time for two years in a hotel [where] oral English was the major tool [...] I hardly did any paper work during that period, not to mention the academic writing." She also commented positively on the in-class writing opportunities.

After I finished this course and look back, the practice that we did in workshops help me to improve [...] We did hand writing exercises almost every class. At first, I found very hard to start and do not know what to say. In contrast, in the last "think before you read" exercise I wrote a short story about a woman's life before read the story about Miss Brill.

Feedback

While students were encouraged to write openly and critically in their reflection at the end of the course, it was only the practice of peer feedback that elicited a degree of criticism.

Getting feedback from our classmate was one of the practices along the course. If I want to be honest and express my opinion, I must say that, I did not really like it and were not happy with that. Because we all were doing the [...] course to learn how to write so I do not think they can be able to notice my mistake and advise me how to correct them.

It was more common, however, for students to demonstrate an evolving appreciation of some benefit from peer feedback, as the course progressed.

Although at first I think this session did not help me much, but at the end of the course I realized that's quite useful to get feedbacks from others about our writing. For instance, in my second essay my peer reviewer suggested me to write about the effect of the improvement in China women's life to the country as my conclusion. However, I forgot about it and used my own idea which seems like new information in my conclusion. As a consequence, it was wrong as it is one of the four mistakes that should be avoided in the conclusion handout.

Similarly:

> Though, the feedback I obtained from my classmates was of little help but it was worth giving feedback to my class partners because it has provided me with the opportunity and the importance of proof reading.

Both these examples are typical of a number of students who commented on a growing awareness of their own strengths and weaknesses as writers. This is also seen in a third example, from a student who viewed peer feedback altogether more favorably.

> Similarly, another principle of feedback has become an indispensable part of my writing. When I worked with my peers, they always give me some specific suggestion that might be improved on the ideas and organizations. Simultaneously, when I read my peers' essays, and gave the responds to them, I would reconsider whether I have made the same mistake as they did. For example, I still remember last time [X] pointed out some mistakes of the in-text reference I used within the essay. This failure on using the reference did give me a deep impression that I would not make it twice time in the future.

Awareness

As the examples above suggest, the course had some success in helping learners become more aware of their own strengths and weaknesses as writers. For some students the evidence for this lay in their ability to transfer new learning about writing to other courses.

> ...after making some observation, I realize that I can use the introduction technique for my abstract in my lab report. Even though it is not an academic essay but I can improve my abstract [...] because it almost likes the introduction of an essay especially on the thesis statement.

Other students demonstrated this through changes in the goals they set themselves during the course.

> ...the most significant goal I established at the beginning of the course was to reduce my grammatical errors. In my mind, the essay would be perfect if they had the good ideas an accurate expression. In the first lecture, however, I acquired the core word for the English writing from my tutor. It was "awareness". I re-thought about the main differences between Chinese and English writing...

For one student, at least, there was a hint of epiphany about her growing awareness.

> When I started [WRIT] I believe that I primarily needed to improve formal aspects of writing, such as spelling and grammar. As I progressed through the course, I have come to understand that my problems were more fundamental. I first needed to learn how to think.

Discussion

The principal concern for the course designer and the writing teacher is the extent to which a new course meets its goals, and to a large extent the evaluative comments on this new curriculum suggest that it appears to have been successful. In their reflections on the course, many students demonstrated evidence of a growing awareness of themselves as writers, of the transferability of writing skills from WRIT to other courses, and of the writing process. While it would be misleading to claim that all were now confident, competent writers, many did seem to have moved some way along the path to becoming writers who, as Casanave (2002, p. 277) describes it,

> do not view their writing problems as insurmountable. Instead, they recognize ... that they cannot escape complexity and ambiguity and that they must develop strategies for trying to construct a coherent self and a set of practices in spite of the impossibility of finding the One Right Way.

From the learners' perspective, the most contentious issue of the course was the use of peer feedback. Although, for many students, there was a growing acceptance of the practice's usefulness, as discussed earlier, a view that it was only of benefit to less proficient learners did persist.

> Thus, I think responding and getting feedback from classmates will be more helpful for the classmates who are weaker. Classmate with stronger writing skill may help the weaker classmates but not contrary.

The impact of peer feedback on the two parties involved, the giver and the receiver, is still relatively unexplored in the field of second language writing, although Lundstrom and Baker (2009) found greater benefits for the givers than the receivers. Overall, then, the decision to use – and to retain – peer feedback in the course is one that is most influenced by the Principles outer circle in the curriculum design model.

The decision to use literature as input material and to give attention to voice, at least insofar as learners were encouraged and expected to base their argument on their individual response to and understanding of the texts read, also appeared to be vindicated by the evaluation measures. The lack of any negative comment also allayed any concerns that the use of literary texts may have lacked face validity for these academically-focused students. There was no evidence to suggest, however, that learners had been motivated to read texts of the type used in the course independently. Successful reading – and enjoyment – of one short story by Witi Ihimaera did not, in other words, lead students to read other stories by the same author. It is doubtful, therefore, that students were exposed to a sufficient quantity of text to derive any of the benefits for their writing that have been demonstrated in studies of extensive reading (Hafiz & Tudor, 1989; Tsang, 1996).

Language proficiency development is one of the benefits that have been claimed for extensive reading, and this did remain an issue for a number of students. One likely future change in the course as a result may be the inclusion of more deliberate consciousness-raising activities, such as error logs (Lee, 2005) and Dictogloss (Dung, 2002; Wajnryb, 1990), as suggested by Ferris (2004, p. 59). As students frequently mention grammar improvement when engaged in goal-setting exercises in the early stages of the course, such activities could be included without difficulty, and would be compatible with the course goal. More explicit training in vocabulary learning strategies (Nation, 2001) could also be helpful.

Conclusion

The intention of this chapter was to explore the process by which evaluation of a curriculum, in this case a second language writing curriculum, contributes to re-development of the course, allowing the course to remain dynamic. It is this process that is of interest, not the curriculum itself, for every curriculum will differ. Indeed, a curriculum is only "good" insofar as it is appropriate to its specific context. The differences in curricula, their individuality, result from decisions taken as a result of the needs and environment analyses, and the application of principles derived from theory and research. In so doing, the course designer makes justifiable, principled decisions about many aspects of the curriculum. Decisions taken at the initial planning stages, however, may not always be the correct ones and so, as part of the process of curriculum design, ongoing evaluation measures need to be in place to ensure that the course remains responsive to student needs, to changes in the teaching–learning environment, and to new developments in relevant research and theory. By following a process such as that outlined in this chapter, teachers and course designers should be able to create and maintain courses that effectively facilitate their learners' language development.

References

Casanave, C.P. (2002). *Writing Games: Multicultural case studies of academic literacy practices in higher education*. Mahwah, NJ: Lawrence Erlbaum Associates.

Chandler, J. (2003). The efficacy of various kinds of error feedback for improvement in the accuracy and fluency of L2 student writing. *Journal of Second Language Writing, 12*(3), 267–296.

Dung, K.N. (2002). Dictogloss: Using dictation to teach grammar. *Guidelines, 24*(1), 29–32.

Ferris, D.R. (1999). The case for grammar correction in L2 writing classes: A response to Truscott (1996). *Journal of Second Language Writing, 8*, 1–10.

Ferris, D.R. (2004). The "grammar correction" debate in L2 writing: Where are we, and where do we go from here? (and what do we do in the meantime . . .?). *Journal of Second Language Writing, 13*(1), 49–62.

Grabe, W. (2001). Reading–writing relations: Theoretical perspectives and instructional practices. In D. Belcher & A. Hirvela (Eds.), *Linking literacies: Perspectives in L2 reading–writing connections* (pp. 15–47). Ann Arbor, MI: University of Michigan Press.

Guenette, D. (2007). Is feedback pedagogically correct? Research design issues in studies of feedback on writing. *Journal of Second Language Writing, 16*(1), 40–53.

Hafiz, F., & Tudor, I. (1989). Extensive reading and the development of reading skills. *ELT Journal, 43*(1), 4–11.

Hansen, J.G., & Liu, J. (2005). Guiding principles for effective peer response. *ELT Journal, 59*(1), 31–38.

Hirvela, A. (2001). Connecting reading and writing through literature. In D. Belcher & A. Hirvela (Eds.), *Linking literacies: Perspectives in L2 reading–writing connections* (pp. 109–134). Ann Arbor, MI: University of Michigan Press.

Horowitz, D. (1990). Fiction and nonfiction in the ESL/EFL classroom: Does the difference make a difference? *English for Specific Purposes, 9*(2), 161–168.

Ihimaera, W. (1972). The beginning of the tournament. *Pounamu, Pounamu* (pp. 7–13). Auckland, New Zealand: Heinemann.

Ihimaera, W. (2003). The beginning of the tournament. *Ihimaera: His Best Stories* (pp. 200–207). Auckland, New Zealand: Reed.

Lee, I. (2005). Why burn the midnight oil? Marking student essays. *Modern English Teacher, 14*(1), 33–40.

Lundstrom, K., & Baker, W. (2009). To give is better than to receive: The benefits of peer review to the reviewer's own writing. *Journal of Second Language Writing, 18*, 30–43.

Matsuda, P.K., & Tardy, C.M. (2007). Voice in academic writing: The rhetorical construction of author identity in blind manuscript review. *English for Specific Purposes, 26*(2), 235–249.

Matsuda, P.K., & Tardy, C.M. (2008). Continuing the conversation on voice in academic writing. *English for Specific Purposes, 27*(1), 100–105.

Nation, I.S.P. (2001). *Learning vocabulary in another language*. Cambridge, UK: Cambridge University Press.

Nation, I.S.P., & Macalister, J. (2010). *Language curriculum design*. New York, NY: Routledge/ Taylor & Francis.

Rollinson, P. (2005). Using peer feedback in the ESL writing class. *ELT Journal, 59*(1), 23–30.

Spack, R. (1985). Literature, reading, writing, and ESL: Bridging the gaps. *TESOL Quarterly, 19*(4), 703–725.

Stapleton, P., & Helms-Park, R. (2008). A response to Matsuda and Tardy's "Voice in academic writing: The rhetorical construction of author identity in blind manuscript review". *English for Specific Purposes, 27*(1), 94–99.

Truscott, J. (1996). The case against grammar correction in L2 writing classes. *Language Learning, 46*, 327–369.

Tsang, W.-K. (1996). Comparing the effects of reading and writing on writing performance. *Applied Linguistics, 17*(2), 627–642.

Vandrick, S. (2003). Literature in the teaching of second language composition. In B. Kroll (Ed.), *Exploring the dynamics of second language writing* (pp. 263–282). Cambridge, UK: Cambridge University Press.

Wajnryb, R. (1990). *Grammar dictation*. Oxford, UK: Oxford University Press.

Comment

In this chapter, John Macalister has illustrated the important role that evaluation can play in contributing to course design and re-design. It reminds us that responsible curriculum design includes ongoing evaluation of a course. Evaluation can be either summative or formative. It allows us to determine whether a course is successful, and to identify areas that may need improvement. In this case study, both are present. The audience here was primarily the course designer/teacher, but other audiences are often involved, and sometimes these are major stakeholders. Evaluation and its effects have been mentioned in several of the other case studies in this collection; it is always worth asking who the evaluation is for, and what is its purpose. It is also worth checking in any report of a curriculum design that there is provision for appropriate evaluation. Without it, a course can lose its dynamism.

Tasks

1. The evaluation presented in this chapter focuses on the students' subjective experiences of the course. Consider how evidence of actual outcomes (in terms of writing improvement) could be brought into the model. This will involve formulating more concrete "aims" (or expected learning outcomes) within the process of curriculum design.

2. Evaluation can be done for different audiences and different purposes. The audience in this chapter was the course designer/teacher. Consider how the evaluation might differ if the audience changed.

TABLE 10.2

Audience	Purpose	Tools
Scholarship provider for international students		
Student association for new student information handbook		
Academic adviser in a faculty requiring students to take WRIT		

3. What makes a "good" course? A range of meanings can be attached to "good" (see *LCD*, p. 11). Which of the following possible meanings were important to John Macalister in this case study? A "good" course . . .
   a. attracts a lot of students
   b. makes a lot of money
   c. satisfies the learners
   d. satisfies the teachers
   e. satisfies the sponsors
   f. helps learners gain high scores in an external test
   g. results in a lot of learning
   h. applies state-of-the-art knowledge about language teaching and learning
   i. is held in high regard by the local or international community
   j. follows accepted principles of curriculum design.

11

LOCALIZING SPANISH IN THE ANN ARBOR LANGUAGES PARTNERSHIP: DEVELOPING AND USING A "TEACHABLE" CURRICULUM

Donald Freeman, Maria Coolican, and Kathleen Graves

Introduction: A "Teachable" Curriculum

This chapter discusses the development of what we are calling a "teachable" curriculum in the Ann Arbor Languages Partnership. This notion of "teachability" integrates two somewhat contrapuntal elements: on the one hand, the curriculum needed to address the language needs of elementary (primary school) students learning to use Spanish in the world; on the other, it needed to support new teachers as they were learning to teach language to elementary students. Thus the curriculum had to effectively scaffold on two levels – student learning of the new language and teacher learning of the new professional practices involved in teaching that language to these students.

The Ann Arbor Languages Partnership is a collaborative undertaking of the university and the local school district to "support improved educational attainment of children and their social participation in school, local, and global communities through the delivery of clinical teacher preparation in languages" (A2LP Executive Summary, 2009). Begun in 2007 as an educational exchange of services between the district and the university, the Partnership began providing Spanish language instruction to some 1,225 district students in Grade Three (ages 8 to 9) through a carefully structured teacher education program run by the university. The Partnership is organized around four core value propositions intended to guide both policy and practice:

1. *Language pluralism and effective transnational citizenship*: The Partnership activities are based on the proposition of "plurilingualism," that language competence is partial, dynamic, and driven by users' needs. The curriculum and assessments are documented through the Common European Framework of Reference for Languages and Learning (Council of Europe, 2001a).

2. *Learning in and through experience*: Experience provides a common foundation for students who are learning new language(s) and for the Apprentice Teachers who are learning to teach them. These experiences are embedded in one another so that the experience of students learning a new language is supported through the experience of professional learning of the new teachers who work with them. Together, this view of learning and teaching propels *community engagement* that can reposition languages from being simply school subjects to becoming assets of social capital (Putnam, 2000) in an increasingly transnational world.

3. *Documenting and making public language learning and use*: Documentation is critical to build these language assets into social capital. In plurilingual learning, this documentation process needs to be "user-driven." It involves capturing what learners *want to do* with the new language and monitoring what they *can do* against those goals. The Partnership plans to document student goals and uses through the Language Portfolio process derived from one now in use throughout the European Community (Council of Europe, n.d.).

4. *Collaborative work*: The Partnership brings together the respective interests, needs, strengths, and resources of the school district and the university in a fully collaborative undertaking to support and extend language diversity and learning, by building a clinical teacher preparation program in language teaching.

Part I: "The Time Before the Beginning"

As is often the case with educational initiatives that are complex and systemic, it is very difficult to actually pinpoint the beginning of the Partnership. There was a constellation of social factors and organizational elements that contributed to how it was conceptualized, and subsequently launched. Taken together, these influences loosely comprise "the time before the beginning;" they created a social and educational environment that was productively disposed to this novel design that combined student language learning with teacher education. This section focuses on three of these factors that shaped both the overall Partnership and more specifically its teachable curriculum: community support, reform of teacher education at the university, and experience with new models.

Community Support

Language instruction in US schools has typically been hard to sell, particularly in times of heightened focus on accountability in literacy and mathematics coupled with shrinking public sector resources. The Ann Arbor community was no different, having recently suffered in 2007 a significant economic downturn, and schools faced a persistent gap in academic achievement among different groups in the system. It was in the context of these wider social factors that the district had to undertake a participatory planning process aimed at engaging the wider community in creating and sustaining interest in and commitment to the school system. In 2007, there were a series of community-based conversations that culminated in a new strategic plan for the district.[1] The plan, which was endorsed by the school board and district administration, was explicit in two goals that became central to the Partnership: the need to strengthen the recognition of diversity – including language diversity – for all students in the district and the commitment to extend instruction in additional or new languages into the elementary schools. The district plan stated that they wanted to enhance current curricula to prepare students to be successful in a global society.

Reforming Teacher Education at the University

At the same time the district was involved in a planning process that articulated the commitment to language diversity, the university was engaged in an examination of how it provided teacher education. The reform has focused on how beginning teachers learn "the work of teaching" (Ball and Forzani, 2009, Cohen, Raudenbush and Ball, 2003) and how that work might be parsed into specific learnable and assessable classroom practices (Lampert, 2001). This has led to thinking differently about classrooms as settings for professional learning and about the roles of faculty, teachers, and others who might support this learning (see Freeman, 2009). While the university's teacher education programs, and the World Languages area, had enjoyed cordial working relations with many schools in the district, the level of systemic commitment to providing classroom instruction contemplated by the Partnership was new. The university was interested in developing new settings for practice and exploring new forms and models for teacher induction and support.

Experience with New Models

There is certainly no lack of models through which districts and universities collaborate in instruction and/or teacher preparation. Ranging from laboratory schools to professional development school designs, these models generally focus on creating hybrid institutional structures to address the intersection of needs and interests of both parties. Thus both "laboratory" and "professional development" schools differ in basic ways from schools *per se*, through the roles of university faculty and/or school personnel, and/or the students they serve. This hybridity

---

[1] "A 32-member Strategic Planning Team – representing parents, students, teachers, administrators and community members – drafted the Ann Arbor Public Schools Strategic Plan. It is a plan that includes beliefs, mission, objectives and strategies." *AAPS Strategic Plan 2007–2012.* Ann Arbor: Author.

can be both a strength, in creating a new social and professional structure, and a liability, in that such structures are often vulnerable because they lie outside the core mission of each group. In a real sense, these arrangements, as innovative as they are, oftentimes prove to be fleeting.

The Partnership began with a different premise: that the university and district could develop an educational "exchange of services" towards the common goal that made language diversity a key element of social capital in district classrooms and in the community. To enact this common goal, each institution had a primary need: In order to address its strategic plan and meet commitments to parents and community, the district needed to add Spanish language instruction in elementary grades; to build its language teacher preparation capacity and to pursue new models of teacher preparation, the university needed access to extended clinical settings.

The complementarity of interests that led to the Partnership seemed somehow different from other models in that each partner had a concrete need that was directly connected to its particular core mission. The district's commitment to language diversity and its interest in expanding instruction in new languages in elementary schools and the university's initiatives in rethinking teacher preparation created a rather unique design opportunity. It is probably fair to say that neither set of factors alone would have led to the depth of systemic thinking and design that came to characterize the Partnership. But taken together, the district's interest in new language instruction and the university's interest in developing new forms of teacher preparation created a complementary set of institutional concerns that provided the foundation for working differently together.

District and university leaders agreed that it would be useful to have a proof of concept, an instance in which this "exchange of services" model had been used. The example could show that a different design was indeed feasible and, perhaps more importantly, it might also help to anticipate some of the implementation

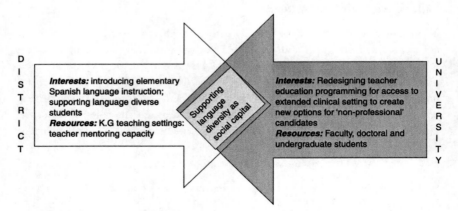

FIGURE 11.1 The partnership design as an educational 'exchange of services'

issues that were bound to arise. We found this proof of concept in a similar program design, the Windham Partnership for Teacher Education that Freeman and his colleagues had developed in the early 1990s. The Windham Partnership brought together eight rural elementary schools in southeastern Vermont with the graduate language teacher education program at the School for International Training to provide French and Spanish instruction by teachers-in-training who were supervised and supported by mentor teachers in the elementary classrooms in which they taught (Rodgers and Tiffany, 1997).

These elements of community planning and engagement coupled with ongoing reform of teacher education at the university generated a fertile environment in which the exchange of services concept that undergirded the collaboration could take hold and grow. However, realizing this new design depended on developing a teachable curriculum that would connect the respective institutional goals of student language learning and teacher professional learning.

Part II: Setting out the Parameters for a "Teachable" Curriculum

To develop this teachable curriculum, a steering group made up of key district administrators and university faculty developed the curriculum framework and sequence of lessons. As with any curriculum, a number of factors guided its creation. These factors stemmed from the needs and concerns of the partners, the school district on the one hand, and the university on the other. The district determined both the new language to be taught, Spanish, and the entry grade level, grade three. The district chose grade three as the starting point on the basis that by then children have developed a basic level of literacy in English, the majority first language and language of instruction, and this can serve as a base for developing literacy in the new language. The results of the 2006 community survey overwhelmingly supported Spanish as the first choice of new language, largely because Spanish is the dominant second language in the United States. An important byproduct of this choice, however, was to position the third-graders who speak Spanish as a first or home language as experts, where many might often be positioned as English language learners in general instruction.

Both the district and the university were committed to an approach that did not treat language as a school subject, but as something living, developmental, and usable in the world (Larsen-Freeman and Freeman, 2008). Since many adults have had less-than-positive language learning experiences as students in US schools, the steering committee wanted to challenge the notion that languages are essentially unlearnable in school. Thus in order to sustain interest in and commitment to the curriculum, student progress in learning needed to be transparent to both children and families. It was for this reason that the steering group decided to base the new language curriculum on the Common European Framework (CEFR) as a performance-based, internationally validated framework that is coherent across multiple languages.

The CEFR focuses on what learners "can do," thus allowing students to document their new language abilities in ways that are understandable to peers, parents, and community members, and are portable throughout their time both in and outside of school. In this way, we felt the documentation would be transparently understandable in a non-technical way in multiple settings of school and employment. Beyond documentation, both partners agreed that the curriculum would need to be appropriate and engaging for children as young language learners. The university was particularly concerned that it be readily teachable by new teachers. Unlike conventional designs in which "student teachers" work under the direct supervision of "cooperating teachers" in their classrooms, in the Partnership design, the Apprentice Teachers would be the Spanish language teachers in the classroom.

The steering group expressed this group of factors as three design parameters: the curriculum needed to be *credible*, it had to focus on real language learning; it needed to be *embedded* in the general school curriculum, not an add-on subject or something available only to a limited group of students; and it needed to be *teachable* to young learners by new teachers. These factors together reminded us in the development process that the focus needed to be on how the curriculum would be enacted in the classroom (Graves, 2000).

A Credible Curriculum

In considering credibility, the steering group took into account several dimensions: credibility to parents and the broader community, credibility to children, and linguistic credibility (Graves, 2008). Often foreign language learning at the elementary level is rendered simply as a string of topics, what we called the "colors and numbers" syndrome, with little attention to the ongoing development of young learners' underlying language competence. In contrast, the CEFR orientation, which recognizes, develops, and documents language competences, offered the credibility we were seeking so that parents could see their children progressing as language learners and users over time. The descriptors of CEFR A1 level of competence provided a starting point for developing a sequential Spanish language curriculum that would span the upper elementary grades, and the assessments and Language Passport would provide a means for documenting progress. During its first year, the Partnership planned to adapt a version of the Language Portfolio used in Britain in the ASSET Languages Project and designed specifically for early learners.[2] Thus the district third-grade students would have an opportunity to capture their emerging sense of their own plurilingualism and to document the development of their Spanish language knowledge throughout the project and beyond.

---

[2] For information about ASSET Languages see <http://www.assetlanguages.org.uk> (accessed October 14 2010).

An Embedded Curriculum

A second issue that the steering committee grappled with had to do with the perceived relevance of foreign language study in US schools (Magnan, 2007). Oftentimes, foreign language in elementary school, or FLES, curricula are seen as extra "add-ons," sometimes available to subsets of the school population as in "gifted and talented" programs; thus programs can be labeled as superfluous and become easy to cut when resources diminish. Thus to be sustainable, particularly in a period of shrinking resources in terms of school time and finances, the steering committee determined that the Partnership curriculum needed to be embedded in the overall elementary school curriculum. We were heartened that there seemed to be a natural affinity between the Michigan social studies curriculum that focuses in grades kindergarten through three on self, family, and community and the A1 descriptors of the CEFR. As children learned about these expanding social circles, that learning could be complemented and expressed in Spanish as a new language. Thus in a strategic sense, the Partnership curriculum was not about learning Spanish; rather, it was positioned as helping students learn to use Spanish when communicating about their social environment, as captured in the state social studies framework.

A Teachable Curriculum

In a certain sense, the Partnership was based on a calculated gamble: that new teachers who were proficient in Spanish but likely with little or no experience teaching it, could, with intensive preparation and ongoing support, do a credible job of teaching the language to third-graders. Thus in addition to the parameters just discussed of credibility, and the embeddedness that helped to achieve it, the curriculum developed in the Partnership needed to be teachable. This meant it needed to be constructed in such a way that the new Apprentice Teachers would feel comfortable and productive as teachers from the outset. To be teachable for and by them, the curriculum needed to be structured around elements of predictability and consistency. It needed to be highly explicit about what the teachers and students were to do and say in each lesson, and the supporting classroom materials needed to be easy to prepare and to use. In essence, the curriculum needed to be well scaffolded, so that newly minted Apprentice Teachers could pick it up and teach it.

Part III: The Curriculum Development Process

With these parameters in mind – that the curriculum be *credible, embedded,* and *teachable* – the development process was begun in earnest in the fall of 2008. The process itself fell rather naturally into three phases, outlined in Figure 11.2. The first phase focused on customizing or localizing the CEFR level descriptors to the district context and state social studies curriculum, and then creating lessons and units on that basis. In the second phase, a small group of Apprentice Teachers piloted

Phase One October 2008–August 2009	Phase Two Summer 2009	Phase Three September 2009–June 2010
University team in consultation with district 'localizes' the CEFR Level Descriptors to create Partnership indicators, and then lessons and units	Apprentice Teachers pilot lessons with elementary students in district summer school; lessons refined on that basis.	Full launch in which 36–40 Apprentice Teachers teach 1,225 Grade 3 students in 63 classrooms.

FIGURE 11.2 The **phases** of the curriculum development process

these lessons with third-graders in the district's summer school to get a sense of how the lessons played in the hands of new teachers with students. Then in the third phase, the Partnership was launched across the district in September 2009.

Localizing the CEFR Descriptors and Creating Lessons and Units

The first development task was to work with adapting the CEFR level descriptors for use in this particular setting. Because the CEFR has been constructed as an "open source" document, it is customizable for local use (Morrow, 2004). The steering group looked at ways in which this localization process had worked for groups in other language settings. Three major challenges emerged. The first had to do with the manner of localization: we had to determine the ways in which the relevant CEFR level descriptors could be customized to the Partnership context and expectations. The second challenge addressed the context of localization more fully in how the Spanish curriculum would connect to and become embedded within the larger scope of third-grade student learning outcomes in the district. And the third challenge involved determining the level of scaffolding necessary for the curriculum to support the Apprentice Teachers in developing the pedagogical skills needed to deliver these lessons.

The actual development process began by examining the CEFR A1 level descriptors and determining the ways in which those "can do" outcomes statements could be customized – or localized – within the Partnership to what we termed "indicators."[3] In undertaking this task, the goal was that the curriculum be perceived as enabling productive language learning and language use for the young

---

[3] Although the CEFR documents use the term "level descriptors," the Partnership chose to use the term "indicator" because it was more familiar terminologically in the US standards-setting discourse. While we agree completely with the notion of "describing" performance in CEFR, general US standards and curriculum terminology seem to favor the notion of indicating, perhaps in a more prescriptive sense, what that performance *should* be. Given the goals of credibility and embeddedness, we decided to adopt the latter term. In essence, though, the two terms refer to the same thing: a statement of performance outcome.

learners, which we termed a credible curriculum. To this end, the steering group turned to the state grade three social studies curriculum, thus tying this objective of credibility to wider instructional goals through the fact that the Spanish curriculum would be embedded within the larger grade-level curriculum.

As mentioned previously, the state social studies curriculum for kindergarten to grade three focuses on expanding circles of self-knowledge. In kindergarten, students learn to talk about "myself and others;" in first grade, they focus on "families and schools;" and in second grade, on "the local community." In the development process, we saw the clear opportunity to build on these expanding concepts of knowledge of self in the world in Spanish. If this new language curriculum could be aligned with these expanding concepts, it would allow third-grade students to review and build on what they had explored in social studies in earlier grades. Fortunately, the CEFR readily supported this progression as the A1 level focuses on concepts associated with family and local community, and on being able to interact with others in simple ways.

Figure 11.3 shows A1 level descriptors drawn from different scales in the CEFR (see Council of Europe, 2001b) displayed in the left-hand column, and the localized A1 indicators for Spoken Interaction (SI) (listed on the right); key terms have been bolded to show the connection. Both descriptors and indicators are phrased as "can do" statements. The first four localized SI indicators in the right-hand column are closely linked to the CEFR descriptors, while the fifth local SI indicator has been added to capture appropriate school-based language for children.

The steering group examined ways in which these localized Spanish language outcomes, which we had called "indicators," could be linked to existing third-grade standards in social studies. These standards, known as "GLCEs" or "grade level content expectations," are a regular part of the curricular and instructional discourse in the district at the grade and school levels. In third grade, the social studies curriculum focuses on "Michigan studies." The scope of these GLCEs includes opportunities to study various aspects of civic engagement. The third grade GLCE states that:

> In extending students' civic perspective beyond the family, neighborhood, and community to the state, the third grade content expectations prepare students for their role as responsible and informed citizens of Michigan. . . . Building on prior social studies knowledge and applying new concepts of each social studies discipline to the increasingly complex social environment of their state, the third grade content expectations prepare students for more sophisticated studies of their country and world in later grades.
>
> (Grade Level Content Expectations, Social Studies, 3rd Grade, p. 11)[4]

---

[4] See also <http://www.michigan.gov/mde/0,1607,7–140–28753_33232—-,00.html> (retrieved October 14, 2010).

CEFR A1 Level Descriptors (from Council of Europe, 2001b)	Partnership Grade 3 A1 Spoken Interaction [SI] Indicators
CEFR Global scale Can understand and use **familiar** everyday expressions and very basic phrases aimed at the satisfaction of needs of a concrete type. Can **introduce him/herself and others** and can ask and answer questions about personal details such as **where he/she lives, people he/she knows and things he/she has.** Can interact in a simple way provided the other person talks **slowly and clearly** and is prepared to help.	*Spoken interaction* **SI 1:** I can introduce myself, somebody else, and use basic greetings and leave-taking expressions.
Conversation **Can make an introduction and use basic greeting and leave-taking expressions.**	**SI 2:** I can be understood when I say certain simple, familiar sentences, but I am dependent on my partner to help me when the sentences are more complicated.
Self-assessment grid I can interact in a simple way provided the other person is prepared to repeat or rephrase things at a **slower rate of speech** and help me formulate what I'm trying to say. I can ask and answer simple questions in areas of immediate need or on very **familiar topics.**	**SI 3:** I can ask people questions about where they live, people they know, things they have, etc. and have many such questions addressed to me provided they are articulated slowly and clearly. **SI 4:** I can handle numbers, quantities, cost, and time. **SI 5:** I can understand simple directions asking me to stand up, sit down, line up, speak, or listen when they are addressed carefully and slowly to me.
Goal-oriented cooperation **Can handle numbers, quantities, cost and time.**	

FIGURE 11.3 Linking the CEFR A1 descriptors to the localized Partnership language indicators

In nominating Spanish in the 2006 community survey, many parents had said that they wanted their children to learn "the fastest growing language in the state" and "to be able to understand and interact with the regional Spanish-speaking population." By linking GLCEs to Spanish language indicators, the Partnership could demonstrate how language and cultural knowledge could be useful and usable in becoming "responsible and informed citizens of Michigan." Closely connecting the Spanish to these GLCEs served to embed the new curriculum not only in the larger grade-level curriculum, but, perhaps more importantly, in the social and professional discourses, or "local language" about teaching and learning in the district.

The connection between the Spanish language goals expressed through the CEFR A1 level descriptors as adapted and the state GLCEs in social studies focused on interaction skills. The CEFR conceptualizes language competence according to skills of listening, reading, writing, spoken production, and spoken interaction, while the social studies grade three GLCE, "Public Discourse, Decision Making, and Citizen Involvement," talks about communication in general terms:

> ...students continue to develop competency in expressing their own opinions relative to these issues and justify their opinions with reasons. This foundational knowledge is built upon throughout the grades as students develop a greater understanding of how, when, and where to communicate their positions on public issues with a reasoned argument.
>
> (Grade Level Content Expectations, Social Studies, 3rd Grade, p. 23)

Taking civic engagement skills as a wider or macro-frame for the more specific language skills in the CEFR, the steering committee developed this connection. The argument that "... how, when, and where to communicate their positions on public issues ..." included becoming able to express basic information about self, home, and community in language other than English was embraced and accepted. In this way, the connection could be further detailed through explicit linkages among language skills in Partnership indicators for the third grade as Figure 11.4 illustrates.

	Speaking	Listening	Reading	Writing
Indicator #4	I can describe my home, family, moods, and likes	I can understand common questions about my name, age, home, family, mood, and likes	I can understand information about people's names, ages, homes, families, moods, and likes when reading a piece of writing about them	I can write sentences and simple phrases about myself and my home, family, moods, and likes
Indicator #5	I can give personal information such as my name, age, birthday, address, and telephone number	I can understand most of another person's statements about their name, age, birthday, address, telephone number, home, family, moods, and likes, provided the speaker articulates carefully	I can understand a questionnaire that asks me basic information such as the date, my name, age, birthday, address, and telephone number	I can fill in a questionnaire with information such as the date, my name, age, birthday, address, and telephone number

FIGURE 11.4 Linking skills among the Partnership indicators

Creating Units and Lessons

Having aligned the now localized A1 level Partnership indicators with the third-grade social studies GCLEs, the next step was to organize content into units and, eventually, lessons. The units were designed to focus on topics that emerged from both the localized indicators as well as grade-level social studies topics. They were crafted around topics such as family, personal information, and school subjects. The lessons themselves are designed to be 30 minutes long, with two lessons taught per week, or 51 lessons for the school year. The lessons follow a standardized sequence that begins with an opening song and ends with a goodbye ritual, all entirely in Spanish. Because they are short, the lessons are sequenced such that students re-encounter and re-use previously learned material. This routine structure helps to support the goals of credibility and teachability. Arguing that a key aspect of credibility lies in using the language, the aim was to have the lessons taught almost entirely in Spanish, which they could more readily be when classroom management was scaffolded through routine patterns of interaction. Likewise, this predictability in lesson structure enhanced its familiarity for students and thus its teachability for the Apprentice Teachers.

Learning from Practice

The original bank of lessons was designed in fall 2008 and early winter 2009. These lessons became, after some revisions, the enacted curriculum used in the Apprentice Teacher training laboratory in summer 2009. Each summer, the district runs a summer program, the Summer Learning Institute, for elementary students who need academic support and remediation in order to be able to begin the next school year "at grade level." In July 2009, the district was able to include Spanish in the summer school, which opportunity allowed for piloting lessons to get feedback from elementary students and from Apprentice Teachers. The subtitle of this section, "Learning from Practice," refers to two kinds of learning that resulted. The first had to do with learning about the lessons themselves, while the second referred to what the new teachers learned from teaching the draft lessons. As this was the first training opportunity with Apprentice Teachers, this trialing provided a context for understanding what such induction would need to include.

Piloting the lessons offered direct and immediate insight into the teachability of the curriculum. Through observation and verbal feedback from both teachers and students, it quickly became clear that if these thirty-minute language learning experiences were to be useful and relevant, we would have to embrace the notion that "less is more" when designing these lessons. The lessons as piloted in July 2009 were, quite simply, too full of content and overly ambitious instructionally, a message brought home through the feedback process.

To address this problem, the curriculum team decided to create a lesson structure that became a template for all 51 lessons. Each lesson now features a core objective;

there is an opening procedure to engage students in using the new language immediately and directly. This is followed by a series of activities that introduce and/or extend the lesson topic in a variety of ways intended to address and engage multiple learning styles. Finally, there is a closing procedure that features a song or other habitual closure activity. Figure 11.5 includes an example of this format.

In some ways, this lesson appears as a classic elementary language lesson. The focus is on being able to share information about birthdays, which follows to the Speaking Indicator, *I can give personal information such as my name, age, birthday, address, and telephone number,* and the Listening Indicator, *I can understand most of another person's statements about their name, age, birthday, address, telephone number, home, family, moods, and likes, provided the speaker articulates carefully.* The lesson connects and extends student learning in the social studies by using prior experience of learning about "myself and others" and "families and schools" to give the students the opportunity to learn to communicate personal information and mutual understanding in Spanish. The activities are oriented to young language learners, using games with which they are familiar to create multiple and iterative learning opportunities within the larger lesson.

Even with strong initial training, the predictable lesson structure alone is not sufficient to scaffold new teachers to work productively with students. Additional information needed to be included that made explicit the instructional moves involved in the simple lessons. Therefore, versions were developed that included directions to the Apprentice Teachers to scaffold their teaching. The intent is to help them to draw on what they know about young learners to make decisions that support manageable communicative interaction among their students. Simple instructional moves, along with the reasoning behind them, are laid out to guide the enactment of the lesson. Figure 11.6 shows the details around the "ball toss" activity.

In terms of learning how to support new teachers, the summer school provided an opportunity to implement an iterative cycle of teaching and learning for the Apprentice Teachers. The mornings were spent studying key concepts in teaching young learners such as child development, second language acquisition, and principles of communicative language teaching. These concepts were then directly linked to teaching in the second part of the morning when the Apprentice Teachers worked with the lesson plans they would teach at midday. Each lesson was modeled by the university trainer, and then deconstructed into teaching moves. Following this analysis, the Apprentice Teachers rehearsed the lesson as they had seen it with a teaching partner and received immediate and focused feedback from the university trainers. The Apprentice Teachers were assigned to teach in pairs both in the summer school and subsequently throughout the school year, although the pairs might differ. These pairings offered multiple opportunities for peer coaching and feedback in this rehearsal process (Lampert, 2009). When the time came to teach the lesson in the afternoon, the new teachers had had immediate practice, coaching, and reflection on both its process and content. Following the actual lesson with the elementary students, the Apprentice Teachers

Date taught:

Name: Lesson 19 Unit Review *los meses y el cumpleaños*

Length: 30 minutes

Class Information: 3rd graders at _____

Content: months, dates, birthdays

Objective(s): Students will be able to tell when their birthdays are and their ages.

Assume already know: *How to say the months, tell the date and ask and answer about their birthdays*

Time in minutes	Stage	Procedure	Purpose	Materials	Language
5	Opening	Song ¡*Buenos días!* Repeat 2 times. Review months Model first, and then ask the date of at least 5 students.	Warm up Review, reactivate Help them to predict what is coming (the date question) and be prepared	Month poster Calendar	Song lyrics Months ¿*Cuál es la fecha de hoy? Hoy es* …
4	Practice	Ball Toss	Practice telling birthdays	• Ball and expressions poster • Posters with dates of month; months of year	¿*Cuándo es tu cumpleaños?* *Mi cumpleaños es el ___ de ___.*
11	Practice - Production	**Conecta Cuatro:** Divide class in 3-4 teams. Each team chooses a square and answers the question. Teams take turns. If a team answers question incorrectly another team tries to answer to gain the square. The first team to correctly answer 4 squares that are connected wins.	Review introducing oneself, giving age, birthday and the date.	Connect 4 chart	¿*Cómo te llamas?* ¿*Cuántos años tienes?* ¿*Cuándo es tu cumpleaños?* ¿*Cuál es la fecha de hoy?* Numbers
5	Two production activites one with your choice of content	Teléfono **OR** Alphabet Chant assisted by a student(s)	Review introducing oneself, giving age and asking/answering birthdays	Expressions posters Alphabet poster	¿*Cómo te llamas?* ¿*Cuántos años tienes?* ¿*Cuándo es tu cumpleaños?* ¿*Cuál es la fecha de hoy?* Numbers, etc.…
5	Closure	San Fermín song *Adíos* song		San Fermín poster	

FIGURE 11.5 Sample lesson (Lesson #19 – Dates and birthdays)

Stage	Procedure	Materials	Language
Practice	Toss ball or hand out numbers and go in order or simply announce that you are going to call on five students and they can ask for help from you or another student if they want to. Have the students think about: the date first then the month then put together *el* ___ *de* ___ Model this on the board, the building of this chunk of information. After this scaffolded 'pre-thinking', students should be more ready to answer the question. It will help separate the cognitive load of figuring out their birthday in Spanish from how to say the complete sentence in Spanish.	• Ball and expressions poster • Posters with dates of month; months of year	*¿Cuándo es tu cumpleaños?* *Mi cumpleaños es el __ de ____.*

FIGURE 11.6 Explicated 'ball toss' curriculum activity

debriefed what they had done with each other and with trainers who had observed them, and on that basis they prepared for the next day.

In this very real sense, the summer school provided a means to test the core premise: the extent to which a teachable curriculum had been developed. The piloting foreshadowed the extent to which the curriculum would be appropriately teachable to grade three students by new teachers in the first academic year of the project.

Launching the Partnership

In September 2009, the Partnership was launched in the district schools. About 40 Apprentice Teachers prepared to teach approximately 1,225 students in 63 third grade classrooms in all 20 of the district's elementary schools. The principal focus in this first year was on ensuring that the curriculum was indeed teachable. The steering group felt fairly certain that we had developed a curriculum that was credible, based on early reactions, and the fact that it embedded social studies foci. However, the extent to which the curriculum would be fully teachable was, up until the launch, not really known. While the summer training had given some sense of how the curriculum would unfold, it would not be until Apprentice Teachers were in classrooms for the full academic year that it would become clear whether the curriculum was teachable.

As the first year progressed, it became evident that the effectiveness of scaffolding in the curriculum (see Figure 11.6) depended on larger social structures.

To develop autonomy, the Apprentice Teachers had to follow the curriculum closely, even as they were growing increasingly flexible within it. Too much flexibility too soon made for sloppy, incoherent, and uneven teaching; too little flexibility over time made for formulaic lessons that were not engaging for students. Striking this developing balance between structure and autonomy became a central issue in the first year. Having achieved significant academic success as university students by passively waiting for professors to share information, many of the Apprentice Teachers came to teaching quite comfortable with the idea of being told what to do. In the Partnership, however, as they had to continually reflect on the efficacy of their own teaching they became active agents in their own professional learning. Some new teachers responded to the situation as an invitation to learn in new and exciting ways, while others found it a challenge that was at times cautiously exciting and at others daunting and even threatening. The challenge of the first year became one of continual calibration: how to scaffold the work for each Apprentice Teacher to move the individual along a continuum of increasingly independent and active professional learning.

For the third grade students, while the curriculum was indeed teachable, the effort to maintain it that way was significant. It proved easier in many ways to develop a curriculum that is credible and embedded than one that is readily teachable to students over time. This dimension of teachability requires constant adaptation both in the moment and over time. In the moment, there is adjustment to the differing demands of particular third grade classes as understood by their individual Apprentice Teachers. Then as the learning and teaching unfolds over time, with students and their teachers becoming more proficient – the one in language and the other in teaching – there is the push for more autonomy.

As the Partnership moves into its second year of implementation, a new grade level will be added, which will double the numbers of students, classrooms, and Apprentice Teachers. The focus will be on maintaining this teachability of the curriculum as we, as designers, become more adept and experienced at predicting where calibration for teachers and adjustment for students will be needed, and hopefully more skilled at making those adaptations. There is a "just-in-time" quality to the work which is at once exhilarating and exhausting; but to end with a curriculum frozen in activity will defeat the goal of the undertaking: developing in students and new teachers an appreciation, commitment, and capacity to work with language as a tool for social diversity.

References

Ann Arbor Languages Partnership [A2LP]. (2009). *Ann Arbor Languages Partnership Executive Summary*. Ann Arbor, MI: Author.

Ball, D.L. and F. Forzani. (2009). The work of teaching and the challenge for teacher education. *Journal of Teacher Education, 60*(5), 497–511.

Cohen, D.K., Raudenbush, S.W. and Ball, D.L. (2003). Resources, instruction, and research. *Educational Evaluation and Policy Analysis, 25*(2), 119–142.

Council of Europe. (2001a). *Common European Framework of Reference for Languages: Learning, teaching and assessment.* Cambridge, UK: Cambridge University Press.

Council of Europe. (2001b). *Structured Overview of all CEFR Scales.* Strasbourg: Council of Europe.

Council of Europe. (n.d.) European Language Portfolio. Accessed August 18, 2010 at <www.coe.int/portfolio>.

Freeman, D. (2009). The scope of language teacher education. In A. Burns and J. Richards (Eds.) *The Cambridge guide to second language teacher education.* New York: Cambridge University Press, pp. 11–19.

Graves, K. (2000). *Designing language courses.* Boston, MA: Cengage-Heinle.

Graves, K. (2008). The language curriculum: A social contextual perspective. *Language Teaching, 41* (2), 149–183.

Lampert, M. (2001). *Teaching problems and the problems of teaching.* New Haven, CT: Yale University Press.

Lampert, M. (2009). Learning teaching in, from, and for practice: What do we mean? *Journal of Teacher Education, 61* (1–2), 21–34.

Larsen-Freeman, D. and D. Freeman. (2008). Language moves: The place of "foreign" languages in classroom teaching and learning. In J. Greene, G. Kelly, and A. Luke (Eds.) *Review of Research in Education, 32,* 147–186.

Magnan, S.S. (2007). Reconsidering communicative language teaching for national goals. *Modern Language Journal, 91,* 249–252.

Morrow, K. (2004). *Insights from the Common European Framework.* Oxford: Oxford University Press.

Putnam, R. (2000). *Bowling alone: The collapse and revival of American community.* New York: Simon and Schuster.

Rodgers, C. and Tiffany, P. (1997). Teacher thinking and the Windham Partnership Reflective Teaching Seminars. Paper presented at the Annual Meeting of the American Educational Research Association (Chicago, IL). ERIC Document #411219.

Comment

In this chapter, Donald Freeman, Maria Coolican, and Kathleen Graves have reported on an exciting interaction between a school district and a university which has resulted in an elementary level language class that seems far removed from the more standard offering of lashings of cultural content with a light sprinkling of linguistic items.

The approach to course design in this and many other case studies in this book is essentially a "waterfall" model, a sequence of carefully planned steps. This is possible when there is plenty of time and resources available, the ideal conditions for curriculum design. One of the interesting features of this "teachable" curriculum, however, is the incorporation of the teacher as course designer, for the design team needed to accommodate the teachers' increasing confidence in the classroom as well as their awareness of their own learners' needs. This accommodation certainly ensured the new curriculum remained responsive to the teaching–learning environment, even in its initial implementation. The training of teachers in the Languages Partnership is the subject of Chapter 12.

Task

1. Read the chapter again and analyze it in terms of the curriculum design model outlined in Chapter 1.

TABLE 11.1

Parts of the course design process	Ann Arbor Languages Partnership's procedure
Environment analysis	
Needs analysis	
Application of principles	
Goals	
Content and sequencing	
Format and presentation	
Monitoring and assessment	
Evaluation	

12

LEARNING TO TEACH SPANISH: IDENTIFYING, INDUCTING, AND SUPPORTING APPRENTICE TEACHERS IN THE ANN ARBOR LANGUAGES PARTNERSHIP

Donald Freeman, Maria Coolican, and Kathleen Graves

Introduction: Bridging Teachability to Teacher Preparation

In the previous chapter, we discussed the development of the curriculum in the Ann Arbor Languages Partnership. The key feature of this curriculum was what we defined as "teachability," which meant that the curriculum needed to be accessible for students learning Spanish and well scaffolded for the Apprentice Teachers who would teach it. Accessibility for students was based on two main features of the curriculum: that it would be *credible* to students, parents, and community members in how it captured and represented language in the world, and that it would be *embedded* in the general curriculum such that Spanish would not become simply a 'subject language' (Larsen-Freeman and Freeman, 2008). These features of teachability for students were critical to the Partnership's goal that learning new languages could visibly and transparently support and contribute to language diversity as a form of social capital within the community and district. To realize these goals, the project drew on a young and largely inexperienced teaching force: a group of about 40 students in the first year, most of whom were university undergraduates studying for degrees in Spanish, and/or heritage or mother tongue speakers of the language, who would teach the Spanish language curriculum in 63 third grade classrooms in the district's 20 elementary schools.

We referred to these new teachers as "Apprentice Teachers" for several reasons. While they were new to classroom teaching, bringing a certain passion for Spanish and for working with young learners, the majority had had no formal training in language teaching. Unlike "student teachers" at the university who are part of the formal teacher certification sequence, many of the new teachers in the Partnership were not seeking state certification as elementary teachers. In large measure they seemed to view teaching in the Partnership as a commitment to giving back to

the community in Spanish and to volunteerism in the best sense, and were ambiv-
alent as to career preparation,[1] a point we will return to later in this chapter.

There are two additional features that distinguished the "Apprentice Teacher"
role, both of which center on the teaching they did. New teachers in the Partnership
are placed in "teaching pairs," so that the great majority co-teach with a fellow
Apprentice Teacher. Together, this teaching pair is responsible for the Spanish instruction in the classroom. Whereas "student teachers" at the university are placed with
master or cooperating teachers in their fieldwork and work closely with this teacher
to learn the culture and specific teaching practices of that particular classroom, the
new teachers in the Partnership, although they work under the supervision of a
certified teacher, are, by design, the sole teachers of Spanish in their elementary
classrooms. For these reasons, we determined to name the role for what it was: an
apprenticeship in learning to teach Spanish; as such it needed to be carefully scaffolded to prepare and support these new teachers to credibly enact the Spanish
language curriculum. The concept of "teachability" then became a bridge between
student learning of Spanish and teacher learning of how to teach that language.

As a systemic project, the Partnership embraces three levels of learning. Central
to the design is student language learning, as discussed in the previous chapter.
This learning is enacted through the work of new or Apprentice Teachers with
the teachable curriculum as they are learning to teach it. Together, these two levels
of learning support a larger goal of engaging the wider community to consider,
and hopefully support, language diversity as an element of social capital (Putnam,
2000). As partners in the project, the district and the university seek to promote
values of transnational civic involvement across languages and cultures through
the recognition of plurilingualism (Council of Europe, 2001a) and autonomous
learning through experience. To engage these values, the Partnership is committed
to transparently documenting language learning and use in the community,[2] and
working collaboratively to realize these ends (see Chapter 11). Figure 12.1
captures the interaction of these three levels of learning and engagement.

This chapter addresses Apprentice Teacher learning in the Partnership, and
specifically how that learning was scaffolded in three major phases: how Apprentice
Teachers were *identified* to participate in the Partnership, a process which included
recruiting and selecting these participants from the wider university community;
once selected, how they were *inducted* into the approach to language learning and
teaching on which the Partnership is based. This induction involved initial intensive training with extended follow-on work. So the third phase details how the
Apprentice Teachers were *supported* as they taught throughout the school year.
From the standpoint of teacher education, we viewed the entire three-phase
experience as a single professional learning environment, although within that

---

[1]   In fact, of the 37 apprentice teachers in the 2009–2010 cohort, 13 were in the formal teacher
   certification sequence.
[2]   See Chapter 11 on the language portfolio process.

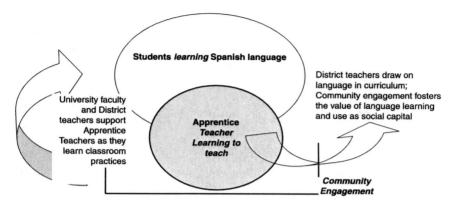

FIGURE 12.1 Levels of learning in the Ann Arbor Languages Partnership

environment each phase marked distinct moves in the learning trajectory. This view of teacher preparation stands in stark contrast to the more conventional one of "learn then apply" or "prepare then teach" on which much teacher education is based (see Darling-Hammond and Bransford, 2005).

Conceptualizing and enacting this vision of a year-long professional learning process involved rethinking many of the structural elements of conventional teacher preparation, including the connection between preparation and practice – what is sometimes called "courses versus fieldwork;" the notion of back-grounded versus foregrounded knowledge – sometimes called "foundation courses" (social processes and history of education, educational psychology) versus "content or methods courses" in the discipline; and the types of scaffolding and support these new teachers needed to begin working productively. These elements evolved within, and were shaped by, the context and values commitments of the overall project (see Chapter 11). In the next section, we turn to the parameters that shaped the development of the training design to prepare Apprentice Teachers.

Part I: Developing the Training Design

Teacher education designs that closely affiliate universities with schools face many challenges. The irony is that, even with the shared broad goal of education, the institutional interests of universities and schools often diverge more than they align. As those interests multiply and become more concrete, it often seems that they become more distinct – and even conflicting (see Sarason, 1993). For this reason, arguably the central problem in designing such programs is to establish a common ground in which the goals and needs of each institution are directly addressed and hopefully met. Locating this shared platform that would be the foundation for Partnership activity began with the premise that each party had concrete needs as well as something to offer in the joint undertaking. So if the complementarity or fit of these needs could be mapped, the resources would follow. Put another way, if each party did not find a proposition of concrete and immediate value in the design – a need that could not readily be otherwise met – it would be unlikely that we could evolve a sustainable design. And the inverse was also true: If the need could be clearly identified and met through the new design, it would be in each party's interest to use reasonable resources to achieve it. We came to call this premise an "exchange of services" (see Figure 11.1 on page 131).

Developing an Exchange of Services Model

As explained in the previous chapter, each institution had a primary need: To address the strategic plan developed in 2006 and to meet commitments to parents and community under the plan, the districts needed to add Spanish language instruction in the elementary grades. To pursue new models of teacher preparation, build its language teacher preparation capacity, and attract a broader and more diverse population to teaching, the university needed different program options and extended access to classrooms as settings for clinical learning (Grossman, 2009). The complementarity of fit between these two needs under-girded the Partnership: The district would receive the Spanish language instruction through a new teacher education program that the university would develop and run. This translated into an exchange of services in which the district received and supported Spanish language teaching for approximately 1,200 grade three students while the university had access to and supported 63 grade three classrooms as professional learning environments for 40 new Apprentice Teachers.

New Roles and Learning Environments

To realize this design and implement this exchange of services, we needed to make sense of the conventional functions of teacher preparation differently. The organizational theorist Karl Weick (2001) describes sensemaking in complex environments in this way: "The basic idea of sensemaking is that reality is an ongoing accomplishment that emerges from efforts to create order and make retrospective sense of what occurs." Rethinking how teachers are prepared in this design depended on articulating new roles and developing new learning environments for students as they learned Spanish and Apprentice Teachers as they learned to teach it. The term "new" here could be misleading, however, since in each case the roles and the environments existed in the ecologies of district class-rooms and university lecture halls; but they had to be made sense of in new ways. This process entailed giving new definitions to some of the existing elements in each institution, understanding that these "new" definitions would carry in them different, potentially new, ways of thinking and operating for the individuals involved.

Part II: Implementing the Training Design

Identifying, Inducting and Supporting the Apprentice Teachers

The exchange of services – elementary Spanish language instruction as a teacher preparation programmatic environment – outlined the formal training design. As with any complex undertaking, however, the specifics played out in unique ways. We turn now to how these elements of the training design worked in practice in the first year. This discussion is organized around the central processes of the training design: identifying, inducting, and supporting the Apprentice Teachers.

Who are the Apprentice Teachers?

The undergraduate students who make up the majority of Apprentice Teachers are "millennial" students. They come from a variety of liberal arts disciplines, and are generally not intending to devote their careers to teaching. Rather, they are Spanish speakers – native speakers, heritage speakers, and university Spanish majors or minors – who want to share their knowledge of the Spanish language and cultures with children. They are interested in learning how to teach in this limited context, and are willing to spend time on training, weekly field seminars and twice-weekly teaching for which they receive academic credit.

During the last two decades, the time period in which today's university students have grown up, forces of globalization, and technological innovation have dramatically changed the career opportunities and expectations in the United States; this dynamism seems likely to continue. As the US society has moved towards a knowledge economy (Uhalde, Strohl, and Simkins, 2006) ethnic, racial, and linguistic diversity has increased markedly in US classrooms (Educational Testing Service, 2007). Pedagogically, today's university students have grown up with different pedagogical methods than the generations before them. Their "apprenticeship of observation" (Lortie, 1975) has been shaped by slogans about teamwork and making a difference (Pinder-Grover and Groscurth, 2009).

The millennial generation, defined as those born between 1982 and 2002, is described as having notable differences in experience, with technology and virtual interaction, for example, and interests in social commitment and collaborative work. These millennial students tend to be team-oriented, interested in working with others on projects or to solve problems.[3] This group orientation seems to encourage volunteerism, and particularly working with groups for social or civic causes (DeBard, 2004).[4] Millennials' technological literacy has allowed them to

---

[3] See Pew Research Center, *Millennials*, retrieved on October 14 2010 from <http://pewre-search.org/millennials/>.

[4] It is interesting to consider the US program "Teach for America" in light of these characteristics. The program recruits highly selectively, taking about 15 percent of its applicants, then provides intensive induction and places them in difficult-to-staff urban and rural public schools around the United States. The University of Michigan is the largest sending institution to Teach for America.

Principles for Teaching Millennial Students *(from Pinder-Grover & Groscurth 2009)*	The Partnership activities that address the principle...
Facilitate cooperation among students.	Co-planning and teaching lessons Dialogue with peers through structured peer feedback sessions
Prepare students for diversity and cross-cultural interaction.	Training for, experience with, and reflection on working with diverse elementary students – ESL, special learning needs, heritage speakers, etc. Working with peers outside their university field of study supports interdisciplinary perspectives and solutions
Cultivate knowledge creation.	Cooperation with classroom teachers Dialogue with peers and university trainers Reflections on experience, iterative lesson planning
Promote active engagement inside and outside the classroom.	Explicit participatory models in training Discussions of past and anticipated experiences with individual students and whole cohort Engagement in Partnership's broader goal of language as an asset for social capital by introducing new language and culture to students early in their schooling

FIGURE 12.2 Educating "millennial" students – Principles and Partnership practices

address social problems via web-based technologies, and they are accustomed to communal efforts that create and institutionalize online knowledge, as with Wikipedia for example. These students are used to accessing information quickly and connecting with people easily and often through a variety of social media such as Facebook and Twitter. Pinder-Grover and Groscurth (2009) summarize these trends in four principles, which they argue can lead to teaching millennial students productively: "Facilitate cooperation among students; prepare them for diversity and cross-cultural interaction, cultivate knowledge creation; [and] promote active engagement inside and outside the classroom."

The Partnership drew on these principles explicitly in identifying, inducting, and supporting university undergraduates as Apprentice Teachers. Figure 12.2 summarizes these training moves, which are elaborated in the following sections.

To begin the process, candidates for the role of Apprentice Teacher had to be identified, recruited, and selected, which we discuss in the next section.

Identifying Apprentice Teachers: Recruitment and Selection

A large, complex research university presents both opportunities and challenges to recruiting candidates to participate in a project like the Partnership. On the one hand, the potential pool is large and varied; on the other, accessing that pool is not easy, and there are myriad competing projects and opportunities for undergraduate students, so finding the key features that will connect with candidates is centrally important. The steering group made use of conventional channels such as contacting education students and undergraduates pursuing degrees in Spanish or visiting upper level Spanish lectures to present the program. We also used other, somewhat less conventional, channels such as advertising the Partnership on Facebook or seeking out various clubs and organizations that represented heritage Spanish speakers on campus or involved undergraduates in tutoring in the local Spanish-speaking community. These latter channels offered a productive match with the millennial interest in community service.

Once they expressed interest, candidates attended one of several informational sessions to learn the details of the project. It was at these sessions that members of the steering group were able to connect directly with individuals and to gauge their level of interest and understanding in the project. The informational sessions began a selection process that was essentially one of mutual winnowing down. The project wanted candidates who understood its goals and were willing and able to commit to the full year. Likewise the candidates wanted to grasp the full level of involvement that was expected given that the program was atypical in combining induction and fieldwork for a year's worth of undergraduate academic credit.

Actual selection involved two interviews. The first was a Spanish language interview, conducted by Spanish language professors from the Arts and Sciences Faculty, and the second interview was run by Maria Coolican, the Partnership director, and a senior doctoral student who serves as Partnership manager. In both interviews, candidates worked in groups of four to six as this setting provided a better opportunity to gauge their Spanish proficiency and to observe their styles of interaction with peers, both qualities crucially important to the Partnership's teaching pair format. While both interviews had a gatekeeping function, the second was focused on the extent to which the candidate exhibited the "habits of mind" (Sizer, 1986) that supported the Partnership. These might include flexibility, interest in service opportunities, and evidence of an ability to make a long-term commitment. In conjunction with these interviews, candidates provided academic transcripts and letters of recommendation. With this composite information, the Partnership director made the initial selection decisions.

Inducing Apprentice Teachers: Delivering Intensive Training to Meet Teaching Outcomes

During this first year of the Partnership, the process of winnowing and self-selection continued in earnest in the induction, which ran for a very intensive period of eight to ten six-hour days. This intensity was intentional as it mimicked the level of commitment and interaction that would be central to Apprentice Teachers' successful teaching. Building on the understanding of millennial students described above (see Figure 12.2), we faced two challenges in preparing these new candidates to be able to teach productively in third grade classrooms. The first challenge involved determining the outcomes or competences Apprentice Teachers were expected to meet through the year-long program of professional preparation and support. These outcomes then shaped both the induction and the ongoing support they would receive; they would also help to determine programmatic judgments about individual teachers' progress and learning. Since the academic credit awarded by the university was based on the year-long trajectory, it was further important for the project to articulate an overarching set of learning outcomes.[5]

The outcomes, which are detailed in Appendix A, are meant to frame Apprentice Teachers' professional learning across the entire trajectory of school year, and thus to scaffold connections between the intensive induction and the weekly seminar and observation work throughout the year. They are organized in four categories or "strands:" teaching, student learning, language(s), and school and community. Each strand has two goals, a "professional practice goal" and a "professional growth and development goal;" the former addresses what Apprentice Teachers must be able to do to teach productively in the project, while the latter is explicit about the ongoing learning process in which they are expected to engage throughout the year. This bifurcation is meant to capture defined standards for immediate performance (professional practice) in relation to clear expectations for development (professional growth and development). Each statement is further specified by defining the key verbs within it, which is intended to make acting on the statement more explicit for all parties.

These professional learning outcomes for Apprentice Teachers (see Appendix A) are intentionally phrased as "can do" statements similar to the Partnership student language learning outcomes, which are derived from the Common European Framework of Reference (see Chapter 11). The alignment supports candidates as they review and document their learning as new teachers in ways that parallel the goal-setting and assessment processes the students use to document their learning of Spanish.

The second challenge was one of implementation, and particularly designing and carrying out the intensive induction. There were several constraints that shaped the induction design, including scheduling, connecting the practical elements with district teaching resources, and then staffing the training design appropriately. In terms of schedule, the induction needed to take place when students were available to attend, given that it did not carry university academic credit independently but as part-and-parcel of the year-long experience. We experimented with three intensive schedules: the first was a month-long training in July 2009 held in conjunction with the district's summer school, as discussed in the previous chapter. The second was a week-long induction in late August 2009, just before the beginning of the

---

[5] This decision to award academic credit for the entire trajectory from induction through teaching was a complex one, informed by many factors. Chief among these was the instrumental reasoning that candidates would be more likely to stay engaged if they were working towards credit for the whole experience. Philosophically, the steering group believed that the design depended on an experience of professional learning that closely integrated input and practice with reflection and critique, and therefore needed the opportunity to learn and improve practice across the year.

district's school year. The third design, which is preparing candidates for the Partnership's expanded second year of work, was held for two weeks in May 2010, before the end of university term. This third design will become the annual training opportunity for candidates who are joining the Partnership.

Although they differed in duration, the three schedules share a common design. Since the majority of candidates have never taught, the aim of the induction is to make them comfortable with teaching generally, and conversant with the designed lessons, as they work with third grade students. To this end, the induction design centers on actual teaching. It is built around an iterative cycle of teaching and learning in which Apprentices first experience the sample lesson; they then deconstruct it by describing the steps of the lesson and the teaching moves the university trainer made to enact it (see Grossman et al., 2009). They discuss the lesson, how it was organized and implemented, and then they practice the lesson with each other.

More broadly the training design includes readings, discussion, mini-lectures, and modeling specific classroom practices, as well as lesson planning, practice teaching, and feedback on all practice sessions. Throughout the process, candidates' engagement in doing teaching leads to their learning of teaching. This approach is based on the premise, which has been widely elaborated in the teacher education literature (e.g. Richards and Lockhart, 1994; Farrell, 2007), that reflection on experience is the strongest and most persuasive source of learning. This commitment to experiential learning is based on the notion that one learns best by doing, when that activity is supported by structured analysis and reflection, followed by the opportunity to apply what has been gleaned from that reflection, combined with feedback from skilled others, to develop emerging skills (Kolb, 1984).

Supporting Apprentice Teachers: Building the Ongoing Work of Teaching

Once the induction has been concluded, Apprentice Teachers enter directly into the field, which is where the third phase – supporting ongoing professional learning and development – takes place. This support in the Partnership is built around three key roles: the Apprentice Teacher, the trainer or seminar instructor from the university, and the mentor teacher from the district. Each role has specific responsibilities within the project design, and simultaneously has new learning/professional opportunities associated with it; these are summarized in Figure 12.3.

When put together, the roles generate four main "learning relationships," which are core to the training design. These "learning relationships" are understood as structured interpersonal engagements between individuals who have different roles in the project; or, if individuals have the same role, as with Apprentice Teachers in their teaching pairs, they bring and exploit their different backgrounds and experiences in these engagements. It bears pointing out that the relationships *per se*, absent any structured form of interaction, would not necessarily lead to professional

	Apprentice Teacher	University trainer	Mentor teacher
Institutional Role	University undergraduate student	Education doctoral student	District grade level or specialist teacher
Partnership Responsibilities	Teach two 30 minute lessons/week/class [Most Apprentice Teachers teach 2–3 groups/week] Plan and collaborate with teaching partner in Teaching Pair Attend induction training and weekly seminar Be observed regularly and participate in debriefing	Co-plan weekly seminar Deliver seminar (3 hours weekly) Observe and debrief individual Apprentice Teachers Coach/trouble-shoot Teaching Pairs	'Cover' class as certified teacher Introduce and support teaching pairs in understanding local school culture and expectations Offer informal liaison with school community
Professional Learning Opportunities	Deepen understanding of teaching new languages to young learners Become a professional member of local school community Work in close collaboration in the Teaching Pair	Become proficient in training model (which includes intensive induction and on-going coaching) Use Partnership work for own professional work and research Develop close relationships with district personnel	Position Spanish language in general curriculum Observe third grade students in a new learning environment, which may highlight different capacities Deepen understanding of informal mentoring

FIGURE 12.3 Roles in the Partnership

learning. Although no doubt people would and do learn from one another when they work together, it can be a random and serendipitous process. In these learning relationships, the explicitly designed use of venues and of training activities within those venues serves to catalyze the learning, since the different roles have to use professional discourse to navigate and advance their work together.

Figure 12.4 maps the four learning relationships that form the foundation for professional learning of teaching in the Partnership design. Each of these relationships supports professional learning since the two protagonists bring different experience and professional discourses or "local language" to the interactions (see Freeman, 1996). It is a basic equation of interaction: Each person in the dyad knows some things and needs to know others, and this imbalance provides a basis

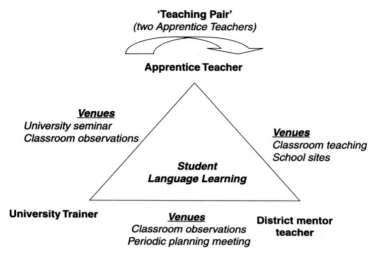

FIGURE 12.4 Learning relationships and learning environments

for their work together. For example, in the Apprentice–Mentor Teacher dyad, the Apprentices know Spanish and the specific curriculum and lessons to be taught, but need to know about the third grade students and classrooms, and the schools in which they are teaching. The Mentors know the children and the school, and the general curriculum, but in most cases do not know Spanish and have not taught a new language to young learners. Similar dynamics apply in the Apprentice–Trainer learning relationship, in which the Trainers are better versed in language teaching and in the language curriculum than the Apprentices, but do not know the specific learning trajectory of the third grade class or children in it as the Apprentices do. These learning relationships play out through specific activities in several venues. We turn now to detail two major instances: the weekly seminar and the regular observation/feedback interaction.

The Weekly Seminar

Apprentice Teachers take part in a weekly three-hour seminar, facilitated by one of the three university trainers. The seminars have three major activities: trainer input to address the knowledge base for teaching languages to young learners; reflection on the participants' teaching practices; and creating action plans to address their particular teaching issues in the upcoming Spanish lessons. Readings and activities in the seminar input sessions include such topics as student motivation, second language acquisition and child development, the role of heritage speakers in the classroom, communicative language teaching, classroom management strategies and building a classroom community.

Apprentice Teacher Generated Content | Portfolio: *Two Possible Tables of Content*

First Idea: TIME *By the week...*	Second Idea: ARTIFACT *By the document type*
<u>Week of MONTH/DATE</u> • Lesson scripts w/ action plan • Weekly reflection • Observation notes <u>Week of MONTH/DATE</u> • Lesson scripts w/ action plan • Weekly reflection *[THIS CYCLE REPEATS EVERY OTHER WEEK]* • Collected action plans • Learning statement • Additional documents	• Lesson scripts (all term) • Weekly reflections • Observation notes (biweekly) • Collected action plans • Learning statement • Additional documents • Self evaluation • Pictures of school/classroom site; Scans of student work

FIGURE 12.5 Alternative Portfolio organizations

Co-teaching and Observation/Debriefing

The heart of the Apprentice Teachers' work is teaching, which they do twice a week for thirty minutes per third grade class. Because most schools have multiple class sections of third grade, a teaching pair is likely to teach more per week either within or across schools. In the Partnership's first year, most teaching pairs taught two to three third grade classes each week, for a total of four to six 30-minute lessons. Working primarily with their partners in the teaching pair, the Apprentice Teachers interact to plan, deliver, and debrief their lessons. They do so both formally, in the venue of their weekly field seminar, and informally in traveling to and from school and outside the classroom. They also interact with a university trainer both in the field seminar, which is held once a week for three hours, and when they are observed every two weeks while teaching. While the teaching pair is in their school, they have regular contact with the school's mentor teacher, a district teacher who is responsible as the legally certified teacher of record for the classroom. The university trainers and mentor teachers interact informally at the school site, and have periodic general meetings.

The teaching pairs are observed regularly by the university trainer; this second set of eyes is key to providing data for their reflective work and planning in the seminar and supports their professional learning. Each pair is observed every other week, so there is close tracking of the Apprentice Teachers' development and maximum accountability is built into the system. The observations follow a protocol that focuses on following the Partnership lesson format (see Appendix B;

see also Figure 11.3) and how students are engaging with the lesson; developing and using effective classroom norms; and the extent to which instruction is entirely – or nearly entirely – in Spanish. Following the observed class, the Apprentice Teacher debriefs with the university observer and responds to the observer's notes. The Apprentice Teacher also responds to a reflective prompt focusing on a specific aspect of teaching that grows out of his or her action planning in the seminar. In this way the observation works to tie the teaching closely to the weekly seminar and thus to sustain the overall learning trajectory of the year.

The Learning Portfolio

To map their professional growth and aggregate lessons learned throughout the year, Apprentice Teachers generate a Learning Portfolio. The portfolio has two principal functions: it serves as a reference guide, personalized through experience, for the individuals as they plan and reflect on the lessons they teach; and it is the vehicle of year-long assessment. In both senses then, the portfolio offers a tool through which Apprentice Teachers can develop reflective practice (Bailey, Nunan, and Curtis, 2001). By articulating their professional learning processes, the doing of teaching becomes the learning of teaching.

In developing the portfolio, documentation and collection of materials begins immediately. Apprentice Teachers start with an analysis of their own language learning and language skills (see the Language strand in the professional outcomes framework, Figure 12.6). Then, as their teaching progresses, they include lesson scripts for the lessons that have been observed by the trainer and bi-weekly observation notes and weekly reflections that have been exchanged with the Trainer. They also include Final Learning Statements as the capstone documents for each semester. Other documents may include notes from the mentor teacher, additional activities and materials for particular lessons that the Apprentice might create, called "back pocket activities," or perhaps a YouTube video to supplement a lesson objective. The intent is to provide data that will document candidates' experiential learning process (Kolb, 1984) as they develop professionally.

Capturing the learning trajectory in the Learning Portfolio blends clearly structured and expressed expectations with choice of format. Apprentice Teachers need to understand the academic requirements, even as they are pushed to think carefully about how they represent their work and learning across the year. Figure 12.5, which is drawn from the Partnership's *Teacher's Handbook*, suggests two options for how a portfolio can be organized.

The organization on the left follows the time sequence of the teaching experience, while the option on the right clusters the different types of learning opportunities in an organization that compiles like documents and artifacts. Both options require the same documentation, and each includes a summative Learning Statement.

Conclusion: Lessons Learned from the Partnership's First Year

In the second school year, the Partnership will double the number of Apprentice Teachers and the classrooms in which they teach. The project will add a grade level, following students who were in third grade last school year into grade four, and it will continue to teach third grade. Thus the current curriculum will be retaught to a new cohort of third graders, and a new set of lessons will be extended into grade four. This transition is an opportunity to examine the past year and engage in some systemic reflection similar to the process asked of Apprentice Teachers.

A couple of points bear discussion in closing this chapter. The first has to do with continuity of participation. Of the original 40 Apprentice Teachers, 14 – or about a third – have signed on for a second year. In the initial design, we had generally assumed – admittedly without much thought – that Apprentice Teachers would be in the Partnership for only a year. Interestingly, we can see no reason to limit participation since the design can serve multiple years as both a service opportunity and a professional learning environment. So beyond the basic affirmation of the project, this continuity of participants represents an opportunity to reconsider each of three elements reported here: how the Apprentice Teachers are identified, inducted, and supported in their professional work.

In terms of identifying new candidates, in a year in which activity will double in size, bringing back this pool of more experienced participants will clearly strengthen the project. Further, in working with the interests and motivations of the millennial student population discussed earlier, the group that is the Partnership teaching force, we need to better understand what about the experience of doing the Partnership inspires this significant number of Apprentice Teachers to return for another year.

The intensity of induction training has been one of the more vexing aspects of the first year. As described earlier, we experimented with three different induction schedules and determined that the May training design is the most viable. This timing – after the university's second term classes are over, but before students' summer jobs and internships typically begin – seems the most feasible. Even at this time of year, however, candidates face competition with other priorities, so having a continuing group of Apprentice Teachers may reduce some of the problems of timing.

Another area of work involves the roles within the Partnership (see Figure 12.4), which we believe can be further developed and deepened to support professional learning. The continuity in the cohort creates greater stability and deepened learning and engagement among the second year participants. There may be new possibilities for peer support by leveraging the experience that they will bring as continuing Apprentice Teachers through "near peer" collaboration (see Murphey and Arao, 2001) and peer coaching, for example. The roles also include the teaching pairs and the mentor teacher–university trainer relationships. Together, they offer promising settings in which professional discourse can be practiced and learned, thus enhancing classroom work (Freeman, 2004).

Apprentice Teachers are placed to teach in pairs for pragmatic as well as philosophical reasons. While the rehearsal and coaching designs for paired teaching work well in induction, they seem to become somewhat less efficacious in the regular classroom. This may be related to an unintentional and unexamined assumption by Apprentice Teachers, that paired teaching equates to team teaching. There are definite pedagogical benefits to working in pairs, which we have not fully explored: from expanded classroom management and better use of group work, to modeling the new language between two fluent speakers and increased possibilities for student practice. The Apprentices seem to recognize that team teaching is a sophisticated skill, although it is not one that is explicitly addressed in the induction or seminar training. Because to date we have seen the pairs primarily as professional interlocutors who support one other as they reflect on their teaching and develop action plans, we have not focused as much on the pedagogical possibilities as we could.

There is much that can be done in inducting and supporting Apprentice Teachers on how to teach as a member of a pair. In the first year, some teaching pairs seemed to thrive, while others did not. Without close analysis, a key here seems to be organizing more intentional matches. At present, given the logistical complexities and the scale of classrooms to be staffed, matches are made more based on availability. Introducing an element of choice into the process might better support professional learning; it would, however, be an extremely complex undertaking.

Likewise there is more that can be done with the role of mentor teachers, who in the second year will all be third or fourth grade classroom teachers. This will offer a more obvious and potentially deeper opportunity to connect the social studies and Spanish curricula. There are some risks to seeing the mentor teacher as the "local expert," however (Fieman-Nemser and Parker, 1992), particularly from the standpoint of teaching socialization as well as our goal that new language learning be plurilingually based. Since many of these teachers will have not experienced this orientation, either in learning new or "foreign" languages in schools or even in using them in the world, many aspects of the pedagogy and approach may seem different. There is the possibility, with the best of intentions, that a mentor teacher may push the classroom instruction towards treating Spanish as a "subject language" with all the social and pedagogical assumptions and practices that entails (Larsen-Freeman and Freeman, 2008), which is not the goal. While we are eager to explore a deeper and more connected relationship between the third and fourth grade curricular standards and the foci of the Partnership Spanish lessons, it is important not to lose sight of the larger goal of making languages a visible and usable asset of the social capital of the school and the community.

References

Bailey, K., Nunan, D., and Curtis, A. (2001). *Pursuing professional development: The self as source.* Boston: Cengage-Heinle.

Council of Europe. (2001a). *Common European Framework of Reference for Languages: Learning, teaching and assessment.* Cambridge, UK: Cambridge University Press.

Council of Europe. (2001b). *Structured Overview of all CEFR Scales.* Strasbourg: Council of Europe.

Darling-Hammond, L. and Bransford, J. (2005). *Preparing teachers for a changing world: What teachers should learn and be able to.* San Francisco: Jossey-Bass.

DeBard, R. (2004). "Millennials coming to college" In M.D. Coomes and R. DeBard (Eds.), *Serving the millennial generation.* New Directions for Student Services, No. 106. San Francisco: Jossey-Bass. pp. 33–45.

Educational Testing Service. (2007). *America's perfect storm.* Princeton, NJ: Educational Testing Service.

Farrell, T.C. (2007). *Reflective language teaching: From research to practice.* London: Continuum.

Feiman-Nemser, S. and Parker, M. (1992). Mentoring in context: a comparison of two U.S. programs for beginning teachers: NCRTL Special Report. East Lansing: National Center for Research on Teacher Learning, Spring 1992.

Freeman, D. (1996). Renaming experience/reconstructing practice: Developing new understandings of teaching. In D. Freeman and J.C. Richards (Eds.) *Teacher learning in language teaching.* New York: Cambridge University Press, pp. 221–241.

Freeman, D. (2004). Language, socio-cultural theory, and second language teacher education: Examining the technology of subject matter and the architecture of instruction. In M. Hawkins. (ed.) *Social/cultural approaches to language learning, teaching, and teacher education.* Clevedon, UK: Multilingual Matters.

Grossman, P. (2009). *Learning to practice: the design of clinical experience in teacher preparation.* Washington, DC: American Association of Colleges of Teacher Education/National Education Association Policy Brief.

Grossman, P., Compton, C., Igra, D., Ronfeldt, M., Shahan, E., & Williamson, P. (2009). Teaching practice: A cross-professional perspective. *Teachers College Record, 111*(9), 2055–2100.

Grossman, P., and McDonald, M. (2008). Back to the future: Directions for research in teaching and teacher education. *American Educational Research Journal, 45,* 184–205.

Kolb, D.A. (1984). *Experiential learning: Experience as the source of learning and development.* Englewood Cliffs, NJ: Prentice-Hall.

Larsen-Freeman, D. and Freeman, D. (2008). Language moves: The place of "foreign" languages in classroom teaching and learning. In J. Greene, G. Kelly, and A. Luke (Eds.) *Review of Research in Education, 32,* 147–186.

Levine, M. and Trachtman, R. (1997). *Making professional development schools work: politics practice and policy.* New York: Teachers College Press.

Lortie, D. (1975). *Schoolteacher: A sociological study.* Chicago: University of Chicago Press.

Murphey, T. and Arao, H. (2001). Reported changes through near peer role modeling. *TESL-EJ,* retrieved October 14 2010 from <http://tesl-ej.org/ej19/a1.html>.

National Academy of Sciences Committee to Review the Title VI and Fulbright-Hays International Education Programs. (2007). *Executive summary, International education and foreign languages: Keys to securing America's future.* Washington, DC: National Academies Press.

Pinder-Grover, T., and Groscurth, C.R. (2009). Principles for teaching the millennial generation: Innovative practices of University of Michigan faculty. *CRLT Occasional Paper # 26.* Ann Arbor, MI: University of Michigan Center for Research on Learning and Teaching.

Putnam, R. (2000). *Bowling alone: The collapse and revival of American community.* New York: Simon and Schuster.

Richards, J.C. and Lockhart, C. (1994). *Reflective teaching in second language classrooms.* New York: Cambridge University Press.

Sarason, S. (1993). *The case for change: Rethinking the preparation of educators.* San Francisco: Jossey-Bass.

Sizer, T. (1986). "Rebuilding: First steps by the coalition of essential schools." *The Phi Delta Kappan, 68* (1), 38–42.

Uhalde, R., Strohl, J., and Simkins, Z. (2006). *America in the global economy: A background paper for the new commission on the skills of the American workforce.* Washington, DC: National Center on Education and the Economy.

Weick, K. (2001). *Making sense of the organization.* Malden, MA: Author.

Appendix A

Strand	Professional Practice Goal	Professional Growth and Development Goal
Teaching	*The Apprentice Teacher can effectively plan, implement, and assess lessons that follow the Spanish curriculum.* **Specified:** **Plan** involves structuring the lesson in response to student progress and needs and making effective use of resources and materials **Implement** means carrying through the lesson 'in real time' responding to what students are doing and need to in order to learn **Assess** means making reasoned judgments, based on evidence, about how the lesson went and what students can/cannot do in Spanish from the lesson	*The Apprentice Teacher can document and analyze his/her own classroom practice, set goals based on that analysis, and monitor his/her progress towards those goals.* **Specified:** **Document** means the Apprentice Teacher is skilled at several ways to capture what goes on in his/her lessons **Analyze** means the Apprentice Teacher is able to 'decompose' these records using one or more analytic approaches and/or tools **Monitor** means that the Apprentice Teacher is able to track his/her progress towards goals s/he undertakes sets or agrees to)
Student Learning	*The Apprentice Teacher can monitor and assess student progress.* **Specified:** • **Monitor** means that the Apprentice Teacher structures learning opportunities in the lesson so as to be able to see what students can/cannot do with help and independently. • **Assess** means making judgments about student performance as monitored against external criteria	*The Apprentice Teacher understands and applies basic concepts from second language acquisition and developmental psychology appropriate to elementary student learning.* **Specified:** • **Understand** means the Apprentice Teacher is conversant with the professional concepts, terms, and discourse • **Apply** means that the Apprentice Teacher can use the above to accurately and appropriately describe and interpret student performances and their work
Language	*The Apprentice Teacher can monitor and use language (Spanish and English) appropriately to teach lessons and manage the class.* **Specified:** **Monitor** and **use** means that the Apprentice Teacher recognizes, tracks, and adjusts language choice and use in teaching and managing the class	*The Apprentice Teacher sets his/her own Spanish language learning goals and monitors progress towards them.* **Specified:** **Set** here refers to using the CEFR and ELP process to establish individual language learning goals **Monitor** means that the Apprentice Teacher can capture and document progress, using the ELP process.
School and Community	*The Apprentice Teacher can interact effectively and appropriately with members of the school and with community members connected to the children s/he teaches.* **Specified:** **Interact** means that the Apprentice Teacher is able to accomplish the work s/he needs or wants to do in the school	*The Apprentice Teacher understands and applies basic professional concepts related to school culture and school-community and teacher-parent-child interaction.* **Specified:** **Understand** means the Apprentice Teacher is conversant with the professional concepts, terms, and discourse **Apply** means that the Apprentice Teacher can use the above to accurately and appropriately describe and interpret interactions, interests, and phenomena in school and community

FIGURE 12.6

Appendix B

Lesson ##: Lesson Name _____

My students already know:

Problematize this:

Action Plan:

Time (min)	Interaction Pattern	Stage	Procedure	Purpose	Materials	Language
		Opening				
		Presentation				
		Practice				
		Production				
		Expansion activity				
1" Total =30"	e.g. T-Ss	Closure	Sing 'Adiós' song.	Whole group closure		Song lyrics

FIGURE 12.7 Lesson format

Comment

The world is littered with instances of well-designed, well-intentioned curricula that have been poorly implemented. A new, or a revised, curriculum is an opportunity for change, and the onus for bringing about that change, a change in the learning experience, typically rests on the teacher. Perhaps it is inevitable, then, that when course designer and implementer are not the same person there may be a gap between what was intended and what is experienced. Sometimes the method of inducting teachers into the new curriculum is clearly at fault. In this chapter, however, the Ann Arbor team has described a well-designed training program for implementing the curriculum they introduced in Chapter 11. Their training program results from a careful environment analysis, particularly of the teachers segment of that particular circle in the design model. While an evaluation of the effectiveness of the training program is yet to be completed, this chapter suggests that it is very likely to have delivered on its promise.

Tasks

1. In an influential book on curriculum innovation, Markee (1997) suggests a very useful list of guiding principles (see *LCD*, pp. 179–180), among which he includes the following:
    a. Good communication among project participants is a key to successful curricular innovation.
    b. The successful implementation of educational innovations is based on a strategic approach to managing change (e.g. short-, medium-, and long-term strategies; different strategies at different times).
    c. It is important for implementers to have a stake in the innovations they are expected to implement.
    To what extent are these three principles evident in the Ann Arbor Language Partnership?
2. How would you evaluate the success of the Ann Arbor Language Partnership from
    a. the school district's perspective?
    b. the university's perspective?
3. In many parts of the world, communities express a desire for their languages to be taught in the education system. One of the reasons why the languages are not taught is a lack of suitably trained teachers. Think of a situation where this may be the case. Would the Ann Arbor model of teacher training work in that situation?

Further Reading

Markee, N. (1997). *Managing curricular innovation*. Cambridge, UK: Cambridge University Press.

13

NEGOTIATED SYLLABUSES: DO YOU WANT TO?

Andrew Boon

Introduction

As I begin to write this, I sit in front of a blank computer screen to conjure up words and second-guess what you may want to take away from investing your time in the reading of this chapter. In a similar way, during the process of syllabus design, I try to imagine what my students may want, lack, or be required to know so that I can decide on the goals, content, materials, and assessment criteria of the particular course to increase its value for and address the needs of the learner. However, more often than not, the learners (or potential learners) are absent from the key decision-making process as the teacher works alone to predict, interpret, and map out a pre-designed syllabus; an "integrated series of teaching-learning experiences, whose ultimate aim is to lead the learners to a particular state of knowledge" (Hutchinson & Waters, 1987, p. 65) over a certain period of time. The problem here is that as the syllabus is put into action and both teacher and learners begin to co-construct the teaching–learning process on a lesson-by-lesson basis, there may be "an unfolding compromise" (Breen & Littlejohn, 2000, p. 9) between what has actually been written down and stated and what actually may take place in the classroom; a myriad of syllabus interpretations which have "the potential to inhibit, disrupt or delay" (Breen & Littlejohn, 2000, p. 9) the ultimate achievement of course goals. With pure negotiated syllabuses, on the other hand, the learners become actively involved in negotiating the purposes, content, management, and means of assessment of a particular course (Breen & Littlejohn, 2000). The syllabus document remains a blank page; it is fluid and flexible; a retrospective product of the discussions, decisions and directions taken jointly by the learners and teacher.

Negotiated syllabuses are likely to increase student motivation and involvement in the learning process (Breen & Littlejohn, 2000; Davies, 2006; Nation & Macalister, 2010). However, learner and teacher reservations towards either gaining or relinquishing control of syllabus design decisions can often mean that negotiated syllabuses are difficult to implement (Clarke, 1991) or are even unwanted. This chapter will look at three different teaching contexts in which I have implemented negotiated syllabuses or courses with in-built elements of negotiation and will examine the question of whether teachers and learners really want to share in the syllabus decision-making process together.

Short Business English Courses

A few years back, I was involved in designing and teaching short business English courses to Japanese employees from a number of different companies who volunteered to take and self-finance a ten-week period of English instruction (Boon, 2005). As time was very limited, these courses needed to provide the learners with a high surrender value (i.e. students feel they have benefitted although having studied for only a short time) and were therefore wholly client-centered. The first lesson was structured to enable the teacher to elicit students' needs and to involve all participants in negotiations with one another and the teacher as to the overall design of the course.

Needs Assessment Questionnaire

At the beginning, the learners were asked to complete a needs questionnaire (Appendix 1) and then share their answers with the group. During the group discussion, I could obtain vital information and ask follow-up questions, if required, to help me design the course. Students started by discussing whether or not they currently used English in their job (target situation analysis) and from this we could identify possible activities and situations to cover in the course. If needs were not so immediate, as many students who undertook these voluntary courses did so in order to enhance future career prospects by improving their current level of English, we could concentrate on eliciting potential business situations that class members might later become involved in or had an interest in studying. The questionnaire also asked learners to comment on their attitudes to and expectations of the learning process. Learners discussed previous positive and negative learning experiences and preferred ways of learning, which helped me to determine materials and aids, groupings, teaching techniques, assessment, and homework tasks (if any) that may or may not work with the particular group. Finally, students were asked to create a learning goal to achieve by the end of the course. By sharing learning goals, it was possible to identify any further desired learning outcomes of the group for possible inclusion over the ten-week course.

The Pick and Choose Sheet

In the first lesson, it can often be difficult for learners to give concrete answers on what they really want. In the short business courses, I found that my learners were unsure of their needs or were only able to express vague ideas of what to include. Therefore, I designed a "Pick and Choose Sheet" (Appendix 1) which listed twenty self-contained business lessons covering a variety of topics and learning objectives which I had prepared and taught on previous courses. Students were instructed to work together and decide whether these lessons would be useful to study or not and were encouraged to come up with their own alternative business lesson ideas. Students were then asked to choose individually the three most important lesson ideas for them and write each one on a separate piece of paper. The pieces of paper were then spread over the table for all students to see and they worked together to discuss, justify choices, negotiate, compromise, and reduce the lesson ideas to the number of remaining lessons available on the course. During the negotiations, I could ask questions directly to students to clarify any ambiguities and then write the results of the discussion on the chalkboard. Modifications could then be suggested by all participants regarding the proposed content and sequencing before reaching a final agreement.

The Feedback Sheet

As needs are in a constant state of flux, negotiation should be an ongoing process rather than a one-off event. Thus, I provided students with a feedback sheet (Appendix 1) to be completed and emailed to the teacher at specified periods throughout the duration of the course. After experiencing a number of classes (and therefore being in a position to make more informed comments), students were asked to provide feedback on the course, the content, the activities, and their learning goal and to suggest modifications to the syllabus drawn up or goal decided upon in lesson one of the course in light of any changing needs.

Negotiated Syllabuses: Did we Want to?

As the teacher of a short business course with limited contact time, self-financing students with a range of needs, and no suitable published course material that could cater for the areas requested and the time available, it was essential to involve the learners in the negotiation of syllabus design in order to maximize what they could take away from the learning experience. The initial needs assessment lesson itself was a valuable part of the learning process whereby group members could begin to establish class relationships by interacting together in the second language (L2) to make authentic and democratic decisions that would provide a "working" syllabus for the remainder of the course. Having become an integral part of the decision-making process, learners then felt able to voice their opinions via the feedback sheet to have further says in course direction and to make changes and suggestions, if they so desired. In post-course evaluation interviews and questionnaires, students stated that courses had been enjoyable, had included useful topics and "I liked being able to choose what I could study because the lessons met my purpose very well."

Extension Center Courses

Currently, I work at a Japanese university that has an extension center program and offers a variety of courses to people in the local community. During spring 2010, I was asked to teach six-lesson English conversation courses to two groups of Japanese learners comprising retirees, homemakers, and one self-employed individual (a pre-intermediate group of seven students and an intermediate group of five students). The only information provided to me prior to the start of the first class was the specified dates of the lessons and the names of the students in each class.

Finding out What Students Want

After introductions and a get-to-know-you icebreaker game, students were asked to complete a short needs assessment task on the lesson handout: see Figure 13.1.

Students then worked in pairs or small groups to interview one another about their needs in English. After this activity, I elicited answers from each group member, writing them on the board so learner needs were clearly visible. Learners had many different reasons for taking the conversation course: for travel purposes, to help grandchildren with their English homework, to be able to communicate with and write letters to foreign friends, and as a retirement activity. In question 2, learners tended to respond with areas that gave them the most difficulty such as listening, vocabulary, and speaking. Answers to what they would like to study in the class were really vague (e.g. "Speak English, listen to the teacher, learn English

---

Task 2: Finding out about English:

1] Why do you want to study English?

2] What do you find easy / difficult about studying English?

3] What would you like to study in this class?

1. _____   4. _____
2. _____   5. _____
3. _____

FIGURE 13.1

TABLE 13.1

Class 1	Class 2
1. Introductions and needs assessment	1. Introductions and needs assessment
2. Restaurants	2. Talking about the news
3. Shopping	3. Movie reviews
4. Giving directions	4. UK and US differences
5. Daily conversations	5. The generation gap
6. Review and feedback	6. Daily situations/feedback

conversation, travel English") and required me to ask further questions to establish the particular situations, topics, functions, or skills that students wanted to cover over the remaining five lessons. Through a process of group discussion and teacher support, a working syllabus was drawn up on the board and then agreed upon democratically by the students: see Table 13.1.

Although negotiations between learners successfully resulted in the creation of a course road map, there were a number of problems with the needs assessment procedure. Firstly, some of the information gained in the first lesson was still too ambiguous to enable me to prepare lessons and material that would match learner needs exactly. I tended to resort to teacher intuition and created open-ended material to allow for flexibility and input of student voice during each lesson. Secondly, although several students had indicated in the needs assessment that they studied English to communicate to overseas friends by email or letter, interestingly, no student selected writing as a topic to be studied in the course. Finally, due to a prior engagement, one student asked to take part in lesson one of class one but was to attend class two for the remaining lessons. This meant he contributed to the negotiations for a course he would not attend. Another student was absent for the needs assessment lesson and therefore lost the opportunity to have a say in the syllabus decision-making process.

Ongoing Needs Assessment

As learners often lack the experience to participate fully in syllabus decision-making from the beginning of a course, it is important to establish "an ongoing dialog between teacher and learners" (Nunan, 1988, p. 5) to keep determining content and learning objectives. Thus, the negotiated syllabus co-created in lesson one was printed at the top of the lesson two handout for each class and students were given the opportunity to comment on and modify it, if necessary. The extension center lessons were prepared to maximize student involvement in shaping their content and direction. For example, in the "talking about the news" lesson, I asked students to brainstorm current news items on the chalkboard, introduced them to structures to start conversations about the news (*"Hey! Did you hear about . . .?"*), and they worked in pairs to choose items from the board to discuss. Finally, comments were invited from students in the last five minutes of each lesson regarding their thoughts on the particular day's learning experience, allowing me the opportunity to adjust my teaching accordingly and to probe for further information about the requested topic for the following week. In fact, one student was able to voice her concern that the upcoming lesson theme (Class 2: Lesson 6) was too vague and suggested that we change it. After further negotiations, we decided to do a short review task and to have an end-of-course potluck party during class time instead.

Negotiated Syllabuses: Did we Want to?

As a prior needs assessment was not conducted by the institution and students were the major stakeholders in terms of investing their time and money to improve their English within a short six-lesson course, it was essential to involve them in the negotiation of the syllabus design from the beginning. In the final lesson, I conducted a questionnaire in which students could give course feedback and comment on the role of the negotiated syllabus in the course in either Japanese or English (Appendix 2). Students stated that the course had covered what they had originally wanted to study:

> *I had some opportunities to speak English.*
> *The class was fun and useful. I wanted to study for a whole year!*

Most students also believed that both teacher and learner should play a role in deciding the course content:

> *The teacher asked us what we wanted to do and followed the answer. The class could evolve from that and this was good.*
> *Both teacher and student should agree but the teacher should lead the others.*

However, students had mixed answers regarding the negotiation of course lesson aims, sequencing, material, homework, evaluation, groupings, and techniques for error correction:

> *The teacher needs to decide the direction.*
> *The teacher is leader and should decide but all should discuss and the teacher needs to take into consideration what learners say as everybody is in the class.*
> *The teacher should encourage students to take an active part in the class.*
> *I don't like homework but if the teacher gives it to me I can't refuse.*

With class members having such varied opinions regarding the areas that should be negotiated by all or decided only by the teacher, it is vital for the teacher to monitor individual learner needs on an ongoing basis (Nunan, 1988), to offer a variety of options that help the learners to recognize what their own particular preferences for classroom language learning may be, and to be ready to modify the course accordingly.

University Courses

University syllabuses for the new academic year need to be designed, written, and submitted by teachers in late January for classes that will begin in April. A syllabus includes the course title and brief description, its overall aims and objectives, the method of assessment, the materials or coursebook to be used, and a description of each lesson including the lesson title, planned activities, and homework to be given. With such detailed information having to be decided and committed to up-front before actually meeting the students and finding out their subjective needs, syllabus design can end up being little more than an educated guess.

Negotiation in Pre-designed Syllabuses

Pre-designed university syllabuses, nevertheless, do not have to be written in stone. It is still possible to include negotiated elements within the course design to provide learners with the opportunity to take greater control over the direction of their learning (Clarke, 1991). For example:

- I often assess students via project work. This involves students conducting research and presenting their findings via a poster presentation. Students are given the freedom to determine their own research topics with the proviso that foci fall within the parameters of the course and that the formulated research questions are in fact researchable. Students can discuss their ideas with their peers and the teacher and, once they have gained approval, they can proceed with their projects.
- Students are often provided with choices. For instance, in oral communication classes, students can decide which topic they wish to talk about by moving to the designated "discussion space" in the classroom. In writing classes, students can select which topic to write about within the specified parameters of the task (e.g. *Write a paragraph about a family member or a friend*).
- I often label homework tasks as either "optional" or "assessed." Optional homework tasks are left to each student to decide the value in completing them or not. Assessed homework tasks are non-negotiable and must be completed as part of the coursework component of the course. However, deadlines for assignment submissions can be negotiated.
- The methodology I employ to teach a particular group is an ongoing evolution as the teacher and the students interact to construct the teaching–learning event together. Although not always overtly stated, it is a continuous process of implicit negotiation and shared understanding of what will or will not work with particular groups.

- The sequencing of the course is already specified in the syllabus. However, it is possible to modify the order of lessons through discussions with the group so that we can spend longer on a topic or move ahead in the course.
- I tend to use random groupings in my university classes to provide students the opportunity to work with different people and avoid clique formation. However, for project work, depending on the particular class dynamic, I may give the option of student self-selection as opposed to teacher-led random selection of groups.

Negotiated Syllabuses: Do you want to?

I conducted an online survey with 50 teachers (in English) and a graduate student conducted face-to-face interviews with 20 university students (in Japanese and then translated into English) to determine what aspects of the syllabus they may be interested in negotiating. Perhaps not surprisingly, a range of views on every aspect were elicited, as can be seen in the selection of responses to negotiating course content in Table 13.2. A selection of responses to all areas investigated can be found in Appendix 3.

Teachers were by no means in agreement regarding the merits of negotiating a syllabus, or aspects of it, as these three responses illustrate:

It is essential to negotiate courses.
I would like to try it but it is not always possible.
Syllabuses should never be negotiated.

TABLE 13.2

	Course Content
Teachers	☺ – *"Students become more involved / Students can make the most of the learning experience."* ☹ – *"Students do not want to / Not so much with less able or less motivated students / I am too busy / It is not allowed at my institution."*
Students	☺ – *"We are university students, so we want to decide ourselves / If the teacher always decides, it is boring, but we need some good examples".* ☹ – *"Students usually have no idea / Teachers have more expertise than students so it is better that they decide."*

Conclusion

From the responses of both teachers and the business, extension center, and university students, it is clear that negotiated syllabuses are perceived as fostering a more responsible, autonomous, and motivated group of learners. Through negotiation, learners can elevate themselves from a rather passive role to the role of co-participant whose voice resonates through the teaching–learning experience, helping to shape and define the course in its process of becoming. On the other hand, however, there are concerns about learners' ability and willingness to engage in negotiation and syllabus decision-making; that it is a time-consuming process; and about the conventional institutional, instructor, and student expectations that this is in fact the teacher's duty. However, if learners do not receive opportunities to have a say in what goes on in the classroom, their ideas may never be voiced and both teacher and students may lose the potential of what could have been rather than what is. Instead, by experimenting with techniques for our learners to identify and express their needs, to exercise "some degree of control over the way the course proceeds" (Davies, 2006, p. 8), and to provide us with ongoing feedback about the classroom experience, we may find that learners do want to. But, do you?

Acknowledgment

I would like to thank my graduate student, Ms. Yoko Takizawa, for her help in conducting student interviews and translating their responses.

References

Boon, A. (2005). Tell me what you want, what you really, really want! *Modern English Teacher, 14*(4), 41–52.

Breen, M.P. & Littlejohn, A. (2000). *Classroom decision-making*. Cambridge, UK: Cambridge University Press.

Clarke, D.F. (1991). The negotiated syllabus: What is it and how is it likely to work? *Applied Linguistics, 12*(1), 13–28.

Davies, A. (2006). What do learners really want from their EFL course? *ELT Journal 60*(1), 3–12.

Hutchinson, T. and Waters, A. (1987). *English for Specific Purposes*. Cambridge, UK: Cambridge University Press.

Nation, I.S.P. and Macalister, J. (2010). *Language curriculum design*. New York, NY: Routledge.

Nunan, D. (1988). *The learner-centered curriculum*. Cambridge, UK: Cambridge University Press.

Appendix 1

Documents can be downloaded from SlideShare:

1. Needs Assessment Questionnaire
   http://www.slideshare.net/lovesongofprufrock/needs-questionnaire
2. The Pick and Choose Sheet
   http://www.slideshare.net/lovesongofprufrock/pick-and-choose-sheet
3. The Feedback Sheet
   http://www.slideshare.net/lovesongofprufrock/feedback-sheet-4393329

Appendix 2: Course Feedback Form

1. What did you like about the course?
2. What didn't you like about the course?
3. Did the course cover what you wanted to study?
    Very much ———- Yes ——— Kind of ——— Not really ——— Not at all ———
    GIVE REASONS FOR YOUR ANSWER:

Appendix 3

TABLE 13.3

	Course Content
Teachers	☺ – "*Students become more involved/Students can make the most of the learning experience.*" ☹ – "*Students do not want to/Not so much with less able or less motivated students/I am too busy/It is not allowed at my institution.*"
Students	☺ – "*We are university students, so we want to decide ourselves/If the teacher always decides, it is boring, but we need some good examples.*" ☹ – "*Students usually have no idea/Teachers have more expertise than students so it is better that they decide.*"

	Lesson Aims
Teachers	☺ – "*When students give an explicit request/It makes everyone engaged and influences group dynamics.*" ☹ – "*It could get tedious for each lesson and take up too much time/Students are too disinterested/Even when I offer small choices the answer is the teacher should decide.*"
Students	☺ – "*I like to decide/We decide but it depends on students' levels.*" ☹ – "*If decided for us, we can see what we really need to study/I'm lazy to decide lesson aims/Students cannot decide and this is not good to change after registering for the class.*"

	Sequencing
Teachers	☺ – "*I especially like to do this to accommodate students (responding to topics, questions that arise)/Students are often grateful that the teacher is responsive to students interests.*" ☹ – "*Students do not have knowledge in this area/Students want a ready-made package.*"
Students	☺ – "*Teacher should decide but accept what students want if requested.*" ☹ – "*Teachers know better how to carry on the class, if students decide it would be a mess/Teachers are experts/We can feel comfortable if it is already decided.*"

	Material
Teachers	☺ – "*I would like students to bring in their own materials/Students choose topics of own interest to discuss in class.*" ☹ – "*Not really as I develop my own materials on a weekly basis/Ordering and time requirements to obtain material make it impossible/I would like to but my school says no.*"
Students	☺ – "*It is a good class if we discuss materials and resources between teacher and students/I would like to choose by myself, if I could/Textbooks without color decreases my motivation.*" ☹ – "*Students do not know what material is good/I decide the course by who is going to teach it and the materials that are going to be used.*"

	Homework
Teachers	☺ – *"Yes as this gives ownership to students/Students need to work around a schedule/I give two tiers of compulsory and optional homework."* ☹ – *"I think students would probably say 'no homework'/This is the domain of the teacher as students will minimize what they say they need."*
Students	☺ – *"Students have different time available. We need to discuss this otherwise we can hate the class and the teacher. If the teacher gives us too much, it is not good/I would like the teacher to listen to the students' opinions."* ☹ – *"If students decide, they never study/If students choose it, we would choose the easy way/The teacher should decide so that it links to the next lesson."*

	Evaluation
Teachers	☺ – *"To some extent as in getting students to say what aspects they think they should be evaluated on/Yes as it becomes less about the grade given and more about where the students are."* ☹ – *"This must stay within the teacher's control/This is dictated by the university/I cannot change the assessment criteria once the course is under way."*
Students	☺ – *"Teacher assessment is important but we can also assess each other as this is important, too."* ☹ – *"This is NOT what students can decide/If students do it, we would try to give each other a good score/The teacher is the expert, students cannot judge the level."*

	Methodology
Teachers	☺ – *"I would welcome student ideas/I take this into consideration after students' evaluation of the first term."* ☹ – *"Students have limited knowledge of methodology/If they wanted me to teach grammar-translation, I could not bring myself to do it/No, we are experts."*
Students	☺ – *"We can have fun if both teacher and student discuss this/It is boring if it is always decided by the teacher."* ☹ – *"We have no idea/We choose our classes based on teachers' styles we like or do not like so I want the teacher to do it his or her own way and we will follow."*

	Groupings
Teachers	☺ – *"I give students the option of forming their own groups in accordance with their wishes."* ☹ – *"No as this can cause problems if there is a student that nobody wants to work with/It takes too long and takes away the suspense/Students need to learn to communicate with a variety of people."*
Students	☺ – *"We can gain skills if we make groups ourselves/I prefer a group I know rather than strangers."* ☹ – *"If students decide, we always sit in the same groups/If we make groups with our friends, we start using Japanese."*

	Error Correction
Teachers	☺ – *"Yes as this encourages autonomy/It is necessary in my context as students want the teacher to correct every mistake. If you delay feedback, they think you are not doing your job."* ☹ – *"Students would like me to correct every error/It is too much work/I have a large number of students."*
Students	☺ – *"It is not always best if the teacher tells us our mistakes."* ☹ – *"I would like to know the right answer."*

Comment

The situation that Andrew Boon describes in this chapter will be familiar to many teachers – the class is about to meet for the first time, you know very little about the students ... what will the course look like? In this case study, elements of negotiation have been introduced into three different types of course, most strikingly perhaps in the university context. Very often, however, we find in the language classroom that it is a matter of the students needing to fit the course rather than the course fitting the students. One challenge for the teacher is to find the balance between what the subject or curriculum requires and what the students want. This balancing act recalls the divisions of the needs analysis circle – lacks, necessities, and wants.

Tasks

1. Consider the elements of negotiation introduced into the university course in this chapter.
    a. In terms of the curriculum design model, where is negotiation being introduced?
    b. Can you suggest other negotiable elements that could be introduced into a course like this?
2. Andrew Boon has discussed negotiation in three different contexts. For each context, identify the factors that favored negotiation, and any constraints that made it difficult.

TABLE 13.4

	Business course	*Extension center*	*University*
Factors in favor of negotiation			
Factors working against negotiation			

3. In your own teaching/learning context, or one that you are familiar with, do any of the factors you have identified in Task 2 exist? What potential for negotiating elements can you identify in this context?

14

ENHANCING CONSUMERIST LITERACY PRACTICES IN AN URBANIZING COMMUNITY

Moses Samuel and Saratha Sithamparam

Introduction

The school-based ESL curriculum project, which is the focus of this chapter, was part of a university-school partnership in which we, as university researchers, worked with teachers to develop curriculum units that were responsive to the needs of students. The project was carried out in two broad phases: (a) an analysis of the environment in which English was taught; and (b) the development of curriculum units based on the environment analysis. The rationale for this project stems from concerns that students in rural Malaysia were not motivated to learn English because they did not see the need for the language in their daily lives.

This curriculum project was carried out in the township of Banting, which was undergoing economic transformation. Banting, located about 20km from Kuala Lumpur, the capital of Malaysia, has historically been an agricultural area with rubber, oil palm, and tea plantations. However, economic development resulted in the establishment of a number of small and medium-scale industries as well as multinational palm oil processing and electronics factories. These developments resulted in higher incomes for people in the community, and with this came changes in consumerist literacy practices and lifestyles.

The curriculum project aimed to develop units that were relevant to the literacy practices of the community. In order to understand how literacy is used in communities, Street (2001) suggests the use of "field work methods and sensitized ways of discovering and observing uses and meanings of literacy practices." (p. 1). He notes:

> . . . before launching into [the design of] literacy programs . . . it is necessary to understand the literacy practices that target groups and communities *are already engaged in*. (p. 1, italics added)

This chapter reports on how one curriculum unit from the project was designed. This unit on "food labels" aimed to enhance the literacy practices of students as young consumers.

Environment Analysis

In designing the curriculum unit on food labels we began with environment analysis (Nation & Macalister, 2010) or situational analysis (Richards, 2001) in order to identify (a) constraints which would affect the implementation of the curriculum, and (b) potentials from the situation that could be used to infuse local relevance in the English curriculum so that students would find lessons meaningful. In their model of the curriculum design process, Nation and Macalister (2010) list three factors in environment analysis: situation, learners, and teachers. In Table 14.1 the constraints and potentials of environment are presented in terms of these three factors.

The Situation

In analyzing the situation we focused on both the national syllabus as well as features of the local setting in which the school was situated (Holliday, 1994; Nation & Macalister, 2010).

The National Syllabus

The teaching and learning of English, which is the official second language in Malaysia, is driven by a national syllabus. This document focuses on the skills of listening, speaking, reading, and writing, as well as grammar, vocabulary, and pronunciation. The document is organized according to topics which provide the context for language development.

TABLE 14.1 Environmental constraints and potentials

Factors	Constraints	Potentials
The situation	The national syllabus prescribes generic content	Teachers may supplement the national syllabus with local content
	The use of English outside school, especially in the family was limited	Urbanization of the community resulted in an increased role for English
The learners	Learners did not find English lessons stimulating or directly relevant to their lives	Learners were interested in the changes occurring in their community
The teacher	The teacher relied on the textbook and modeled exercises on national examination papers	The teacher was trained and confident in her use of English

The unit on "food labels" covered the following items in the national syllabus:

Item 1.19: Ask for and give information in labels on packages and tins
Item 2.9: Read and locate information in labels on packages and tins
(Source: Ministry of Education Malaysia,1989)

In implementing the syllabus, the prescribed textbook was the primary resource for many teachers. In the textbook used by the school, the chapter on food labels comprised mechanical exercises involving questions such as "What is the brand name of the product?" and "What is the expiry date?" which were based on a fictitious food label. The textbook also included exercises on discrete items of grammar and vocabulary. The students routinely worked through these exercises but found them uninteresting.

The mandated syllabus developed by the Ministry of Education could be seen as a constraint in that it specified generic content which did not address the particular experiences of learners in different communities. However, when viewed as a framework, the syllabus allowed teachers and curriculum developers working at the local level to include specific content relevant to students' experiences. We saw this as offering potential for the curriculum process.

The Local Setting

An analysis of the local setting allowed us to identify the literacy practices in the Banting community so that we could include aspects of these practices in designing the curriculum. Changes in consumerist practices in the town could be seen in the way in which goods were bought and sold in the community.

Traditionally, provision shops provided the neighborhood with its variety of goods. The provision shop was basically a one-shop retail outlet that sold products as varied as fresh food, stationery, kitchen utensils, aspirins, and cough syrups. These products were tightly packed into every conceivable space in the shop, on racks and shelves, and piled high on the floor. Brooms, mops, and feather dusters could be seen hanging from hooks on the ceiling. There was little room to move around and when a customer wanted to purchase something, he or she would usually tell the shopkeeper what was needed. The shopkeeper would then get the item for the customer. As a member of the community, the shopkeeper knew the consumer profile of the neighborhood, what brands would appeal to different people, and what they could reasonably afford. Talk was an important part of the shopping experience and these oral exchanges could be in Malay, Chinese, or Tamil, which were the languages spoken in the community.

Around the time of the project, a large supermarket opened in the town. This event was widely talked about as a sign that the town had "arrived." Shopping trolleys parked outside the supermarket signaled a different kind of shopping experience from what the community was accustomed to. A range of consumer products packaged in cans, jars, bottles, and cartons was now available on shelves along aisles, with signs displaying categories of products such as food, detergents, and toiletries. Shoppers at the supermarket did not reach their goods through the shopkeeper, but had direct access to products on shopping aisles. Unlike the provision shop experience, which was mediated by the shopkeeper, the supermarket experience was mediated by the customers' readings of texts including advertisements, product labels, and posters announcing special offers, which were often in English and Malay, as both imported and locally produced goods were sold.

In moving from provision shop to supermarket, consumerist decision-making moved from being largely talk events to being primarily literacy events, involving reading and interpreting informational texts like product labels as well as persuasive texts like advertisements. Confronted with the sophistication of marketing strategies involving a range of persuasive texts and the need to exercise choice unmediated by a shopkeeper, there was now a greater need in the community for consumerist literacy.

The analysis of the local setting indicated that the community was urbanizing, and this was reflected in changes in their consumerist practices. In terms of language use English was playing a larger role, and as may be seen in the example of shopping in the supermarket, literacy was becoming increasingly important. This had implications for the curriculum we were designing.

The Learners

The curriculum was designed for students in their first year of secondary school. While the language of instruction in secondary schools in Malaysia is Malay, students have the option of attending primary school where the main language of instruction is Malay, Chinese, or Tamil. In both primary and secondary schools English is taught as a subject. Interviews with the students indicated that, except for about a quarter of the students who spoke English at home, the use of English by the rest of the students outside the classroom was limited. In addition, the students did not find their textbook-based English lessons stimulating or useful in their day-to-day lives.

However, with access to cable television and the Internet, as well as the opening of the supermarket, the students recognized that English was becoming increasingly important in their lives. Despite their generally limited proficiency in English, the 14-year-olds were excited about the changes taking place in their town. This had potential for curriculum design, as this interest could be tapped into by providing the learners with materials relevant to their situation.

The Teacher

The teacher we worked with, like many teachers in the school, relied heavily on the textbook. Exercises that were set for her class were modeled on national examination papers. While her teaching approach was a constraint, this teacher was, however, trained in the teaching of English as a second language and was also a fluent speaker of English. Workshops for teachers that were run alongside the curriculum development process helped the teacher to explore alternative ways of teaching. These workshops aimed at helping teachers to become sensitive to the social situatedness of literacy (Barton & Hamilton, 2000) and the changing nature of texts and literacy practices (New London Group, 1996).

The Curriculum Unit

The environment analysis pointed to the need to enable students to develop literacy skills in English in relation to the increased range of products and new ways of shopping in the community. While the national syllabus outlined a framework, this had to be further elaborated on by designing concrete activities around authentic artifacts and texts that would engage students in meaningful literacy practices.

The curriculum unit on food labels focused on breakfast foods and drinks. It involved the use of authentic food products, as well as simulations of real world purposes in buying and selling food. In implementing the unit, a breakfast bazaar, comprising a display of authentic breakfast products (such as cartons of milk, cereal boxes, and loaves of bread) was set up in the classroom.

Table 14.2 lists the curriculum focus and the activities that were developed. The focus of the curriculum progressed from awareness-building to the development of skills needed in consumerist activities, as shown in the table. As a result of the opening of the supermarket, new products had entered the community. In our curriculum, therefore, students were introduced to vocabulary related to food and drink items (e.g. cornflakes, yoghurt, and creamers), and forms of packaging (e.g. cans, cartons, and jars). In addition to learning new vocabulary for products and their packaging, students learned to classify food items (e.g. wheat, rice, and oats were forms of grain, while walnuts, almonds, and pecans were nuts). Building on this vocabulary, students progressed to develop skills for reading consumerist texts. They learned to read labels on food packages for information. The label is a non-linear text as information is presented in sections and boxes; readers focus on different sections for different kinds of information. In addition, information on labels is also signaled through the use of fonts of different types and sizes, images, as well as colors. Students learned to read the labels on food packages for information. As they examined the labels, they learned to identify the ingredients used, their nutritional value, and directions for use. As consumers they learned to take note of prices and expiry dates of products.

After the activity involving a close reading of labels, the students went on to learn to use the information obtained so that they could recommend products to potential customers based on their personal profiles. For example, in recommending a snack to Sofiah, a weight-conscious Muslim teenager, students chose a

TABLE 14.2 The curriculum unit on food labels

Focus	Activity
To develop awareness of the range of food and drink products available as well as introduce related vocabulary	Students name and classify products displayed in the breakfast bazaar.
To develop awareness of various forms of food packaging as well as introduce related vocabulary	Students name various types of packaging and match types of packaging with food products.
To read labels as informational texts to find out more about the product	Students examine words and images on the packaging of a particular product (e.g. a cereal box) and identify details such as the ingredients used, their nutritional value, directions for use, its price and its expiry date.
To make decisions about the purchase of products based on the profile and needs of particular consumers	In groups, students analyze cards containing the profiles of individual consumers, including their personal preferences and needs, in order to suggest items for purchase from a display of food products set up in the classroom.
To design labels that are informative and persuasive	Students design a label for a traditional breakfast item containing details about the content, nutritional value, price and shelf life of the product.

food item that was both halal (i.e. permissible for Muslims) and had low caloric value.

In the closing activity of this unit, students designed labels for a traditional local breakfast food which they were familiar with – such as *thosai* (savory rice and lentil pancakes), *pau* (dumplings), and *nasi lemak* (coconut rice with spicy anchovies) – which were typically not labeled when sold. The activity encouraged students to ask questions about the ingredients used, the nutritional value and the shelf life of the product. The purpose of this activity was to help students develop certain ways of thinking about food products to enable them to engage with nutritional and consumerist information. This curriculum therefore went beyond the national syllabus: it extended items specified in the national syllabus by making connections to the literacy and consumerist practices now impacting the community.

Conclusion

The starting point for the curriculum project was the concern that students did not find English lessons engaging. The environment analysis which examined the situation, the learners, and the teacher highlighted the fact that real world texts and the literacy practices of the community did not figure in the English classroom. While the analysis pointed to constraints in relation to each of these three factors, it also suggested potentials that curriculum developers could draw on. In the project we identified changes in the consumerist practices in the urbanizing community and saw the need for finding spaces within the existing national syllabus to incorporate texts and practices from the social worlds of learners and their communities.

References

Barton, D. & Hamilton, M. (2000). Literacy practices. In D. Barton, M. Hamilton & R. Ivaniĉ (Eds.). *Situated literacies*. London: Routledge, pp. 7–15.

Holliday, A. (1994). *Appropriate methodology and social context*. Cambridge, UK: Cambridge University Press.

Ministry of Education Malaysia (1989). *English language syllabus: Form 1*. Kuala Lumpur, Malaysia: Curriculum Development Center.

Nation, I.S.P. & Macalister, J. (2010). *Language curriculum design*. New York: Routledge.

New London Group (1996). A pedagogy of multiliteracies: Developing social futures. *Harvard Educational Review, 66*(1), 60–91.

Richards, J.C. (2001). *Curriculum development in language teaching*. Cambridge, UK: Cambridge University Press.

Street, B.V. (2001). *Literacy and development: Ethnographic perspectives.* London: Routledge.

Comment

One of the truisms in curriculum design is that courses cannot be static. They need to respond to changes, such as in the proficiency of learners entering a program, or to technological innovations. Several of the chapters in this volume have captured this dynamism; for example, Susan Smith's experience of designing and delivering a course to Peruvian officials (Chapter 6) and Patrick Foss's account of incorporating blog writing into a program at a Japanese university (Chapter 16). In this case study, however, Moses Samuel and Saratha Sithamparam have described how social change provided an opportunity to introduce meaningful language use into the classroom. Their environment analysis identified constraints that needed to be worked within but also found the potential to adapt the mechanical exercises in the prescribed textbook into locally relevant, meaning-focused activities.

Tasks

1. Consider your own teaching environment. What types of changes have occurred in your local situation in the past five years? How has the curriculum responded to those changes? If the curriculum has not responded, how could it be adapted?

2. Here are some topics of modules in a coursebook. For each topic suggest an activity that relates it to the world outside the classroom in a teaching/ learning context you know. (You might want to consider how you'd expect a coursebook to deal with the topic first.)

TABLE 14.3

Topic	Suggested activity
Important firsts	
Special occasions	
Ambitions and dreams	
Take care!	
Money, money, money	

(These topics come from Sarah Cunningham and Peter Moor with Jane Comyns Carr, *New Cutting Edge Pre-intermediate*, Harlow, UK: Longman, 2005.)

3. Learners can play an important role in adapting a coursebook. Using the shopping topic described in this chapter, suggest how learners could supply materials and information for classroom activities.

15

THE TEACHER AS INTERMEDIARY BETWEEN NATIONAL CURRICULUM AND CLASSROOM

Kevin Parent

A poll conducted in an in-service training program for high school teachers in South Korea saw that 64.3 percent of the 28 respondents felt that training in curriculum design was irrelevant to them as teachers. When asked to elaborate, the fairly unified opinion was that it wasn't their job to decide what to teach, which should be left to those who had a view of the larger picture. Only two of the remaining respondents felt strongly that it had a place in a teacher's education. In Korea, as in many countries around the world, education is governed by a national curriculum. Decisions regarding what children need to know and when it should be learned are made by a dedicated branch of the national government. Although not a universal model, national curricula are established in the United Kingdom, Japan, China, and many other countries. In Australia, education policies are made by the states or territories although a national curriculum may be adopted in the future. Education policies in the United States are also left to the states; even the hotly contested No Child Left Behind Act of 2001 (Meier & Wood, 2004), a piece of national legislation, allows standards to be set by the individual states. But in all these countries, education policy is the domain of elected or appointed officials. Teachers, then, are the executors of policy. While writings on curriculum design generally acknowledge that any teaching situation has constraints of various kinds, much of what is written applies largely to models where the instructor has a far greater degree of freedom than the public school teacher. Without accounting for the academic freedom associated with higher education, undergraduate programs, for example, are frequently the final step in English education for many learners, a situation that accords its own degree of freedom. By examining a government-published textbook and its implementation in a South Korean middle school classroom, this chapter examines this imbalance and discusses the limitations and the freedom of the teacher at the terminal end of the curriculum chain.

Background: Lower Secondary Education in South Korea

With the national curriculum (NC) acting as a unifying agent, education differs little from middle school to middle school in Korea. Students enter at about the age of 13 (universal age, which differs from the system used in Korea to express age), after finishing six years of elementary school. Years are reset after entering middle school, and again in high school, so incoming students are referred to as "first year" or "first grade" rather than "seventh grade." For three years, students alternate between five-day and six-day weeks, attending classes for six hours or more Monday through Friday and a half-day on alternate Saturdays. Individual schools may alter this pattern – usually in the form of lengthening the hours – and certain weekdays may be longer than others. Additionally, after-school classes may add two or more hours to the schedule. Semesters run from March to July and August to February. There is no failing and students advance regardless of academic achievement. Middle school is the final level of compulsory education although 97 percent of 25- to 34-year-olds have completed upper-secondary education (OECD 2008).

The perception that Korean students spend all day at school, arriving home after midnight, needs addressing. It is not entirely inaccurate but generally reflects supplemental education. Traditionally, this has generally come from the private sector, either privately-run *hagwons* (cram schools), private tutors, or both. The relationship between the two sectors is sometimes tenuous, with public school teachers famously asking students why they didn't learn a given point from their *hagwon* teacher. To curtail the soaring cost of private education, on which parents spend an estimated US$11,000,000,000 annually, the Korean government in 2009 began instituting after-school programs within public schools, which, as of early 2010, resulted in the closing of 9.3 percent of Seoul-based *hagwons*.

There is no tenure system as such for public schoolteachers in Korea. Teachers are hired not by a school but by the Ministry of Education and deployed to various schools. When first becoming teachers, applicants take a qualification test in the region of their choice, but the ratio of successful to unsuccessful applicants varies considerably from region to region, with larger cities being more competitive, and this becomes an important factor in deciding where to apply. After being assigned to a school, middle school teachers may request a transfer after three years and must move after five, a pattern that repeats throughout their career. Unless otherwise requested, these transfers are to other schools within the same local board of education (the same city or province). Thus teachers may experience a wide range of social-economic statuses, seemingly correlating familial situations and student ambitions, while never becoming entrenched in a single school.

The teaching of English within the middle school system is generally done in tandem by a Korean teacher and a native-speaker teacher and is known as "team teaching." The vast majority of native English teachers come from EPIK (English Program in Korea). Established in 1995, EPIK recruits teachers from countries where English is a primary language and places them in classrooms alongside Korean teachers. Unlike their Korean counterparts, the native-speaking co-teachers are not required to pass a qualifying exam nor have a background in education although some training is provided. In 2009, 3,337 EPIK teachers were recruited for both primary and secondary schools. While most middle schools have a native speaker assigned, not every class can be accorded one, and some native-speaking teachers divide their week between two different schools.

The relative roles of the two teachers vary drastically from school to school and pair to pair. As the native-speaking teachers are reallocated more frequently than the Korean teachers, they are often surprised at the difference of expectations from school to school; they may be viewed as equals at some schools or treated as temporary help at another; the Korean teacher, likewise, may get paired with a foreign teacher showing dedication, unprofessionalism, or any point in-between. Some matches are perfect fits; others are not. While there is a system to register complaints, the initial pairing cannot take personalities into account and native-speaking teachers are assigned to schools based on need.

During the first year, students generally have three English classes per week, three more in the second year, and four in the third year. Many schools, however, add a fourth class to the first-year students' schedule. This class, done by the two teachers, generally will not have a dedicated textbook but may still follow the textbook of the main course, supplementing it with activities developed by the teachers. Although not mandated by the NC, many schools have recently begun dividing classes into low, middle, and high levels and assigning students accordingly.

Textbooks are developed by commercial companies and then authorized by the Ministry of Education (Yoon, 2004). The choice of textbook is made at the school level from a variety of "packages." Each package is a unified series of books for the three years approved by the Ministry of Education. As of 2010 there are 25 such packages, having nearly doubled from 13 in one year. At the school in the case study below, the package was selected by a committee of six Korean teachers. A book is used for the entire school year and is designed in two parts, each of which must be completed within a semester. A class has two books: the main text and an activity book. Each year, students progress to the next book in the series.

Focus: A Middle School English Class

We can now turn our attention to an actual middle school classroom. The school is situated in Daejeon, the fifth largest city in Korea with a population of some 1.5 million, which occupies a geographically central position in the country. The students' families are estimated by the teachers as lower middle class. Each English class has about 25 students.

This case study is informed by observations and discussions with the teachers. The primary teaching team consists of a Korean woman, aged 38, who has been teaching for 13 years, and a 26-year-old woman from the UK who is currently in her second year of teaching in Korea. Both years have been at the same school but she worked with a different teacher the first year; that teacher has since transferred. She has gone from teaching an estimated 50 percent of the class with the previous teacher to 75 percent with the current one. This shift is not related to teaching abilities or dedication but is the result of different personalities interacting differently; the previous Korean teacher was very outgoing and the current one is more withdrawn.

The textbook package employed by the school is called *Middle School English* (Im et al., 2009a). The main text of the first year is a softbound book whose 185 pages are all colorful, containing illustrations, photographs, sheet music, and a mixture of Korean and English scripts, with the latter dominating. Apart from the front and back matter, Korean is used primarily for task instructions but is also used for glosses or to explain words such as *pancake* which do not translate directly. Pronunciation is given in IPA. The characters who appear in the book's dialogues are both Korean and non-Korean. The average length of English sentences containing both subject and verb, drawn from a random sample of 30, is 6.1 words (standard deviation of 2.32).

The two parts of the book contain six and five lessons respectively. After every third lesson is a four-page "round up test." The lessons are organized along notional-functional lines, with such topics as introducing oneself, favorite foods, giving directions, holidays, etc. Each lesson is 14 pages long and constitutes a "block lesson" (Nation & Macalister, 2010), meaning that each unit follows a set pattern. First there is a variety of listening activities in which the learners' responses move from simple matching or checking to writing single words, a variety of speaking activities, reading and answering questions, writing activities, pair-work activities such as information gaps, pronunciation practice (phonemic level), and a game. This text does not have a dedicated vocabulary section although books in other packages do. Some of the vocabulary in the dialogues and activities are Korean words such as names of food and holidays. Grammatical structures occurring in the book include equation via copula, *wh-* questions, use of modal *will*, etc. The accompanying activities book (Im et al., 2009b) is notably larger at 270 pages. The units match those of the main text, and its activities do not differ much from those of the main book. Although "activities book" implies a contrast, it really is more of an extension or supplemental book, offering additional listening activities, readings, and writing assignments of the types found in the main book.

Needs Analysis

When assigned to teach a new EFL class at a university, the instructor may need to assess the level of the students, determine their needs and then choose a textbook, though it is frequently the case that the textbook decision has to be made on a best guess as it needs to be selected prior to the first class. This highlights an important difference between teachers working within the framework of a national curriculum and those working outside it. Within the framework, there is no needs analysis nor is one necessary: the NC cannot be modified to accommodate the results one would produce. While the construction of the curriculum must be informed by a perception of learners' needs, at the classroom level the NC effectively tells students what they need. This is perceived as unfortunate by the teachers, who see the NC as, at best, an averaging or leveling out of individual students needs. "All students have to progress at the same pace," summarized the native-speaking teacher.

Indeed, while teachers are generally happy to have their classes divided according to low, middle, and high levels, the division does not free them from the constraints of the curriculum. All students, regardless of level, must follow the same textbook and do so at the same pace. The teachers feel that the curriculum is designed with the low-level students in mind and note that students in the high-level class begin to get bored and even lose the language-learning passion that had projected them into the advanced class to begin with.

Implementing the Curriculum

In the classroom, then, the book is the curriculum. Its units must be followed in sequence and the amount of time devoted to each is predetermined. At the middle school in Daejeon, whose teachers believe this to be the case throughout the country, there is a hierarchy of activities. First, class time has to be devoted to the main text. Second, additional time may be allocated to the activities book, though this can be assigned as homework to ensure the covering of the main text. Finally, any remaining time may be filled with teacher-developed activities related to the lesson. The amount of time dedicated to each tier is perhaps the biggest practical difference between the proficiency levels. Much of the classroom time in the lower-level classes is devoted to completing the units of the main text; only in the advanced class, whose students either learn more quickly or may already know the material, is there time remaining for teacher-created activities.

Regarding the first and second of these, grammar is generally presented at the beginning of the unit. In the lower-level classes, this is done by the Korean teacher (in Korean); in the advanced classes, the native-speaking teacher does it, generally restricting the explanation to word order, with the Korean teacher stepping in only if needed. From here, lessons move along the path of the coursebook, touching on each of the four skills (first listening, then speaking, reading, and finally writing) before culminating in a game, time permitting. (Interestingly, there are different perceptions by the students regarding being taught in English depending on whether it is by the Korean teacher or the native English-speaking one. While the native English-speaking teacher is not expected to communicate in Korean, when the Korean teacher speaks in English, the students feel she is being mean for opting to use the more difficult classroom code.)

Regarding the third priority in the hierarchy, the teacher-developed activities frequently include PowerPoint presentations, games, or songs. One such presentation includes at the top of each slide the words "I feel . . ." and a graphic of a face, whose expression changes with each slide. Students say the whole sentence, completing it with the adjective depicted by the emoticon, which has been introduced in the main text.

Other presentations prepared by the teachers introduce vocabulary that is not necessarily found in the book. For a unit on eating out, a slide shows an Italian restaurant which is followed by a slide showing the names and pictures of four items one might order there (*seafood pasta, lasagna*, etc.). Subsequent slides do the same for Chinese, Japanese, American, and Indian restaurants. Further slides depict additional restaurant-related vocabulary such as *waiter, bill*, and *leave a tip* (which the teachers explain since this practice is not followed in Korea). After completing the presentation, students may role-play restaurant scenarios.

Some presentations show other ways to use the vocabulary, thus recycling it in various sentences. One, regarding phobias, uses the sentence stem "I have a fear of . . ." then shows various pictures, introducing vocabulary such as *spiders, needles, clowns, foreigners, heights*, etc. It then introduces sentences such as *I'm really afraid of . . ., . . . make me feel strange* and *. . . give me the creeps*, etc. A final slide introduces idiomatic expressions, something the textbook seems to avoid, such as "When I fly, I'm a bundle of nerves," "Dentists make my skin crawl," etc. Since these teacher-created materials are generally implemented only in the high-level classes where the book activities are finished quickly, activities such as these help keep these learners interested by introducing vocabulary and expressions they may not already know, which the textbook alone may not do adequately.

Sometimes the teachers create board games. These involve tokens and dice. Students are placed in pairs, moving their tokens and needing to complete the dialogue with each other in order to remain on the square. Example tasks instruct the students to discuss the day's weather, or order food at a restaurant. These are culled directly from the book. Sometimes songs are used instead of games for variety. In this case, classes get to choose which song they will learn, a sharing of control that is seen to increase their interest.

These activities are generally the extent of classroom decisions, at least in terms of teaching and learning and excluding matters of classroom management regarding, for example, tardy or uncooperative students. The current year has seen a change in school principals, and an accompanying drastic change of styles which shows the extent to which even the level immediately above the teacher can affect teaching and learning. The principal, the teachers conclude, cannot determine what gets taught, since that is set in stone, but has a definite say in how it is taught. The former principal was an enthusiastic leader who genuinely cared about the students and understood the need for free time in learning. The new principal, however, forbids teachers from sitting down or using the microphone and monitors the classroom to ensure these are observed. During a recent inter-school speech contest, he insisted that their school win and demanded the focus of class-room attention be on improving oral ability until the contest had concluded.

The Four Strands

Nation and Macalister (2010) state that a well-balanced course includes approximately equal attention devoted to meaning-focused input, language-focused learning, meaning-focused output, and fluency activities. In this middle school, the balance is not even. Meaning-focused input is provided by teacher instruction and story-based readings in the coursebooks. Many of the books' listening activities cannot be considered meaning-focused as users could complete some of them without comprehending the meaning, and some of the listening tasks have the students choose between two similar-sounding Korean locales. Language-focused learning concentrates on pronunciation in the first year with vocabulary gaining ground by the third and with some grammatical information included. Meaning-focused output is provided by writing activities, which entail writing single sentences (sometimes filling in single words) prompted by pictures in the book. As a supplement to the textbook, they like to assign a topic, tell the students to write five sentences about it, then stand and talk about it, without reading.

Although oral production activities are included in the book, nothing specifically tackles fluency. This is not to say that fluency is completely absent but it is relegated to the activities that comprise the third tier of the hierarchy of priorities. Songs, for example, are initially sung very slowly but repeated with increasing speed until an ideal tempo is attained. But ultimately, fluency is not currently assessed in the university entrance exam nor at any point prior; it therefore is given little to no weight in the classroom. Should this change, there will no doubt be a washback effect that sees it take a place in the curriculum. The goal of classroom instruction may be less one of teaching and learning than one of raising test scores. Note, however, that this does mean fluency activities do not exist in educational services from the private sector. Although the proportions of strands detailed here only represent those observed at one school, the overall balance is determined by the NC and it can probably be said that, at best, fluency suffers in education around the country.

Conclusion

In a widely-viewed speech on TED.com, one of that site's top ten, Sir Ken Robinson (2006) states that "the whole system of public education around the world is a protracted process of university entrance." The teachers agree. The goal of middle schools in Korea is "to prepare students for high school," and the goal then changes to prepare students for the university entrance exam, and enrollment in the more prestigious universities helps secure better jobs.

Returning to the issue of learners' needs, the teachers felt that what is needed, but not provided by the curriculum is a chance to use the language being taught.

Rephrased, much of what is taught is not for immediate use. The first-year course book, for example, includes a unit on directions but the teachers perceive this as irrelevant to the students' needs. People do not approach middle school children asking, in English, how to "get to the bank" often enough to be meaningful to the learners. Further, the unit gives directions via street names, which are not commonly used in Korea, thus implying that the language is for the purpose of overseas travel. Similarly, the first lesson has students introducing themselves when, of course, they are all the same age and have the same "occupation" and most have the same hometown. This is seen to send a message to the learners that what they are to learn are theoretical constructs. It is a bank of knowledge that may, or may not, be tapped at some future point. The teachers agree that when the information really is needed, the grammatical and lexical knowledge is too unstable to be recalled properly.

As the poll question at the start of this chapter shows, there is no agreement that the designing of a curriculum is relevant to teachers. The Korean middle-school teacher saw her role as realizing the NC, putting policy into practice. The co-teacher disagreed, feeling that the NC should inform what happens in the classroom and that, by the end of the year, all students should have learned the same material, but that it is not necessary for all schoolchildren around the country to be almost literally on the same page. There should be, she feels, a national curriculum, but it should be less restrictive and allow the teacher some room and creativity. Part of teaching is deciding what is to be taught, not simply how.

References

Im, B., Song, H., Han, H., Bak, H., Yun, S., An, H., Bak, M., & Pak, H.H. (2009a). *Middle School English I.* Paju, South Korea: Seong-andang.

Im, B., Song, H., Han, H., Bak, H., Yun, S., An, H., Bak, M., & Pak, H.H. (2009b) *Middle School English I: Activities.* Paju, South Korea: Seong-andang.

Meier, D., & Wood, G. (Eds.). (2004). *Many children left behind: How the No Child Left Behind Act is damaging our children and our schools.* Boston, MA: Beacon Press.

Nation, I.S.P., & Macalister, J. (2010). *Language curriculum design.* New York, NY: Routledge.

OECD. (2008). Education at a glance 2008: OECD briefing note for Korea. Retrieved October 15 2010 from <http://www.oecd.org/dataoecd/32/24/41277858.pdf>.

Robinson, K. (2006). *Ken Robinson says schools kill creativity.* [Video file]. Retrieved October 15 2010 from <http://www.ted.com/talks/ken_robinson_says_schools_kill_creativity.html>.

Yoon, K. (2004) CLT theories and practices in EFL curricula: A case study in Korea. *Asian EFL Journal, 6*(3). Retrieved October 15 2010 from <http://www.asian-efl-journal.com/september_04_yke.php>.

Comment

In this chapter, Kevin Parent paints a fairly bleak view of the scope for innovation in the Korean education system. This depiction will no doubt resonate with many teachers working with a national curriculum in the state or public education sector – the teachers whom Parent describes as being "at the terminal end of the curriculum chain." However, as this case study suggests, even here there is potential for the teacher to make changes. Perhaps the most important decision is deciding which of the 25 approved coursebooks to adopt. Having clear, well-thought-out criteria on which to base a decision would obviously be crucial in such a situation. Once a coursebook has been adopted, teachers may also adapt the material presented in a variety of ways, although it is noticeable in this case study that teacher-developed activities were only used with the so-called advanced class.

Tasks

1. When describing his ideal vocabulary course (Chapter 5, this volume), Paul Nation claims that "Even with a very prescribed course, it is possible to balance the strands." Consider how the teacher-developed activities that Kevin Parent describes in this chapter relate to the four strands, and what other activities could be added to achieve a better balance.

TABLE 15.1

Strand	Teacher-developed activities	Other possible activities
meaning-focused input		
language-focused learning		
meaning-focused output		
fluency development		

2. In his exploration of the role of negotiation (Chapter 13, this volume), Andrew Boon demonstrates a number of possibilities for the introduction of change in the curriculum. In a situation such as that described in this chapter, is negotiation equally possible? Think about the components of the inner circle of the curriculum design model, and identify possibilities for negotiation between teacher and learners.

TABLE 15.2

Inner circle	Negotiation possibilities
Goal	
Content & sequencing	
Format & presentation	
Monitoring & assessment	

16

DEVELOPING A BLOGWRITING PROGRAM AT A JAPANESE UNIVERSITY

Patrick Foss

Introduction

Over the past several years, the personal websites/online journals known as blogs have become practically ubiquitous. According to Technorati (2008), a website that tracks and indexes blogs, in 2008 there were at least 133 million blogs worldwide, with nearly a million new blog entries being posted every 24 hours. As noted by numerous others (e.g. Armstrong & Retterer, 2008; Ducate & Lomicka, 2008), a small part of this boom has been fueled by educators, including second and foreign language educators, as more and more of them are introducing a blogging component in their classrooms. The potential benefits of using blogs in language classes are numerous (see Carney, 2009 for a detailed overview). First, initial research into the use of blogs in the classroom seems to indicate that learners view blogs as a "real" form of communication, and that this is motivating for them (Lowe & Williams, 2004; Pinkman, 2005; Ward, 2004). Second, the commenting features present in most blogs can encourage interaction with other learners, leading, hopefully, to a sharing of knowledge (Armstrong & Retterer, 2008; Ducate & Lomicka, 2008; Lowe & Williams, 2004). Third, the fact that initial blog posts, updates, and comments can be published immediately is a further attraction; learning can take place quickly and efficiently, without the time lags that can lead to loss of interest (Kadjer & Bull, 2003). Fourth, the individualized nature of blogs allows them to be used easily as means of self-expression (Ducate & Lomicka, 2008; Farmer, 2004; Thorne & Payne, 2005). Perhaps as a result, blogs may also lead to greater autonomy and self-reflection on the part of individual learners (Mynard, 2007). Sixth, blogs (and other types of online writing) are typically informal and relatively unstructured, which may make them particularly suitable for classroom use with less proficient writers; blogwriting, in other words, may be able to serve as a bridge to academic or more sophisticated forms of writing

(Bloch, 2007; see also Al-Jarf, 2004; Armstrong & Retterer, 2008; Lam, 2000). Finally, blogs may help learners improve their command of vocabulary and grammar (Armstrong & Retterer, 2008; Ducate & Lomicka, 2008).

With some of the above benefits in mind, the instructors at one university EFL program in Japan decided to experiment with integrating student-written blogs into an established writing curriculum. Why and how this was done, and how teachers and students evaluated this experiment, will be discussed in this chapter.

Background: Identifying a Problem

At the Japanese university EFL program described here, freshmen and sophomore non-English majors, most of them with low/intermediate-level English skills, were required to complete two years of basic EAP Reading, Writing, and Communication courses. These courses met for ninety minutes once a week for an average of thirteen weeks per semester. The Writing I and II courses were designed to lead the students from writing simple paragraphs as new freshmen to completing a basic research essay at the end of their sophomore year.

There was concern on the part of some of the instructors that these Writing courses were too academic, too focused on form, and that the students were unprepared to fully participate in them. For example, in a typical series of three to four classes, the instructor introduced a particular rhetorical form (e.g. comparison/contrast), taught key words and introduced sentence-writing exercises associated with the form, and led the students through the paragraph and/or essay-writing process (i.e. brainstorming ideas, producing the first draft, reviewing, editing, and polishing). Although this approach was in accord with the program's academic objectives, some instructors felt that it was also somewhat dry and gave the students little opportunity for self-expression. In addition, there was concern that the drafting/review process was focused too heavily on errors in usage or form rather than ideas; students were perhaps being encouraged by the process to write using a "cookie-cutter" approach and to not take chances. Finally, it was observed that many of the students had great difficulties in completing their written assignments. Part of the problem concerned lack of writing experience. Many of the students' writing classes in secondary school had focused on translating individual sentences from Japanese to English and vice versa; these students had rarely, if ever, written more than two or three consecutive original sentences in English. Another part of the problem concerned lack of vocabulary command and/or confidence. When writing in class, a majority of students referred to electronic or web-based dictionaries, sometimes several times for a single sentence. This often resulted in unnatural sentences that were difficult for other students or the instructors to understand. A final part of the problem concerned lack of typing skills. All writing classes were conducted in computer rooms, and students were expected to type all of their written assignments. However, many students did not have computers at home and/or had never typed anything in English on a computer. "Hunting and pecking" for letters on their keyboards (while at the same time, as noted, referring to dictionaries), some students took several minutes to write a single sentence.

Different instructors had taken different measures to address these concerns. Some instructors spent a few minutes at the start of every writing class on a combination of freewriting and typing practice. Students were given a time limit and instructed to type whatever thoughts or ideas came into their minds during that time, without paying any attention to spelling, grammar, or vocabulary. One instructor had his students write on their own topics and ideas in paper journals in class and at home. Other instructors had students send them paragraphs on general topics via email. Still other instructors had started experimenting with blogs in a limited fashion. However, there were no commonly-used procedures, and there was dissatisfaction with some of the individual procedures. For example, some of the teachers using freewriting felt that while it was useful for building fluency and improving typing skills, it had no communicative purpose. There was also dissatisfaction with the ad hoc way in which procedures were being employed. If there was consensus among the instructors that some form of extensive writing was necessary, then it was felt that it should be officially part of the curriculum and not something for instructors to include in class when and if there was extra time.

Formulating a Solution

The problems mentioned above were discussed at curriculum meetings held by the writing instructors. During these discussions, it was decided that extensive writing *was* something that needed to be part of the curriculum and that the use of student-created blogs was perhaps the best solution. Interestingly, though there were few references to the research literature during these curriculum meetings, many of the arguments concerning why blogs might be beneficial matched those cited in the introduction to this chapter. First, blogwriting seemed to have few conventions; as with freewriting, there were no traditional forms that students would have to adhere to when composing, which would hopefully allow them to practice basic writing skills in a less-demanding environment. Second, the nature of blogwriting lent itself to typing practice. Third, like paper journal writing, blogwriting could be used as a method of self-expression. Finally, that the blogs would be publicly viewable on the Internet and that students would be able to comment on them was highly attractive to a majority of the instructors, as it made blogwriting communicative in a way that freewriting was not and journal writing was to only a limited extent (as only the teacher read individual student journals).

It was agreed, then, to experiment with blogs as an official part of the writing curriculum. In some respects, this was a relatively simple change to enact. No additional equipment was required, given that all writing classes were conducted in computer labs. No major changes to the curriculum were required either. A certain amount of discretionary time was already built into the schedule, and it was agreed to use this time (up to 20 minutes per class period) for blogwriting, though teachers could also simply assign blogs for homework if necessary. Blogs were also assigned a portion of the final overall writing grade; this was to be between 10 and 20 percent, depending on to what extent blogs were used in class.

There was less agreement as to how blogwriting should specifically be incorporated. Individual teachers wanted the freedom to decide how and when to use blogs in their classes. In the end, only a few loose guidelines were agreed upon. First, blogs were to be used as supplementary assignments focusing primarily on building fluency and improving general language use and secondarily on encouraging student interaction. Concerning fluency, blogs were to be written regularly, with at least five assigned over the course of a semester. Also, although blogging would be required and blogs graded, unlike other assignments in Writing I or II, grammar and spelling errors would be ignored. Grades would largely be determined by production; in other words, how many words the students wrote per entry. (Along with hopefully improving learner writing fluency, this policy was seen as having the additional benefit of not overly increasing the instructors' workload). Concerning general language use, blog topics were to be largely non-academic. Concerning student interaction, students were to be encouraged to read and comment on other student blogs.

With the above guidelines in mind, individual teachers were then left to decide how best to incorporate blogs into their own classes. However, this was not typically done in isolation. Most teachers discussed what they were doing with the others and shared ideas and procedures, either casually or during curriculum meetings. In addition, surveys and interviews concerning the use of blogs in the writing classroom were conducted to identify particular procedures and problems and to elicit opinions from the teachers on whether the program could be considered a success or failure. Surveys were also administered to learners, in part to get their opinions on the blog program as well. These procedures, problems, and evaluations will be discussed next.

Implementing the Program: Procedures

At the beginning of the school year, each instructor created his or her own individual blog and guided the students through the creation of their blogs and the formation of class groups. There were a number of similarities and differences concerning how blogs were used in individual classes. These included:

Type of Blog Service Used

Each instructor decided what blog service she or he would use; particularly at the beginning of the program, different services were employed by different instructors (see "Issues and problems" below).

Required Length of Blog Entries

Teachers set word length requirements for their students. For first-year students, the minimum number of words required for a passing grade (60 percent) ranged from 75 to 150. The number of words required for the highest possible grade (100 percent) ranged from 175 to 250. Some instructors used the same benchmarks for second-year students, while others raised them. The minimum number of words required for a passing grade on a sophomore blog ranged from 120 to 200; the number of words required for the highest possible grade ranged from 200 to 300.

Method of Grading

All of the instructors used word count as their primary grading criteria. Students were also expected to complete blog entries on time in the same way as any other assignment. Two instructors used additional criteria as well. One instructor gave points for "writing well and completely" about the topic, including pictures, and making thoughtful comments about other student blogs. Another instructor also required pictures and evidence of effort for students to receive full points.

Frequency of Blog Entries

Some instructors felt it was necessary for students to write on their blogs every week in order for their writing fluency to improve. Others thought that weekly blogs were too burdensome and possibly had a negative impact on motivation. The number of blog entries required for one semester ranged from 5 to 12, depending on the instructor.

Use of Class Time

Most instructors used the first 15 to 20 minutes of class to introduce that week's blog topic and let the students get started and/or comment on the previous week's blogs. However, depending on the week and what else might be on the schedule, some instructors used more or less time or assigned blogs entirely for homework.

Topic Choice

Most teachers alternated between free topics and assigned topics (e.g. "My Favorite Movie," "An Embarrassing Story") in order to relieve students of the pressure to constantly come up with new ideas. However, one instructor believed that student blogs were more interesting for both him and the students when they chose their own topics to write about; this instructor rarely assigned topics.

Use of Models

Some instructors wrote blogs of their own on the topic for that week in order to show their students how a native speaker might approach the task at hand, introduce new vocabulary or target grammatical structures, and/or share information about themselves. Some instructors also tried to include at least one picture related to the topic in order to help students generate ideas. Some instructors did not do either of these things or did so only on occasion. One instructor wrote models at first but as time went on stopped the practice, as he felt that they were too much of an influence on his students.

Connection to Classwork

One instructor made a regular effort at first to connect blog topics to classwork. This chiefly involved introducing concepts or rhetorical patterns in a general way before addressing them more academically in the weeks following. However, he came to feel that he had overdone it, and that students needed more freedom. Most of the other instructors linked blogs and classwork only occasionally.

Degree of Interaction

In order to build camaraderie and foster a sense of audience, all instructors encouraged students to read and briefly comment on other students' blogs. However, some instructors not only encouraged but required students to comment on anywhere from one to three blogs per assignment. Some instructors also commented themselves on student blogs.

The diversity of approaches described above to using blogs in the classroom reflected the diversity of ideas and opinions held by the instructors. As these ideas and opinions were frequently shared and discussed, as mentioned earlier, the instructors were able to learn from each other and refine individual procedures concerning blogwriting when necessary.

Implementing the Program: Issues and Problems

As the blog program developed, issues and problems emerged to be discussed and, when possible, solved. These included:

Choosing an Appropriate Blog Service

The first step for most of the instructors was deciding which blog service to use from among the dozens of free services available. Thinking that all of these services were created equal, some of the instructors put little time into this decision. However, it turned out there were a number of important considerations.

First, how easy was it to set up an account? In order to have their own blogs, students had to create individual accounts with whichever blog service the instructor chose. Depending on the service, the instructors discovered there could be anywhere from one page to several pages of account information to be filled in. As many of the students in the program had little computer experience, it took some of the instructors one full class period (90 minutes) or more to get everyone set up and ready to go. As a result of this experience, some teachers created step-by-step guides for the most user-friendly blog services, which over time became the blog services of choice.

Second, how easy was it for students to interact? Some blog services utilized allowed members to easily organize themselves into groups (e.g. "blog circles"), which made it simple for learners to find classmates' blogs. Services without this feature forced members (and/or their instructor) to individually link to other blogs, which was time-consuming. Some blog services allowed members to comment on other blogs instantly and at will, so long as they were signed in to the service. Other services required members to enter their email address and/or type in an anti-spam code word each time before comments could be published, the process of which was discouraging for low-level learners or those pressed for time. Still other services required comments to be moderated, meaning the owner of the blog had to approve individual comments before they were published. It was thought that while this possibly kept negative messages from appearing and discouraged cyber-bullying, it also impeded the free flow of opinions and ultimately discouraged participation. After a period of experimentation, most instructors in the program gravitated toward services that offered instant, hassle-free commenting.

Third, how customizable was the blog? Some blog services offered only limited, pre-designed templates for users to select. Other services allowed users to customize their blog pages in a variety of ways, be it through use of pictures, avatars, fonts, colors, or other components. Some teachers noted that the more students were free to design their own blog pages, the more ownership they seemed to take of them, and the more care they spent writing their blog.

Fourth, how public was the blog? Initially, most of the instructors wanted all the learner blogs to be public (i.e. viewable by anyone over the Internet). Godwin-Jones (2003) has written that the public nature of a blog may lend to its authenticity; learners may write more seriously and thoughtfully when they are aware that "real people" (not just other learners or the instructor) may read their blog entries. These "real people" may turn out to be others with similar interests, leading to friendships and/or useful connections. However, as Ellison and Wu (2008) point out, public blogs may also be read by family members or present/future employers; words written by a student on his or her blog could therefore have consequences even years later. Because of this possibility, some instructors concluded that if blogs were to be a required part of a class, it was better to use a more private forum, one shielded from all but those invited to join. In addition, even though the networks were private, as student blogs were being shared with other students and classes, learners were advised not to post private or sensitive information.

Finally, were there ads? What kind? Most of the blog services trialed had advertising of one kind or another. However, not all blog services had the same kind of ads. It was found that overtly sexual ads, for example, were more commonly seen on some blog providers than others. These ads made some instructors uncomfortable and led them eventually to switch services.

Dealing with Plagiarism and Machine Translation

As all of the student blogs were composed on computers with Internet access, plagiarism and inappropriate use of web-based dictionaries and translation sites became minor issues for all of the instructors. Regarding plagiarism, all teachers reported occasional instances of students copying paragraphs from other websites and pasting them into their own blogs. Some instructors claimed that these copied passages were usually easy to spot, as they were typically in a different font or size than the rest of the blog and written at a much higher level than the student was capable of writing. More difficult to identify were instances of students copying from other student blogs, although these copied passages also often appeared in a different font or size from the rest of the blog. Students caught plagiarizing were typically given zero points for that blog and asked to write the blog again; in most cases, teachers reported that this was an effective response. Regarding the inappropriate use of web-based dictionaries and translation sites, most teachers considered this a more serious problem than plagiarism (though still minor overall – only one instructor considered it to be a major problem). Machine translation is a relatively new phenomenon, the ramifications of which have perhaps not been fully considered by ESL/EFL professionals (see Berberich, 2006; Cribb, 2000). A small percentage of learners were occasionally caught typing whole paragraphs of Japanese into a translation site and copying the English produced directly into their blogs. Some instructors believed they could spot the effects of machine translation from Japanese to English (e.g. highly unnatural use of pronouns) even without observing student actions directly; other instructors were less confident and some research in this area seems to indicate that recognizing the work of automatic translation software is indeed difficult (Ruthven-Stuart, 2008). Interestingly, at least three instructors felt inappropriate use of machine translation was more of a problem where student essays rather than blogs were concerned. As blogs were not graded on writing quality and topics were typically simple and/or student-friendly, the pressure or need to use translation for blogs was thought to be less than for essays. In any case, most instructors responded to this problem by giving learners tutorials on how to use electronic dictionaries and translation software effectively and confronting students suspected of using these tools inappropriately.

Maintaining Motivation

Many instructors reported sensing a higher level of interest from students new to blogs than from those who had already had some experience with them. One instructor reported that, over time, blogs became less fun for some students and more like regular assignments. Two others felt that blogs seemed to become less interesting for students during their second year in the program. In addition, some students seemed uninterested in blogs from the beginning, and there seemed to be little that could be done to motivate them. There was no consensus as to how to deal with these issues. Some instructors felt the best solution was to find high-interest topics for students to write about. At least one instructor felt it was better to let students decide most topics for themselves, as this tended to lead to more interesting writing.

Responding to Inappropriate Behavior

Although it was rare, teachers reported that students writing on their blogs occasionally made inappropriate comments, used inappropriate language, and posted inappropriate pictures. It fell to the instructors to moderate all discussion and deal with small problems before they became big ones.

Explaining the Program to New Instructors

After blogwriting had been incorporated into the official curriculum but before it was introduced to all of the students, two new teachers joined the department. The purpose of the blogwriting program was explained and sample procedures introduced. Neither instructor had used blogs before; as a result, both required a lot of instruction and advice. One of the instructors in particular was resistant to the idea of doing blogwriting in class, stating at one point that she thought it was "pointless." At first, rather than having her students write actual blogs, she had them contribute to what was in effect a type of Internet forum. However, she quickly grew dissatisfied with this. Over the course of a semester, she asked other instructors how they were using blogs and was shown a number of different examples. By the time the second semester began, she had changed her mind and begun to use blogs in similar ways to other instructors.

Evaluating the Program: Instructor Opinions

As the second year of the blog program drew to a close, the seven instructors primarily involved were asked to evaluate the use of blogs in their classes. Had the program been a success? Although each instructor mentioned one or more of the problems stated above, all of them felt positively about the program and gave multiple reasons.

The most common reason given (mentioned, in fact, by each instructor) was that blogs helped students to interact with each other in English. As one instructor put it, "they are not by nature interactive with one another . . . this way allows them a safe approach to being interactive in some way. They're working by themselves but yet they're sharing information with the class." Another instructor said: "It lets them get to know about each other . . . it's useful for creating a team atmosphere in the classroom."

Another common reason, mentioned by six of the seven instructors, concerned the unstructured nature of blogs and the relaxed way they were used in class. One instructor said: "(The students) are writing freely and they're just really trying to communicate what they want to communicate instead of worrying about the grammar or the structure, so it's really freeing for them." Another instructor said: "(T)here are a lot more rules for writing an essay, which is more intimidating. . . . (on blogs) they can do whatever they want." Two instructors felt that students actually wrote more deeply and completely on their blogs than in their essays because the blogs were unstructured. One of them put it this way: "(W)hat happens is, in their blogs, they don't think of it really so much as an assignment as an essay, and they don't feel like there are restraints on how they should write, and they don't feel the pressure of being graded, and they feel that they can be more detailed."

Four teachers mentioned that blogs were simply good writing practice. "If you do it frequently and make a routine out of it, students are kind of establishing a habit of writing in English a little every week," one instructor said. "If you think about the sheer volume of English that they're writing over a semester . . . the more you do something, the better you're going to get at it." Another instructor put it this way: "Using blogs helps (students) get used to writing in general."

Other reasons were mentioned less frequently. Three teachers listed typing practice as a reason why blogs were successful in their classes. Three teachers also mentioned self-expression. "Students would like an outlet to express themselves," one of these instructors said, "and since most students are . . . better at writing than at speaking, they can more easily express themselves on blogs." Finally, two teachers felt that students had to "stretch" (as one instructor put it) when writing blogs because they needed to use different words from those in their essay assignments.

Interestingly, even the instructor who was initially resistant to using blogs in her classes was, in the end, very positive in her assessment of the program. She confessed that "I was very skeptical of it at first, I have to admit. I came in with the attitude that this (was) just pointless writing, but after two years of doing it, I am really, really for it now and I think it's really beneficial for the students."

Evaluating the Program: Learner Opinions

Also during the second year of the blogwriting program, more than 500 learners taking the relevant writing classes were surveyed for their opinions on this activity.

At this point, most of the first-year students had experienced at least one semester of blogging; most of the second-year students had been writing on blogs for at least three semesters. On the whole, these learners also evaluated the program positively, though freshmen were more enthusiastic than sophomores.

In response to questions given in Japanese concerning the usefulness of class blogs, nearly 96 percent of freshmen and 92 percent of sophomores stated that they felt blogwriting was useful. Many students simply wrote that they felt it improved their English skills in general. Other students specifically mentioned the benefits of practice. One freshman wrote (this and all subsequent student responses have been translated from Japanese), "When we write on our blog, little by little it becomes easier to write in English." Blogging was also seen as a way of learning and/or remembering words and/or grammar. According to one sophomore, "I can check how to use words in various ways." Many students wrote that blogging helped them to express themselves. Said one freshman, "On a blog I write what I want to say in English, so in the future if I meet a foreigner I will be able to express myself, I think." A small number of students mentioned motivation or other reasons for why blogging was useful. According to one sophomore, "(Blogging) makes English more interesting." According to another, "Blogs help me to type at a faster pace."

A small percentage of students did not consider blogging to be useful. Some of these students felt that this activity did not improve their English. According to one sophomore, "I only write the English that I know, so I don't learn many new words or expressions." Some felt that blogs should be checked by the teacher in the same way as essays. As one sophomore put it, "I like writing on my blog. However, since I don't understand about what kind of mistakes I'm making, I don't think it's so useful."

A majority of learners also considered blogging enjoyable, though to a lesser degree than useful. Nearly 72 percent of freshmen and 56 percent of sophomores wrote that they enjoyed writing on their blogs. Many connected it to their desire to improve their English. One freshman said, "It's fun. Each time I have to use trial and error to decide what words to use, which is good training for the mind, I think." A number of students specifically mentioned interaction with others. According to one sophomore, "I can teach others in the class various things about me, and I can learn a lot about them. I can get involved with people that I don't usually talk to." The freedom of blogging also made it enjoyable for many learners. One freshman wrote, "I can write freely about my thoughts and interests." In a related vein, a small percentage of students felt that blogging was fun because it was easier than other types of writing. As one sophomore put it, "Unlike with essays, I don't have to write grammar perfectly." Writing on a blog also gave some learners a feeling of achievement. According to one freshman, "On the one hand, it takes a long time to complete, but on the other hand when it's completed I have a sense of accomplishment." Finally, blogging was seen to be "fresh" by a number of learners, albeit more freshmen than sophomores. As one freshman wrote, "This is my first experience (writing on a blog), so it's fun."

For the learners who did not enjoy blogging, while some stated that they did not like writing or English in general, more tended to claim that blogging was difficult, troublesome, or took up too much time. One sophomore wrote, "In Japanese, I can communicate what I want to say 100 percent, but in English I have constraints and have to settle on approximations." One freshman had a similar opinion: "If I was writing in Japanese it would be fun, I think. But I don't have much ability to communicate in English, so I can't say it's a lot of fun." Some sophomores (no freshmen) wrote that blogging was not fun because it was homework. As one student put it, "A blog should be written when you have something to write, but this is like an obligation, so it's not fun." A very small number of students wrote that they did not like to write about themselves. According to one sophomore, "I don't like writing about daily events, and I'm a little resistant to other people reading about my personal life."

Conclusion

Based on the positive evaluations given by both instructors and students, it was decided to retain the blogging component of the writing curriculum, though it would continue to be monitored and hopefully improved as time went on. Introducing this component had been a step-by-step process that involved a great deal of trial and error as well as a commitment to departmental communication and respect for a variety of teaching approaches on the part of the instructors involved. Echoing similar conclusions by Armstrong and Retterer (2008) and Ellison and Wu (2008), as with any type of change, blogs are not a magical tool that will suddenly transform a poor writing curriculum into a successful one. However, as these university instructors discovered, a blogwriting program can add variety to an academic writing course and enable learners to both interact with each other and get more practice with written language.

Acknowledgment

A previous version of this paper was presented at the 29th CDELT Symposium (March 14–15 2009), Cairo, Egypt.

References

Al-Jarf, R. (2004). The effects of web-based learning on struggling EFL college writers. *Foreign Language Annals, 37*(1), 49–57.

Armstrong, K., & Retterer, O. (2008). Blogging as L2 writing: A case study. *Association for the Advancement of Computing in Education Journal, 16*(3), 233–251.

Berberich, F. (2006). Sharing our stories: With translation software? In K. Bradford-Watts, C. Ikeguchi & M. Swanson (Eds.), *JALT2005 Conference Proceedings* (pp. 956–963). Tokyo: JALT.

Bloch, J. (2007). Abdullah's blogging: A generation 1.5 student enters the blogosphere. *Language Learning & Technology, 11*(2), 128–141.

Carney, N. (2009). Blogging in foreign language education. In M. Thomas (Ed.), *Handbook of research on language acquisition technologies: Web 2.0 transformation of learning* (pp. 292–312). Hershey, PA: IGI Global.

Cribb, V.M. (2000). Machine translation: The alternative for the 21st century? *TESOL Quarterly, 34*(3), 560–569.

Ducate, L. & Lomicka, L. (2008). Adventures in the blogosphere: from blog readers to blog writers. *Computer Assisted Language Learning, 21*(1), 9–28.

Ellison, N. & Wu, Y. (2008). Blogging in the classroom: A preliminary exploration of student attitudes and impact on comprehension. *Journal of Educational Multimedia and Hypermedia, 17*(1), 99–122.

Farmer, J. (2004). Communication dynamics: Discussion boards, weblogs and the development of communities of inquiry in online learning environments. Retrieved October 15 2010 from <http://incsub.org/blog/?p=3>.

Godwin-Jones, R. (2003). Emerging technologies: Blogs and wikis: Environments for on-line collaboration. *Language, Learning & Technology, 7*(2), 12–16.

Kadjer, S., & Bull, G. (2003). Scaffolding for struggling students: Reading and writing with blogs. *Learning and Leading with Technology, 31*(2), 32–35.

Lam, W.S.E. (2000). L2 literacy and the design of the self: A case study of a teenager writing on the Internet. *TESOL Quarterly, 34*(3), 457–482.

Lowe, C., & Williams, T. (2004). Moving to the public: Weblogs in the writing classroom. In L. Gurak, S. Antonijevic, L. Johnson, C. Ratliff, & J. Reyman (Eds.), *Into the blogosphere.* Retrieved October 15 2010 from <http://blog.lib.umn.edu/blogosphere/moving_to_the_public.html>.

Mynard, J. (2007). A blog as a tool for reflection for English language learners. *Asian EFL Journal, 24*, 1–10.

Pinkman, K. (2005). Using blogs in the foreign language classroom: Encouraging learner independence. *The JALT CALL Journal, 1*(1), 12–24.

Ruthven-Stuart, P. (2008). MT: We can't detect it, but can we accept it? Paper presented at the 34th Annual Conference of the Japan Association for Language Teaching, Tokyo, Japan.

Technorati (2008). State of the blogosphere 2008. Retrieved October 15 2010 from <http://technorati.com/blogging/feature/state-of-the-blogosphere-2008/>.

Thorne, S. L., & Payne, S. (2005). Evolutionary trajectories, Internet-mediated expression, and language education. *CALICO Journal, 22*(3), 371–397.

Ward, J. (2004). Blog assisted language learning (BALL): Push button publishing for the pupils. *TEFL Web Journal, 3*(1), 1–16. Retrieved October 15 2010 from <http://www.esp-world.info/Articles_26/push button publishing ward 2004.pdf>.

Comment

No matter where we live, there are likely to be changes in the way we live and the way we work as a result of technological innovations. Changes may be major, such as the electrification of a remote rural district, or relatively minor, like the availability of a new software program. But, like everyone else, teachers and course designers need to be aware of and respond appropriately to such innovations. It would, of course, be poor practice to make changes simply because a new way of doing something is available. In education teachers should consider how the use of new technology contributes to course goals and the extent to which it is in keeping with course principles. One of the major questions that should be asked is whether better technology leads to better teaching (Salaberry, 2001). In this case study, Patrick Foss has clearly demonstrated that it can.

Tasks

1. Introducing a change such as blogwriting to a course does, however, require buy-in from teachers, and from students. Even in the university situation described in this chapter, there was some resistance to change. To what extent did different change strategies (see *LCD*, pp. 177–9) facilitate the introduction of blogwriting? Try to find at least one of each of these strategies in this chapter.

TABLE 16.1

Power-coercive	*Rational-empirical*	*Normative-re-educative*

2. The successful introduction of a change is more likely if certain steps are followed (*LCD*, p. 173). How well were these steps followed in this case study?

TABLE 16.2

Make sure that the change is really needed
Plan the type of change so that it is not too great and not too small
Make sure that enough people see that the kind of change is possible
Use a wide range of change strategies
Be prepared for the change to take a long time

3. How would you evaluate the success of the blogwriting program?

Further Reading

Salaberry, M.R. (2001). The use of technology for second language learning and teaching: A retrospective. *The Modern Language Journal, 85*(1), 39–56.

INDEX